T0331869

Digital Business
Security Development:
Management Technologies

Don Kerr, *University of the Sunshine Coast, Australia*

John G. Gammack, *Griffith University, Australia*

Kay Bryant, *Griffith University, Australia*

BUSINESS SCIENCE REFERENCE

Hershey · New York

Director of Editorial Content:	Kristin Klinger
Director of Book Publications:	Julia Mosemann
Acquisitions Editor:	Lindsay Johnston
Development Editor:	Julia Mosemann
Publishing Assistant:	Travis Gundrum; Jamie Snavely
Typesetter:	Keith Glazewski; Travis Gundrum
Production Editor:	Jamie Snavely
Cover Design:	Lisa Tosheff
Printed at:	Lightning Source

Published in the United States of America by
Business Science Reference (an imprint of IGI Global)
701 E. Chocolate Avenue
Hershey PA 17033
Tel: 717-533-8845
Fax: 717-533-8661
E-mail: cust@igi-global.com
Web site: http://www.igi-global.com

Library of Congress Cataloging-in-Publication Data

Digital business security development : management technologies / Don Kerr, John G. Gammack, and Kay Bryant, editors.
      p. cm.
   Includes bibliographical references and index. Summary: "This book provides comprehensive coverage of issues associated with maintaining business protection in digital environments, containing base level knowledge for managers who are not specialists in the field as well as advanced undergraduate and postgraduate students undertaking research and further study"--Provided by publisher. ISBN 978-1-60566-806-2 (hardcover) -- ISBN 978-1-60566-807-9 (ebook) 1. Electronic commerce--Security measures. 2. Business enterprises--Computer networks--Security measures. 3. Computer security. I. Kerr, Don, 1952- II. Gammack, John G. III. Bryant, Kay, 1954- IV. Title.

   HF5548.32.D538 2010
   658.4'78--dc22

                              2010024585

British Cataloguing in Publication Data
A Cataloguing in Publication record for this book is available from the British Library.

Editorial Advisory Board

Table of Contents

Detailed Table of Contents

    Don Kerr, University of the Sunshine Coast, Australia
    John Gammack, Griffith University, Australia
    Richard Boddington, Murdoch University, Australia

This chapter provides an overview of digital business security. It is informed by a contemporary analysis of perceived threats through the eyes of information technology managers both from a representative public institution (a University) and from a private company (a retail sales company). A brief overview of malicious software leads into more general consideration of the risks and threats of security breaches, which are analysed from both a company and a customer perspective. Common to both sectors is the requirement to secure corporate records and other digital information and management and policy guidance is provided here. Cyber-crime remains rife, but is both under-reported and under-prosecuted. As managers may become involved in legal issues associated with information technology security breaches, this chapter also overviews the special nature of digital evidence.

Chapter 2

Richard Boddington, Murdoch University, Australia

Digital evidence, now more commonly relied upon in legal cases, requires an understanding of the processes used in its identification, preservation, analysis and validation. Business managers relying on digital evidence in the corporate environment need a greater understanding of its true nature and difficulties affecting its usefulness in criminal, civil and disciplinary proceedings. This chapter describes digital evidence collection and analysis, and the implications of common challenges diminishing its admissibility. It looks at determining the evidentiary weight of digital evidence that can be perplexing and confusing because of the complexity of the technical domain. Digital evidence present on computer networks is easily replaced, altered, destroyed or concealed and requires special protection to preserve its evidentiary integrity. Consequently, business managers seeking the truth of a matter can find it a vexing experience, unless provided with a clear appraisal and interpretation of the relevant evidence. Validating evidence, that is often complex and incomplete, requires expert analysis to determine its value in legal cases to provide timely guidance to business managers and their legal advisers. While soundly configured security systems and procedures enhance data protection and recovery, they are often limited in the way they preserve digital evidence. Unprepared personnel can also contaminate evidence unless procedural guidelines and training are provided. The chapter looks at the benefits for prudent organisations, who may wish to include cyber forensic strategies as part of their security risk contingency, planning to minimise loss or degradation of digital evidence which, if overlooked, may have adverse legal repercussions.

Chapter 3

Kevin Curran, University of Ulster, UK
Jennifer Caldwell, University of Ulster, UK
Declan Walsh, University of Ulster, UK
Marcella Gallacher, University of Ulster, UK

Authentication is the process of determining whether a user is to be granted access and verifying that they are whom they claim to be. This is generally done via a login system; typically consisting of a user ID and a corresponding password. An intrinsic weakness of this system of authentication is that passwords are easily forgotten, accidentally revealed, can be second guessed, or even stolen. Users today have multiple email accounts; manage their financial affairs, buy, and even sell regularly online. Many sites offer the opportunity to sign up. This can be problematic for managing usernames and passwords and it encourages insecure practices, such as writing them down, storing them electronically, or reusing the same login data on multiple Web sites repeatedly. One of the most common online security issues faced today is that every Web site has its own diverse authentication system that significantly heightens the probability of online crime, such as fraud and identity theft and, furthermore, can compromise the privacy of the individual. A common network identity-verification method is Simplified Sign-On, which allows users to roam between sites without having to repeatedly enter identifying information. Privacy of user's information should be maintained, as only relevant details are passed on to other sites. A number of organizations are already taking Simplified Sign-On on board and have had successful outcomes using this type of system. Some companies, such as Microsoft Passport, have used a Single Sign-On password system but they have had security and privacy issues after the launch. The future for most, if not all, users may be a secure and private single logon to access different sites and accounts on the Internet via Simplified Sign-On. This chapter discusses Simplified Sign-On in more detail.

Chapter 4

An expectation exists in the USA that operators of business-to-consumer (B2C) Web sites will provide public notice of their privacy and security practices in relation to the personal data that they hold. Such documents are referred to in this chapter as Privacy Policy Statements (PPS). The use of PPS has become mainstream in many other countries as well. Privacy and security of personal data are important elements in consumer trust, and hence in a consumer's decision to make purchases using Internet commerce services. PPS could therefore be expected to play an important role in overcoming the impediments to consumer purchases online. This chapter adds to the growing research literature on PPS by developing a research design involving comparison of an organisation's PPS against a normative template developed on the basis of professional practice and laws, policies, practices, and public expectations around the world. A study of six B2C sites was undertaken, in order to assess the practicability of the design, and provide some initial substantive insight into the contributions that PPS currently make to consumer trust. It appears that many organisations' PPS may be seriously inadequate, and hence may be more of an impediment to trust than an enabler of Web-commerce adoption.

Chapter 5

John Campbell, University of Canberra, Australia
Kay Bryant, University of Canberra, Australia

Maintaining the security of information systems and associated data resources is vital if an organization is to minimize losses. Access controls are the first line of defense in this process. The primary function of authentication controls is to ensure that only authorized users have access to information systems and electronic resources. Password-based systems remain the predominant means of user authentication despite viable authentication alternatives. Research suggests that password-based systems are often compromised by poor user security practices. This chapter presents the results of a survey of 884 computer users that examines user practice in creating and reusing password keys, and reports the findings on user password composition and security practices for email accounts. Despite a greater awareness of security issues, the results show that many users still select and reuse weak passwords keys that are based on dictionary words and other meaningful information.

Chapter 6

Raj Gururajan, University of Southern Queensland, Australia
Abdul Hafeez-Baig, University of Southern Queensland, Australia

The application of WLAN (Wireless Local Area Network) technology in the healthcare industry has gained increasing attention in recent years. It provides effective and efficient sharing of health information among healthcare professionals in timely treatment of patients (Collaborative Health Informatics Centre, 2000; Whetton, 2005a). However, there is still a concern among healthcare professionals whether health information is shared safely with WLAN technology. The primary aim of this study is to explore factors influencing healthcare professionals' adoption of WLAN security technology. This study was conducted in regional health settings in Queensland, Australia using a focus group discussion and a questionnaire survey in a mixed research methodology. The outcomes indicate that learning support, user technology awareness, readiness of existing system, and social influence, are four important factors in healthcare professionals' adoption of WLAN security technology. The findings suggest that healthcare professionals prefer to be more informed and prepared on knowledge of WLAN security technology before they decide to adopt it in their work environment. Therefore, their awareness of what the technology can do and cannot do for them, and the support they could get in learning to use the technology, play a crucial role. The healthcare professionals are concerned with how readily their existing system could support WLAN security technology and how people important to them would influence their decision in adopting WLAN security technology. Future research should extend the study in three areas. Firstly, future study should examine factors in this study with more regional areas of Australia. Secondly, future research should also examine the relationship between the factors and the demographic variables. Finally, there is also the possibility of examining the adoption factors with other security technology in healthcare, such as the pairing of WLAN technology and biometric security.

Web 2.0 is a new way of using existing Web resources interactively, and has attracted growing interest from the Web community, and more recently from businesses. However, there are emerging issues associated with security with the use of Web 2.0. This chapter provides an overview of Web 2.0 and outlines the security issues with Mashups and other applications within the Web 2.0 environment.

Chapter 8

ICT systems are expected to be available 24/7 to internal and external users regardless of the circumstances, but the nature of uncertainty in complex and dynamic environments makes Business Continuity Planning more relevant today than ever before. Organisations providing 24/7 ICT availability become strategic dilemmas for decision makers, hence, to ensure operations, managers must balance the costs involved in providing an almost zero downtime infrastructure for information availability with the trust ICT users have on a given organization. Decision makers need to assess possible disruptions and vulnerabilities that can impact on ICT availability to all users. This chapter argues that approaches, such as virtualisation, can provide cost advantages to organizations by ensuring availability and resilience through flexible system implementation, and to achieve this objective, committed strategic managers must have arguments to defend this view.

Chapter 9

Daniel Viney, University of the Sunshine Coast, Australia

This chapter discusses ICT trends of the past decade, the emergence of Web 2.0 technologies, mobile computing (as distinguished from cloud computing), the pitfalls of social networking, security considerations in the workplace, copyright and Intellectual Property considerations, and how to best control threats and vulnerabilities. We are in a period of aggressive technological growth to which there is no foreseeable end. New technologies, such as Web 2.0 and cloud computing, are emerging at an exponential rate, and as a consequence, security threats, controls, and standards are iteratively evolving. As yet, we do not know the security and privacy implications that such a rapid and wide uptake of cloud computing, and other multi-user virtual environment initiatives, and Web 2.0 technologies, will bring. In no way is this cause to panic, instead it is cause to focus on self-education, employee-education, and awareness. To put it simply, these offer our best defense to security threats. By being educated, aware, and vigilant, the majority of threats are nullified, as they are designed to prey upon those who rely on trust when reading emails, visiting Websites, and accessing site content, when navigating the World Wide Web. For example, there are millions of users who are completely unaware of threats, such as phishing, and other forms of Internet-based fraud. More than ever before, the onus is on the individual, both at home and in the workplace, to be responsible for maintaining best practice techniques, while utilizing digital resources to ensure that information security, individual privacy, and applicable legislation are not breached. This can only be achieved through iterative education processes, general awareness, and vigilance.

Preface

INTRODUCTION

There is a widespread perception that conducting business on the Internet has a higher risk than in the traditional face-to-face environment. This is due, in part, to security concerns and to the need for an extra level of trust incurred when paying for goods or services before receiving them. For the majority of consumers, the benefits of immediate access and search capabilities, as well as 24-hour access to businesses on a global scale, outweigh many of these security and trust concerns. Nonetheless, a healthy skepticism of some Web sites, and to deals offered, is essential because for a few people the Internet provides an easy means of concealing illegal and malicious activities.

While there is a common perception that the security of Internet-based transactions is weak, the reality is otherwise. Current security techniques are much stronger than techniques used when conducting transactions via fax or over the telephone. Nonetheless, although the perception of vulnerability is stronger than the reality, digital threats do need to be taken seriously. If an Internet organization is to survive and prosper, it must be fully aware of the threats and attacks (both internal and external) that can be used against it. Both businesses and government agencies operating electronically need to be vigilant against information theft, espionage and liability. They need to establish as many deterrents, defenses, and security measures as necessary, to protect their systems and data, and to understand the principles behind these to counter new threats. Further, the digital business needs to establish an ongoing maintenance program, and good administrative practices, to ensure security measures are kept up to date.

THE OVERALL OBJECTIVES OF THE BOOK

The overriding aim of this collection is to provide managers with an awareness of a range of issues associated with managing and securing the digital business. The specific objectives of the book are to:

- Provide knowledge on the extent of the security threat for Internet organizations
- Build knowledge about the types of threats facing businesses operating in a digital environment and the solutions that will minimize or eliminate those threats
- Identify common mistakes that businesses make in implementing and managing security
- Develop an appreciation of the importance of management strategies and legislation covering security issues in the digital environment.

THE TARGET AUDIENCE

This book contains state of the art research relevant to informing business practice. It provides base level knowledge for business managers who are not specialists in the field; however, the main audience will be advanced undergraduate and postgraduate students undertaking research and further study in the field, or looking towards a specialised career in this area. By providing an overview of the issues, coupled with in-depth chapters on specific key topics, both breadth and depth are addressed for these readerships. We adopt a managerial, rather than a technical focus, since security principles are more enduring than specific technologies.

BOOK CONTENT

The book emphasizes managerial aspects of security and includes the following chapters:

Chapter 1 is an overview of the digital landscape and specifically looks at digital business security issues. It attempts to cover the areas of most concern, according to contemporary interviews conducted with Information Technology (IT) managers from both government and non-government sources. The issues extracted from these interviews are used to illustrate the major points of concern and the interviewees were chosen to represent real decision makers around security issues.

Chapter 2 considers evidence in forensic investigations. This is an important area because, increasingly, managers are being called on to undertake some form of investigative work due to legal disputes, and breaches of personnel regulations or criminal activity. The chapter presents a review of digital evidence to help business managers gain a practical understanding of digital evidence, and to help them to manage this aspect.

Chapter 3 looks at developments in simplified sign-on authentication. Authentication is the process of determining whether a user is whom they claim to be. This is generally done via a login system, consisting of a user ID and password. As users today have a need for multiple sign-on, this chapter discusses the problem of managing usernames and passwords to reduce the need for using insecure practices, such as writing passwords down, storing them electronically, or reusing the same login data on multiple websites repeatedly. These insecure practices can increase the probability of online crime, such as fraud and identity theft and, furthermore, can compromise the privacy of the individual. This chapter discusses a common network identity-verification method, called simplified sign-on, which allows users to roam between sites without having repeatedly to enter identifying information.

Chapter 4 looks at the effectiveness of Privacy Policy Statements (PPS). A PPS is a public notice of privacy and security practices in relation to the personal data held by companies. It is an important element in consumer trust, and in a consumer's decision to make purchases using Internet commerce services. PPS could, therefore, be expected to play an important role in overcoming the impediments to consumer purchases online. This chapter adds to the growing research literature on PPS by describing research involving comparison of an organization's PPS against a normative template developed based on professional practice and laws, policies, practices, and public expectations around the world.

Chapter 5 evaluates user password practice and determines that password-based systems are often compromised by poor user security practices. This chapter presents the results of a survey of 884 computer users that examines user practice in creating and reusing password keys, and reports the findings on user password composition and security practices for email accounts. Despite a greater awareness of security issues, the results show that many users still select and reuse weak passwords keys that are based on dictionary words and other meaningful information.

Chapter 6 looks at a case study of Wireless handheld device and LAN security issues in a healthcare setting. This chapter divides the ICT communications into wired and wireless technologies. The chapter concentrates on wireless technology and provides information on user acceptance of the technology in the healthcare industry. The major barrier to the uptake of wireless technology appears to be user concerns over various security issues including physical, logical, and data security.

Chapter 7 looks at Web 2.0 technologies for business solutions from a security perspective. This chapter discusses the business application of Web 2.0 and the security problems that can occur. Web 2.0 applications are the target for attacks from both external and internal agents and this chapter describes the background, applications, and security concerns of the Web 2.0 technologies used for digital businesses.

Chapter 8 looks at business continuity planning and explores the implications of the expectation that ICT systems need to be available 24/7 to internal and external users, regardless of the circumstances. This chapter discusses the nature of uncertainty in complex and dynamic environments and shows how this makes business continuity planning essential. The chapter argues that approaches such as virtualization can provide cost advantages to organizations by ensuring availability and resilience through flexible systems.

Chapter 9 looks at future trends in digital security. Technological predictions are notoriously uncertain but it is important to look forward and to outline some emerging directions. While it is too early to be definitive about specific technologies still developing, some current areas, such as wireless technology security, along with security policies and technologies around removable media, mobile phones and social networks, are covered briefly, and the applicable management principles are covered more generally within the book.

While this book offers valuable insights into the technologies that can help reduce the incidence of security breaches, in reality, the most important aspect of effective security is the human factor and employees doing the right thing with respect to the use of USB keys, accessing appropriate websites, and being vigilant about email attachments. This is the central message of this collection.

Don Kerr
University of the Sunshine Coast, Australia

John G. Gammack
Griffith University, Australia

Kay Bryant
Griffith University, Australia

Acknowledgment

The authors would like to thank Ms. Maureen Klinkert (Director, ITS - Information Technology Service of the University of the Sunshine Coast), Mr. Barry Mahoney (Manager, ITS - Information Technology Service) and Mr. Barry Pollard (ICT Infrastructure Team Leader - Information Technology Service University of the Sunshine Coast) for their insights into the problem from an educational industry perspective. The authors also acknowledge the work done by Johanna Einfalt in proof reading and copyediting each chapter.

Don Kerr
University of the Sunshine Coast, Australia

John G. Gammack
Griffith University, Australia

Kay Bryant
Griffith University, Australia

Chapter 1
Overview of Digital Business Security Issues

Don Kerr
University of the Sunshine Coast, Australia

John Gammack
Griffith University, Australia

Richard Boddington
Murdoch University, Australia

ABSTRACT

This chapter provides an overview of digital business security. It is informed by a contemporary analysis of perceived threats through the eyes of information technology managers both from a representative public institution (a University) and from a private company (a retail sales company). A brief overview of malicious software leads into more general consideration of the risks and threats of security breaches, which are analysed from both a company and a customer perspective. Common to both sectors is the requirement to secure corporate records and other digital information and management and policy guidance is provided here. Cybercrime remains rife, but is both under-reported and under-prosecuted. As managers may become involved in legal issues associated with information technology security breaches, this chapter also overviews the special nature of digital evidence.

INTRODUCTION

For the majority of consumers, the Internet holds the promise of an environment that provides access to people and businesses on a global scale. For a few however,

DOI: 10.4018/978-1-60566-806-2.ch001

the Internet provides an easy means of concealing illegal and malicious activities. Gold (2008) and BERR (2008) suggest this trend is increasing, as hacking and the development of botnets[1] becomes more of an organized crime than an amateur hobby[2]. The security of digital business is therefore under constant threat, for public and private sector alike.

Digital business security is a very broad topic and a complete overview of the issues would be impossible in one chapter[3]; however, we will attempt to cover the areas perceived to be of most concern, according to interviews[4] conducted with Information Technology (IT) managers from government and non-government sources. These contemporary interviews are reported in this chapter to illustrate the points at issue. While we acknowledge our sample is small, the managers selected were purposively chosen to represent real decision makers concerned with these issues and who may be therefore expected to have concerns similar to many other practicing managers responsible for IT security.

The whole issue of digital business security involves an understanding of the need to account for the use of data both internally, as well as externally. External threats relate to internet security, which can be defined as the protection of the internet account and files from both internal and external threats. At the basic level, this involves passwords, files backups, and setting up file access permissions. In fact, the respondents in the interviews, reported later in this chapter, consider the internal threats, such as the indiscriminate use of USB flash drives, as more of a threat than external factors.

The risks involved in conducting business on the Internet are different from those associated with the traditional face-to-face commerce environment. This chapter will provide an overview of the digital business environment and outline the specific business concerns associated with security for Internet enabled, ecommerce applications, and catering for the demands and rights of existing staff in the internal environment.

Digital security management covers many aspects and these are discussed throughout this chapter. Specific areas of interest include the following:

- Analysis of the risks and threats
- Development of security policies
- Management of the risks and threats
- Planning for possible contingencies
- Business continuity planning in case of a disaster
- monitoring the effectiveness of existing security measures
- Collecting evidence to bring to justice those responsible for the misuse or misappropriation of an organization's information resources.

Before looking in more detail at these aspects we begin by briefly reviewing some typical classes of risks and threats, and associated trends.

Analysis of the Risks and Threats

To commit a security breach cyber-criminals need two capabilities: access to the computer system and knowing how to manipulate it once access is gained. Whether personally initiated or otherwise, malicious software (*malware*) provides one of the most obvious security threats to any organization: a range of types commonly used includes:

- **Virus:** a computer program capable of attaching to disks or other files and replicating itself repeatedly, typically without the user's knowledge or permission
- **Worm:** an independent program that replicates its own program files until it interrupts the operation of networks and computer systems
- **Trojan horse:** a program that appears to be useful but actually masks a destructive program
- **Logic bomb:** an application or system virus designed to "explode" or execute at a specified time and date
- **Keyloggers:** programs that record keystrokes, enabling capture of passwords and other sensitive data

These can destroy or compromise data or processes, and since they occur in many forms there is a constant battle between virus writers and virus protection software companies. Nikishin's (2004) review outlined the history of malicious software attacks prior to 2004 and offered particularly disturbing predictions into the future. In his paper, Nikishin forecast a growth in virus behaviors and in proportion to the growth in the number and magnitude of services provided. In addition, the modes of entry into the system will be many and varied, for example through "email, copying themselves into network resources, attacking server software like Nimda, or a virus which infects files of different operating systems, for example Pelf, which infects the executable files for Windows and Linux" (Nikishin, p. 17). According to Nikishin, antivirus companies have the following problems:

- Unpredictable behavior with respect to methods of penetration of existing strains, as well as new strains of viruses;
- The possibility of new *flash* viruses that have the capability of infecting the World Wide Web in minutes, and this would mean that companies would not have the time to implement infection protection strategies quickly enough.

Nonetheless, protection provided through the services of professional organizations, or open source and free antivirus products are *de rigeur* for most corporations.

Companies may also suffer *denial of service* attacks[5], where vast numbers of requests hit their website simultaneously and servers are unable to cope with the demand. Such attacks typically result in lost business and/or reputation, and even the biggest online companies are not immune. A threat that has become more prevalent since Nikishin's 2004 paper is botnets: a hidden robot network that runs using infected computers often without the user's knowledge. These are often likened to zombies, who rise when their master calls, and can form a vast army to instigate a denial of service attack, or a spam email.

These attacks are beyond human scale, enabled and perpetuated by technological processes, but many other forms of security breach are perpetrated at the human level. For example dumpster diving refers to simply retrieving printouts or other discarded material such as CDs or hard drives that have not been wiped first. Criminal hacking (cracking) is where the intellectual challenge presented by breaking system security (hacking) is used for criminal purposes. Although hacking can be a high level skill, and indeed one prized by banks and governments, in some case only a little knowledge is required, and malicious scripts, (freely available on the internet) can be used by almost anyone, often young teenagers known as script kiddies or script bunnies. Finally, *social engineering* is where a criminal gains an employee's personal trust over time as part of a campaign to eventually abuse it, for example by asking for a system password, or being trusted to be left alone in the room with an unlocked computer.

In addition to these are scams and fraudulent activity, including spoof websites or emails, where the sender or website is forged and not what it appears to be in reality. Phishing and pharming are where official looking emails request personal details such as passwords or bank account numbers, or redirect users to fake websites. Personal details can then be used in identity theft crimes, where a person's credit history, birthdate or other personal details are used fraudulently. This is not just a risk for individuals, but for companies too. Corporate identity theft can also involve credit card abuse, changing directors' name or business addresses and the like.[6]

Gold (2008) has provided an analysis of security issues and offered predictions of imminent issues to be considered. According to Gold, 2008 was a landmark year due to the rapid escalation of web 2.0 technologies, including social networking sites, which has also led to a spate of crimeware that use the technology to provide mechanisms for criminals to take control of computers and computer systems. Gold described the Botnet attack that, according to Kaspersky's lab, was responsible for 5% of Internet traffic over the Valentine's day period.

To provide predictions for the near future Gold (2008) consulted with acknowledged experts in the field from a variety of companies. The following aspects of security were noted:

- Botnets will become more decentralized, making them harder to detect and destroy the source;
- Malicious emails will increasingly use attachments or Web links in an effort to trick end users;
- Software is getting better with detection of unknown malware threats becoming increasingly effective.
- companies will be doing "a lot more with a lot less" and this includes not "undertaking unnecessary upgrades such as Vista" (cited in Gold, p. 26);
- There will be an increasing demand for network access controls and data leakage prevention;
- There will be a surge in "cybercrime reports, mainly due to the downturn in the economy" (cited in Gold, p. 26).

The escalation predicted by Gold is corroborated by reported statistics. A UK survey conducted by Price Waterhouse Coopers for the Department for Business Enterprise and Regulatory Reform (BERR, 2008) showed that 45% of small businesses (with less than 50 employees), 72% of large businesses (with greater than 250 employees), and 96% of very large businesses (with greater than 500 employees), reported security breaches for their business in 2008. As reported by survey respondents the prevalence of four types of incidents where confidential information was exposed to risk, was as follows:

- Detection of unauthorized outsiders within the network (13%)
- Fake (phishing) emails sent asking customers for data (9%)
- Impersonated customers (identity theft) (9%)
- Suffered a confidentiality breach (6%).

The report (BERR 2008) indicated that in many cases companies were not doing enough to protect themselves from these breaches. The breaches that have a major influence on the chances of the above mentioned incidences occurring, and the associated percentage of companies that do not do enough to protect themselves and their customers was as follows:

- Websites that accept payment details but do not encrypt them (10%)
- Companies that spend less than 1% of their IT budget on information security (21%)

- Companies that have no controls over staff use of instant messaging (35%)
- Companies that have not tested their disaster recovery plans in the last year (48%)
- Companies that do not carry out any formal security risk assessment (52%)
- Companies that do nothing to prevent confidential data leaving USB sticks, etc. (67%)
- Companies that had computers stolen did not encrypt hard disks (78%)
- Companies that are not aware of the contents of BS 7799/ISO 27001[8] (79%)
- Companies that do not scan outgoing emails for confidential data (84%).

Clearly security breaches are prevalent, and companies are doing too little to mitigate risk: risks that affect not only themselves, but also their customers.

Risks to Customers

The internet has significantly changed the way consumers engage in trade with businesses, government and enterprises worldwide. With online interaction being promoted by government, businesses and not-for-profit organizations, it can be argued that a duty of care exists to ensure clients of such services are not in danger of being victims of online fraud through the use of online activities. Fraud, especially online fraud, is an emotive issue that attracts significant public attention. Customers are increasingly being targeted by perpetrators of online fraud (Bajari & Hortaçsu, 2004). While an increase in awareness of fraud is occurring (ASIC 2007; Identify Security, 2008; Internet Scams 2008; Scams 2008), much is yet to be investigated. For example, at the time of writing (2009), ten prevalent online scams include (in order of received complaints) fake cheque scams, general merchandise sales (goods purchased but not delivered), auctions, Nigerian money offers, lotteries/lottery clubs, advance fees for loans, prize/sweepstakes claims, phishing, friendship and sweetheart swindles, and internet access services (*Internet Fraud Watch*, 2007). With the numerous ways fraud can occur nowadays, there are many opportunities for abuse.

The United States of America has investigated numerous online frauds received by the Federal Trade Commission (US Federal Trade Commission, 2007). These investigations involved cross-border states within America, as well as international investigations involving many countries. To demonstrate the problems that occur when the investigations go international, and by way of example, we will discuss the case of Australia. Currently, any online fraud prosecutions involving Australian companies, identified by the US Federal Trade Commission, are not enforced due to the costs associated with enforcing an American judgment in Australia. Furthermore, the information gained during the investigation is not able to be turned over to investigating Australian Federal police as there is no authorization currently in place for this to occur (US Federal Trade Commission, 2007).

These problems are not just a concern to customers and consumers of internet services but also to the very companies that provide the services, as the system is built very much on trust. Unlike other business transactions, internet transactions require the customer to pay for the product upfront and the trust required for this type of transaction is much higher than traditional transactions. If this trust is betrayed, the company can find itself in a very difficult situation very quickly.

Risks to the Business

Whitman and Mattord (2009) identify twelve threats to information security in business and these are shown in Figure 1.

These categories of threat represent a combination of technical and human factors and are a good indication of the complexity of the issue with each category having to be considered and understood to varying degrees by managers.

Security breaches can also have a dramatic effect on a company's reputation and even on its share price. The magnitude of the impact is usually a direct reflection on how heavily the company relies on the internet for their business activities. For example, a distributed denial of service attack[9] on Amazon.com would have more severe impacts for the company and its customers, than a similar attack on a website for an oil company. Security breaches can impact on companies through direct effects on share prices, or through a loss of reputation, with respect to customer access or even the security of personal information, like addresses or credit card particulars.

It is difficult to quantify the exact cost of security breaches as companies tend to under report these events and the determining of losses associated with factors other than the breach is often difficult to estimate. However some research has been conducted on the impact of security breaches on companies' share price and reputation and techniques such as event study methodology, have been used to some effect (Garg, Curtis, & Halper, 2003).

Garg et al. (2003) studied the impact of security breaches on the share prices of publically listed companies. In their study of 22 security breach events, the company share price fell by an average of 5.6 percent over a three day period after the security breach event was reported. It is apparent that company losses and net worth reductions of this magnitude could pay for a lot of security initiatives, yet many companies are not spending the required money. For example, the Price Waterhouse Coopers report quoted earlier indicated that 21 percent of companies spend less than 1% of their IT budget on security (BERR 2008).

Garg et al. (2003) also provided case examples of security breaches that affected company reputations and foremost was the denial of service (DoS) attack, especially with companies that are heavily dependent on the Internet, such as eBay and Yahoo. Garg et al.(2003) suggested that the year 2000 was a watershed for internet

Figure 1. Threats to information security in business (Adapted from Whitman & Mattord, 2009)

Category of threat	Examples
Human error or failure	Accidents or mistakes
Compromises to intellectual property	Piracy, copyright infringement
Deliberate acts of trespass	Unauthorized access, unauthorized data collection
Deliberate acts of information extortion	Blackmail of information disclosure
Deliberate acts of sabotage or vandalism	Destruction of systems or information
Deliberate acts of theft	Illegal confiscation of systems or information
Deliberate software attacks	Viruses, worms, macros, denial of service attacks
Forces of nature	Fire, flood, earthquake, lightning
Deviations in quality of service	Internet Service Providers (ISP), power or wide area network (WAN) service issues from service providers
Technical hardware failures or errors	Equipment failure
Technical software failures or errors	Bugs, code problems, unknown loopholes
Technological obsolesces	Antiquated or outdated technologies

security, as the DoS attack demonstrated to companies that the Internet had serious vulnerabilities, and that the true cost of doing business on the Internet included "the cost of downtime, recovery costs (systems and theft of proprietary information) and damage to brand reputation/customer perception".

The purpose of this book is to provide an understanding of these threats from a managerial perspective. To provide an indication of concerns contemporary information technology managers have with respect to security, we interviewed selected individuals in both the public and the private sector. The results of these interviews are described in the following section.

Information Technology Managers' Perspective on Security

In order to gain some insights into the magnitude and complexity of security realities, interviews were conducted with executive staff in an Information Technology Service (ITS) division of an Australian University, and with an Information Technology manager from an Australian nationwide retail company. Their concerns were considered representative of contemporary public and private sector organizations.

A PUBLIC SECTOR PERSPECTIVE ON SECURITY MANAGEMENT

Three IT managers at an Australian University were interviewed jointly. They were the Director of Information Technology Services, the Manager of Information Technology Services (ITS), and the Team Leader of the ICT Infrastructure Team (who is largely responsible for ICT Security within IT Services.)

The views of the director, with respect to security for ITS (Information Technology Services), were introduced as follows:

The most fundamental aspect of security is compliance with legislation and audits of the institution in relation to this…ITS is held responsible for the custodianship of financial data and …ICT security at the most fundamental level in terms of being audited as an organization.

The Director further asserted that "The place that the auditors will go is ITS, to determine how secure the financial data is…This is extended to all assets associated with the university's core business". The Director considered security very important and suggested that there was a fundamental interest in how secure an organization's financial systems are. The Director also suggested that security was very important because the University is audited every year. The Director summarized this line of thought by saying that "Security is about the whole governance regime. You need System Owners to determine who rightfully has access to what."

The University is a relatively young institution and the maturity of the organization was an important factor when assessing security needs. The contemporary security standards suggest that the organization needs to go to a certain level but this has to be tempered against the available resources of the organization. As the Director stated:

[We look at] what are the practices across the organization, what is the maturity of the organization in so far as our ability to adopt that standard and we come back from a particular standard and not adopt it in its fullest extent because we quite simply haven't got the resources.

The institution takes a risk management approach because "we do not have the resources of say a big bank ...We have a balanced approach to allow people to do their job, as well as providing systems security" (Director of ITS).

The Team Leader emphasized the difference between risk avoidance and risk management. He provided an example from the financial sector saying that "in the past financial institutions had a risk avoidance approach [of] locking everything down - buried inside the walls of the institution. Well we are not in an environment like that here". He further went on to say that the University may require sensitive information from a source on the other side of the world and the risk management approach (along with improvements in software) allows the University to undertake this type of activity. He further distinguished between data and information, maintaining that data security is often mentioned but the real need is for information security. Data is not valuable, until it becomes information. The manager went on further to say:

Many of the tools available are based on structured information such as database; however, we not only consider structured digital data but increasingly we must consider unstructured information, such as multimedia content, so it's gone beyond the traditional data processing model. For example, what do we do about email or remote access to email or mobile devices and with people who are increasingly mobile in the global context? (Director and Team Leader)

The Team Leader also suggested that a major challenge for the University was maintaining information security in a mobile world, and this is not so much the technology but the behavior pattern of staff and students. He went on to ask the question "How do we know if the person accessing the information is the person they claim to be?" This problem of identification is further complicated through human behavior with the Team Leader stating that "Human behavior is also a problem, for example walking away from a machine while in an Internet café." This theme was expanded upon by all three respondents with statements, such as:

People have to understand the risks of not having adequate security. There is a great deal of frustration amongst academics in having to unlock a screensaver all the time, and ITS are very aware of this frustration, however, the risks of not doing this must be acknowledged.

The analogy was then given of a finance department and the security provided in terms of locked doors, simply to secure what may only be a small amount of petty cash, but data is accessible from computers everywhere. Not only is the remote access a problem, the fact that it is dynamic, adds further complications to the problem. In addition, people change locations or positions in the organization and these moves require changes in the information systems infrastructure to reflect that. The data manager asked the question "How does ITS know when people have moved on to another role, for example?"

To the question of non-technical security issues, such as email scams, the interviewees spoke about their approach to handling the problem as being one of sensitivity to the requirements of staff. They stated that they do not want to pry or look like they are interfering but they do need to make people aware of the potential scams. The concern they had was that there was a perception amongst some members of the University that ITS should be protecting people from these scams. The reality is that the University cannot protect people from their own decisions relating to these types of scams.

Spam filtering is also a challenge in the University environment and they do use the services of a number of organizations who are acknowledged experts in this area. The University collects information from several sources for third party automated systems and they use AusCERT (Australian Computer Emergency Response Team) from the University of Queensland in Australia, which provides a subscription-based membership.

The University has automatic systems running 24 hours a day, seven days a week. Spam monitoring in general takes a considerable amount of time and effort for a small University, and one full time employee is assigned to this task for a significant amount of time every day. Malware, spam, and phishing (scam) emails are a constantly evolving threat. To provide effective protection, similarly agile and evolving systems are extensively employed. The security manager revealed that "up to 97 percent of emails are dropped every day and the system is being probed every second".

The Team Leader indicated that there were unique aspects to the University environment and in this case, in particular, by suggesting that "under the University environment we have to be more flexible than many other corporate of government environments". This uniqueness was further emphasized by the security manager who suggested that appliances designed to reduce security impacts are available but they cannot work in "set and forget mode" unless the organization has "incredibly simple business rules". The "set and forget" mode will provide around 80 percent accuracy but this organization "expects 99 percent stopping the stuff [inappropriate email and phishing]".

The Director provided an overview of how the security challenges have changed since 2004, with the major security concerns being relatively simple worms, but these are being replaced by sophisticated Botnets (explained by the Director as "methods of gathering PCs to be part of a herd to do some grand organized crime effort". The Director further explained that these Botnets are examples of how the

ITS has a social responsibility, as well as an organizational responsibility, to deal with these things in a reasonable way. She suggested that the University was doing that quite well but there is always more that can be done. For example, Microsoft is doing a lot of work on targeting Botnets and looking to attack before the world of Microsoft itself gets attacked. The indication was that there was a lot more proactive work being done by the vendors now.

Relating to concerns about the relative new area of cloud computing[10], the Director suggested that one of the threats faced by the University was in the multi-user virtual environment world. She went on to suggest that cloud computing is the next threat because, although systems can be locked down within your own environment, the problem is the accountability the University has over a service that is not housed on the campus. IT staff have no capability to control what is done in 'the cloud' by academic staff and students. The IT Director was referring to online multi-user virtual worlds, such as Second Life, and the use of these services for teaching and learning purposes. The IT director suggested that "these worlds exist and your IT group have absolutely no control over them what so ever … so how does the organization control its intellectual property? … That is content that is being distributed through that cloud." Other questions related to who has access to these sites and to the information contained in them and how do you control that? The Director was concerned that nothing is done in "the cloud" until there is a security problem, and then it is fixed, but the industry is always in catch-up mode.

The Team Leader was most concerned about the unknown and he emphasized this through the following statement:

We don't know if a vulnerability exists… it is really those things that are going on … that you don't know about … [for example] if a Botnet gets below the kernel, there is nothing you can do about it because it is below that layer, although the University does run root kit detectors on key exposed systems and have software tripwires installed [the layer of the tools used to detect it in the first place – the tool is sitting above that kernel layer].

A Private Sector Perspective on Security Management

The information systems manager of a large national retail chain was interviewed and asked about his concerns with security. His response to the question, "What is the major concern in your organization with regards to information security?" was:

Generally because we have very corporatized systems for [control of] viruses, [such as] antivirus spyware, malware [and] things like that, our biggest threat is actually internally ... when people put a USB key in [to the computer], that is where we get most of our viruses from. We have files in place [to control external threats], where all but the best hackers would not be able to hack in externally so our threat is internal.

The manager further expanded saying that they have corporate tools that manage viruses, pushes out software to computers, and tells the IT department if any software has been changed without admin rights. The company uses a propriety tool (Cisco works) and any infections are reported back to the central system. In addition, a content filtering system has been built into the proprietary tool. When asked about the use of services like Facebook and MySpace by staff, the response was, "No we have Facebook open, we are liberal with team members here that they are actually allowed to access sites such as banking or Facebook etc, as long as it is on your own time". Like the previous interviews, the key concern was unintentional internal threats and this was exemplified in the following statement:

Some people pirate music or movies etc and bring them into work to share with everyone. Chances they have some spyware, malware[11] Trojans[12], whatever happens to be on it and people have been known to put it on their computer, log into the LAN and infect every computer in the organization, and it might be two days before we can get a patch fit in to fix that.

As mentioned earlier, the company has software arrangements with companies that guarantee that they will manage threats for the company, and if something goes wrong, the provider of the software and service is liable. In addition, the company has an extensive disaster recovery plan, and if something really bad happens, they can "always go back to the tape" from their mirrored site. The IT manager works on the principle that:

Generally you will infect one not both sets of servers so we have always got multiple ways of backing up. We also have the independence of the stores themselves, we have 350 stores around the country... if head office got attacked by something bad they [the stores] can keep on running, the only thing they could not do is an end of day balance. Realistically they could carry on [independently] for a week if they had to.

The company has ecommerce capabilities with a Web store, import store and export store that people can go on and buy goods online if they so wished. This is externally hosted, so the hosting company will "*get hit*", and not the retail company.

This retail company's solution to its security concerns was to have third party provid-
ers to outsource. The IT manager stated, "We have also outsourced our Electronic
Data Interchange (EDI) to a company called GXS[13] inboard and outboard logistic
information is forwarded regularly in a specified format back to us." This effectively
means that all the problems associated with different systems and different trading
partners become GXS's problem. The IT manager went on to say that "big com-
panies like WalMart will only deal with vendors if they go through GXS for EDI".

When asked about the social engineering aspects of security, in particular phishing
attacks and other scams, the manager reinforced the third party propriety software
solution the company had enacted. His response was:

The company has automatic filtering systems that stops a lot of this type of email
traffic... most phishing attacks are targeting government [institutions]. I haven't
to my knowledge not received an email and had to go to our security engineer and
ask to retrieve it... We don't have any missing emails and no junk mail ... in my
previous employment [government institution] there were bouts of up to 50 emails
about Nigerian scams ... haven't had any [here] which is interesting really.

When asked about cloud computing as a follow up from the concerns the director
of ITS from the University had, the response was, "We have gone the VPN (virtual
private network) route with each employee having secure access to the network." The
response to the final question, "Do you feel you have security under control?" was:

Since I have been here [12 months], I have seen one virus that swept through; it
was brought in internally. The security engineer has said they have no high level
security attacks detected like someone trying to hack in ... even if the network is
down our monitoring tools would send you an SMS indicating the attack is occur-
ring ... really it comes down to - we are more at risk from an internal source such
as USB, CD or pirated games.

In summary, the way this company got around its security problems was to
outsource. The final comment was, "Our outward facing Web site is outsourced so
they are not actually attacking us anyway."

Many of the concerns expressed by the respondents in the University interview
are common across the University sector. For example, reports in The Chronicle of
Higher Education confirm the internal threat concern with a study indicating that 21
percent of respondents, in a survey of 182 college officials in the United States of
America, had said that their systems had suffered an intrusion from someone within

their college (Young, 2006). In the same study, 58 percent of those surveyed reported some kind of IT incident and nine percent reported losses of data related to students.

More generally, Gold (2008) predicts an increase in cybercrime due to "The combination of higher sophistication of both the cybercriminals and their crime tools, the low detection and prosecution rate, and the financial stakes [involved]" (p. 26). Protection through ongoing awareness of technical developments is therefore essential. No matter how much is spent on security, however, many initiatives fail because workers are in the main not very conscious of security (Workman, Bommer, & Straub, 2008) who suggest that managers also need to address human behavioral aspects through training and education. The literature and anecdotal evidence (for example from the interviewees quoted in this chapter) indicates that security problems are only going to become more difficult, and thus it is very important that companies keep up to date with the latest in security issues both from a technical and a human point of view. The next section examines these and other policy and planning issues for management.

Management of the Risks and Threats

Security policies and crime prevention are matters for national agencies as well as corporations and both regulation and organization level policies are implicated. For both commercial and government organizations, policies will be generally similar, as they involve a coordinated response to managing security risks associated with IT infrastructure and access. The framework developed through the US Department of Homeland Security[14] provides a comprehensive guide to areas of IT security that remains under continuous review to ensure its currency. This framework can be used at organization level in developing appropriate management and technical competencies and roles in line with wider security policies.

Organizations rely increasingly on computer networks and information management systems to create, store, and transfer the information that forms an essential part of their operations. Threats to the security of digital assets may come from both expected and unexpected sources. Dramatic natural disasters or cyberattacks exist alongside more preventable (and thus manageable) instances of risk associated with technical or physical vulnerabilities. Policy frameworks provide guidance on areas of vulnerability, which require specific technical responses. Management involves generally understanding the potential threats and vulnerabilities in the context of the wider policy and external environment, and ensuring that appropriate technical responses are implemented.

Enterprises require IT security professionals whose competencies span both technical and managerial aspects. The *IT Security Essential Body of Knowledge*

(DHS-NCSD, 2008) comprehensively identifies several functional organizational roles and competencies associated with specific areas of vulnerability that apply to any organizational sector. Management's role generally involves overseeing technical designs and implementations, whilst keeping abreast of technical developments, assessing the changing risk landscape and ensuring compliance with wider policy. Technical developments and standard include cryptographic practices such as public key infrastructure (PKI) and biometrics. PKI allows encrypted data to be exchanged over the insecure public environment of the internet, at a level of security adequate for everyday commerce. Whilst agencies such as America's National Security Agency (NSA) have access to more powerful encryption methods (and the wherewithal to break commercial level PKI codes) PKI provides a global standard for electronic commerce and data exchange. Biometric techniques, which use personal physical characteristics to identify computer users are now becoming commonplace. A simple webcam with face recognizing software for example can prevent unauthorized computer access, and many biometric techniques such as fingerprint readers are becoming affordable and practicable as complementary levels of security to passwords.

Compliance with wider policy may be externally mandated – for example the Sarbanes-Oxley Act affecting public companies in the USA has far reaching implications for IT security (Byrum, 2003)[15]. External industry bodies may also provide specific guidelines that must be taken into account, depending on the organization and a manager's functional role. For example, one identified competency area is "digital forensics", relevant when a security incident has occurred and requires analysis and report. National bodies such as the Association of Chief Police Officers in the UK provide updated guidelines in this area (ACPO, 2007)[16], in which relevant investigators at organization level would be required to be trained and whose practice should consistently follow. Whilst police investigators need to comply to preserve evidence that will be safe in court, many other organizations may also wish to form permanent incident response teams with similar expertise for handling security incidents. In any organization, management competencies and responsibilities in digital forensics might typically include ensuring investigative resources and establishing a specialized forensic team (whether ad hoc or more permanent); ensuring appropriate access levels and overseeing any emerging improvement actions (see DHS-NCSD, 2008, p 8).

In the dynamic area of IT security, however, the specific knowledge required will develop and change, and it is beyond the scope of any framework to detail this. Whilst the Essential Body of Knowledge (EBK) framework specifies the enduring types of competencies required in digital forensic investigation and 13 other fields of IT security, the responsible manager would expect to remain aware of the best current practice and knowledge, in order to organize specific activities in line with the framework's broad areas. Specialized courses, consulting services, publications, websites and conferences can provide relevant guidance. In the case of the digital forensics community, (as with other IT security fields) standards, rigor and consensus on practice is actively debated[17], and shared at specialized fora.

It is important in organizations that security knowledge and sensitive enterprise information is managed and not lost if experts move on – so documentation of processes, policies and resources becomes a management activity, along with sharing knowledge within a trusted community. The security of IT systems and applications is a key area for enterprises, whether the software used is third party or developed in-house, and integrating effective security practices into code development and ongoing risk evaluation is signalled here. Wikis provide a powerful mechanism for knowledge sharing, but there is a risk if identified vulnerabilities are shared before patches are in place, and before a root cause analysis preventing similar occurrences is conducted (Araujo, 2006).

If appropriate, forming a dedicated team can be considered. Such teams are usually called Computer Security Incident Response Teams (CSIRTs), or sometimes Computer Emergency Response Teams (CERTs). For example the computer emergency response team for the Netherlands' Government is called GOVCERT. NL, whilst, for Australia, AusCERT is the national computer emergency response team. CERT is a registered service mark, so the more general and internationally used term CSIRT is preferred here. Detailed guidance on setting up CSIRTs was proposed by West-Brown et al (1998) and was updated in 2003. The European network and Information Security Agency (ENISA) also provides detailed guidance for management setting up CSIRTs (ENISA, 2006)[18] and Killcrece et al (2003)[19] further expand on the variety of models for structuring a CSIRT and selecting a design appropriate to organizational practicalities.

Planning for Possible Contingencies

Management plays a key role in strategic business planning, and through anticipating threats to the business, acting to avoid or mitigate these before they occur. In IT security especially, this includes recognizing the various potential sources of threat, and protecting data and other content through appropriate measures. Good management includes not just technical but also human resource activities: data may normally be behind an enterprise firewall but if transferred to a USB stick and mislaid off-site, it is suddenly compromised. Workforce education and physical as well as technical security measures are indicated.

Unauthorized access to networked resources remains one of the main areas of security breaches. Policies on access within an enterprise will depend on the nature of the work, and who needs to know particular information held within files. Permissions are authorized in line with policies from higher organizational levels, and typically set to operate at individual, group and public levels. Security may be set at a file owner's (e.g. document creator's) discretion, or mandated by an administrator's policy. A file may be set for the owner to read and modify, a trusted group to read only and inaccessible to the general public. A user with higher level clearance (such as a system administrator) can override these access privileges, but issues of privacy and confidentiality can then come into play and cause other problems.

This is a multi-level security approach, and operating systems or network protocols provide standard mechanisms for setting appropriate clearance to read, alter or execute files in a given folder or system area. Whilst both public and individual permissions are conceptually clear for single sites or named workforces, management must decide who belongs to groups with particular access levels, and this becomes further complicated when third-party networks are implicated.

Equally, certain documents may be layered to give permissions for accessibility depending on security clearance policies and associated settings. This facility is important in ensuring original copies are preserved, and not modified accidentally or deliberately. Also at the document level, passwords, encryption and permission settings can be managed for additional security. Products are available that can decrypt documents, using specialized algorithms or brute force if necessary, so access even to documents in encrypted form is another consideration implying any management approach to security must be multidimensional.

Apart from managing access and data and file protections inside an organization, threats from outside, including random or targeted malware attacks, and deliberate intrusions aimed at information theft or vandalism must be addressed. The most recently available Computer Crime and Security survey from the Computer Security Institute (CSI, 2006) found that "virus attacks, unauthorized access to networks, lost/ stolen laptops or mobile hardware and theft of proprietary information or intellectual property ... account for more than 74 percent of financial loss"[20]. Firewalls, anti-malware products and Intrusion Detection Systems (IDS) are well known classes of software designed to mitigate specific threats and are outlined below. Specialist software for analyzing networks to identify security issues has been around for some time, such as SATAN (Security Administrator's Tool for Analyzing Networks) and SARA, (Security Auditor's Research Assistant) based on the classic SATAN model[21], and others. Software permitted to scan a network or computer system must be trustworthy and up to date, since if it can detect a vulnerability it can also pass on this information for subsequent exploitation.

Firewalls are essentially a barrier between the outside (untrusted) and the inside (trusted) environment: often between the internet and the local machine or internal network. Like a physical protective wall a threat is identified and blocked before it affects sensitive material inside the wall. As barriers work both ways, by detecting what is going in and out across the wall it can detect sensitive material escaping outwards to an untrusted or unknown environment.

The malware threats outlined earlier in the chapter each imply specific technical and managerial responses. Specialized software, from leading vendors or otherwise available provides protection against identified viruses, worms and other malware. Professional solutions are often provided together with associated technical information and update services describing vulnerabilities and recommendations for remedial or preventative action. Virus definitions for example are updated continually and thus both a product capable of responding rapidly and a management policy to enforce updates are needed. Applying disk or usage quotas for individual users can limit the amount of resources used by replicating worms. Removing inactive accounts after a grace period removes another potential vulnerability[??]. Monitoring for unusual activity or patterns, using human intelligence or analytic tools also helps identify potentially malicious use. For example Birdi and Jansen (2006) provide valuable insight on the management aspects of Intrusion Detection Systems and make several practical recommendations.

Establishing the risks realistically whilst managing the security budget is a typical management dilemma. Perfect access (no security restrictions) and perfect security (no access possible) are limiting cases between which an optimal position must be found. Mayfield's paradox (Mayfield & Cvitanic, 2001) mathematically characterizes the idea that beyond a certain point spending extra money on security improvements will produce diminishing returns: similarly, increasing the access levels becomes expensive at the limits. Similarly, overspending on security relative to the actual dangers reflects poor management so effective risk assessment in the business context is also signalled.

In considering internet security for businesses, Chang, Hwang, Yen and Huang (2006) reviewed the existing literature and established four factors that need to be considered (in their case in the financial sector, but the principles are more general). These were:

1. **Factors that affect hardware security**. These include:
   ◦ Natural disasters such as earthquakes or storms;
   ◦ Accidents, such as dropping a notebook computer or spilling coffee;
   ◦ Malicious acts, such as deliberate intrusion into computer systems;
   ◦ Hardware defects (bugs or software errors), such as security vulnerabilities found in software.
2. **Factors that affect software security**:
   ◦ Improper design of operating Systems, for example, security loopholes of improper use of software;

- ○ Stealing or illegal copying of application software. Examples of this include, pirating software or other forms of illegal copying.
3. **Human factors**:
    - ○ Human negligence, such as not keeping up to date with the latest virus protection software or failing to install security patches in operating systems or web browsers;
    - ○ Mistakes, such as opening malicious email attachments.
4. **External factors**:
    - ○ Unauthorized intrusions, such as Botnet or denial of service attacks.

These four factors can and should serve as a checklist for planning for any security related contingency that may arise. The planning for contingencies is often referred to as continuity planning, and this book devotes a chapter to this topic: a critical decision area for any business.

Whilst developing policies and plans for managing digital information requires a certain skill set, perhaps one of the most daunting requirements for a manager is the possibility of becoming legally involved in the disputes, breaches in regulations, or criminal activity arising from digital security problems in the workplace. Without awareness of digital evidence issues, cybercrime detection and prosecution will remain low. With this in mind, we conclude this chapter by providing a background to the special nature of digital evidence, vis-a-vis traditional evidence categories.[23]

Digital Evidence

Business managers rarely have a background or expertise in forensic investigations, yet increasingly they may be called on to undertake some form of investigative work in the event of some legal dispute, breach of personnel regulations, or criminal activity arising in the workplace (Stephenson, 2000). The inherent vulnerability of their digital information holdings means that weaknesses in their security exists and are constantly at risk of exploitation from internal and external threats (Stephenson, 2000). Consequently, the rise in computer-based crime and misuse of digital information for improper purposes has resulted in a concomitant reliance on digital evidence in criminal and civil investigations (Etter, 2001a; Palmer, 2001; Thompson, 1998).

Many legal practitioners and courts are still struggling to understand forensic science, notably evidentiary issues with DNA evidence, and more recently have been faced with new challenges posed by digital evidence (Bassett, 2006; Caloyannides, 2001; Edwards, 2005; Etter, 2001b; Losavio, 2006). Similarly, organizations are confused by digital evidence and may not clearly understand its potential benefits and limitations (Jordan, 2005).

Business managers may find themselves involved increasingly in the investigation environment with the responsibility of preserving the crime scene, locating, selecting, and validating digital evidence (Guidelines for the Management of IT Evidence, 2003). Having moved the evidence through the investigation process, business managers are likely to become involved with the process of constructing legal arguments that depend on the presentation of evidence in courts or other hearings. Significant issues also confront the legal fraternity over the use of evidence in court, especially when the evidence is based on digital exhibits.

Digital Evidence in the Legal Domain

Computer crime, or cyber crime, takes a variety of forms including unauthorized use of computers, fraud, forgery, damage and sabotage, unauthorized interception, unauthorized copying of software programs, data misappropriation, posting illegal material, industrial espionage, social engineering, and others (Berwick & Thompson, 1998; Carter, 1995). Recalling the collapses of large corporations, such WorldCom and Enron, that involved large-scale fraud, exemplifies the misuse and concealment of digital information for financial gain. Computers may also be incidental to other crimes by speeding up the computation of information or making it more difficult to detect crimes, such as money laundering and fraudulent banking transactions. The exponential growth of computers has engendered new variations of traditional crimes, such as breaches of copyright and software piracy.

While the Internet and modern communications provide many societies with personal and commercial benefits, users increasingly misuse these facilities for cheating, lying, stealing, and even crimes of violence (Mohay, 2003). So as cyber crime increases, law enforcement agencies try to play catch up with limited success. Increasingly, digital evidence forms an important part of criminal, civil cases and disciplinary proceedings; however, it is often notoriously too difficult to locate and analyze for it to be useful in such processes. The large size, complexity, and changing form of software applications and datasets, challenges experienced investigators. These challenges are normally far greater for legal practitioners and organizations' personnel, who may be involved in collecting and using digital evidence and who possess negligible cyber forensic[24] skills or understanding of the special nature of the evidence. Even with expert help, these investigations can be financially costly and time-consuming exercises that organizations may not consider viable (Sommer, 1998). In the event that such expertise was used, organizations would be well served if they possessed some basic understanding of the technical and the legal complexities of digital evidence.

Digital evidence is information found on a broad range of devices, and generally considered to consist of information held in digital data form, that has some value to the investigator seeking to reconstruct the key events of an incident, and the probative value of the evidence, if it is intended for use in legal proceedings. It is sometimes referred to as IT evidence, electronic evidence, or computer evidence (Ashcroft, 2001; Carrier & Spafford, 2005; Chaikin, 2006; Pollitt, 2001). According to Carrier and Spafford (2004), digital data may be defined as numerical representations, most usually in binary form. Digital evidence may be considered to include any digital data that may be used to establish whether a crime had been committed, or can establish a link between a crime and the victim of the crime, or between a crime and the perpetrator of that crime (Casey, 2000; Saferstein, 1998). Carrier and Spafford's often quoted definition describes digital evidence as *"any digital data that contain reliable information that supports or refutes a hypothesis about the incident"* (p. 3). The definition of what *reliable information* may consist of is examined in more detail in Chapter 3 in the context of evidence validation.

Sources of digital evidence include emails, electronic documents, spreadsheets, databases, system logs, audit logs, application logs, network management logs, network traffic capture, and file system data (Sommer, 1998). Digital evidence is located in files stored on hard drives; memory cards; access control devices, such as smart cards; biometric scanners; answering machines; digital cameras; personal digital assistants; electronic organizers, printers; removable storage devices; and media, such as CD-ROM and DVD discs; telephones; copiers; credit card skimmers; digital watches; facsimile machines; and global positioning systems (ACPO, 1999; Ashcroft, 2001). As new technologies emerge and existing ones converge, new environments, where digital evidence may be found, are created.

Carrier (2003) advocates using conventional crime scene investigation techniques to process digital evidence; however, digital evidence used in legal processes is often problematic as its validity and usefulness may be diminished because of its volatility, the complexity of the digital domain, large datasets, and rapid changes to technology (Mercuri, 2005; Sommer, 2000).

Digital evidence is sometimes considered superior to conventional paper evidence, as it is easier to locate and process (Caloyannides, 2001). Digital evidence normally contains useful metadata, such as key dates, times, and a history of the file, and because of its persistence in recording key data, it can provide proof of past events that an offender may prefer did not exist (Caloyannides; Janes, 2000). Moreover, digital evidence frequently provides metadata recorded from the date of its creation, that is more revealing than paper-based evidence providing potentially valuable information relating to a crime (Flusche, 2001; Janes).

Digital evidence shares characteristics with other forms of evidence, such as paper documents, but its complex technical properties can be problematic for investigators and auditors attempting to collect digital evidence for use in legal cases (Mercuri, 2005; Sommer, 2000). Lawyers and courts are often confused by these technical complexities and may misinterpret digital evidence, potentially resulting in unsound and unfair judgments for various parties involved in legal cases (Caloyannides, 2001; Edwards, 2005; Etter, 2001b; Losavio, 2006).

There are some inherent differences between conventional forms of evidence and digital evidence. Most notable is the ease with which digital evidence may be altered and manipulated, which may be difficult or impossible to detect (Caloyannides, 2001). Digital evidence is mutable and can be altered far more easily than physical records, and consequently, is more susceptible to unauthorized manipulation, making it difficult to validate its admissibility and evidentiary weight in legal proceedings (Akester, 2004; Mattord & Whitman, 2004; Schneier, 2000).

Despite the pervasiveness of computers in society, few legal practitioners have sufficient knowledge about the properties and functions of computers, networks, and digital information to assist them to prepare legal cases based on digital evidence (Mercuri, 2005; Sommer, 2000). The legal fraternity and organizations rely heavily on computer forensic investigators and other computer experts to provide some insight and explanation about digital evidence and its properties (Yasinsac, Erbacher, Marks, Pollitt, & Sommer, 2003).

Digital Evidence and the Public and Private Sectors

There are commonly considered to be two broad categories where digital evidence exists: the public sector investigations, within the domain of criminal law, undertaken by government law enforcement or regulatory agencies; and private sector investigations, initiated by corporations and sometimes by individuals (Enfinger, 2006). Public sector investigations focus on breaches of criminal laws, whereas private sector investigations usually relate to torts and other civil litigation, or disciplinary proceedings against employees. In practice, there is much similarity between public and private sector investigations and it is common for investigations in the public sector to become a civil case, and vice versa.

Public sector investigations seek evidence in pursuit of criminal activity, including fraud, identity theft, blackmail, extortion and most other criminal activity; whereas, private sector investigations may seek evidence of abuse of an organization's assets, such as sending malicious emails or abuse of Internet privileges in violation of company policy, and violations of intellectual property (Enfinger, 2006).

Criminal cases and civil actions rely increasingly on digital evidence for a range of events including theft of intellectual property, blackmail, unlawful access to confidential information, modification of the integrity of information, or making the targeted information unavailable for its intended use (Carter, 1995; Mattord & Whitman, 2003).

Evidence and Digital Evidence

Evidence used in legal cases may consist of witness testimony, hearsay, documents and things, and proves facts that are in dispute through directly proving the ultimate fact without relying on other evidence to prove any intervening, penultimate steps (Anderson & Twining, 1991; Tapper, 2004). Evidence is also used to prove the plausibility of facts from which facts that are being disputed may be understood: most notably, circumstantial evidence (Tapper, 2004). Circumstantial or indirect evidence, which includes documentary and digital evidence, is used to construct inferences that indirectly prove the ultimate fact in a legal case (Anderson & Twining, 1991; Stephenson, 2000).

Evidence of a legal nature proves facts that are in dispute and the weight that may be attached to the facts is examined and tested by various forms of legal argument (Anderson & Twining, 1991; Tapper, 2004). Developing legal argument can be a complex process taking in a broad range of evidentiary issues. Technically complex digital evidence used in constructing compelling legal arguments makes the process significantly more challenging for the stakeholders (Caloyannides, 2001; Mohay, 2003; Tapper; Wall, 2004; Yasinsac et al., 2003).

To Sommer (1998), legal proof relates to the admissibility and weight of evidence and is only distantly related to scientific proof that relies on generally recognized processes of scientific investigation. Evidence should be sufficiently relevant to the issues it is intended to prove to the court; if not relevant, or insufficient, it should be inadmissible (Tapper, 2004). Relevancy in a legal context is not universally defined, but Justice Stephen's nineteenth-century definition, as cited in the Oxford Journal of Legal Studies (Ho, 1999), still holds currency in some jurisdictions and may be helpful when contextualizing digital evidence with other evidence:

Any two facts to which it is applied are so related to each other that according to the common course of events one either taken by itself or in connection with other facts proves or renders probable the past, present, or future existence or non-existence of the other. (Stephen, cited in Ho, 1999, p. 404)

Although no formal universal definitions exist, evidence may be categorized into a range of types depending on the jurisdiction and its stature in the local hierarchy, including direct evidence, indirect evidence, hearsay evidence, and evidence of opinion. The following sections describe the effects that different categories of evidence may have on legal cases, which potentially have implications for business managers.

Direct Evidence and Circumstantial Evidence

Direct evidence, sometimes called witness or testimonial evidence, depends on the credibility of a human witness, and most evidence used in legal cases has traditionally been based on testimony from a range of witnesses, whose credibility may be upheld or refuted if it proves to be fallible (Walton, 2000). Direct evidence that directly proves the ultimate fact in a legal case, such as what the eye-witness saw or heard which is accepted by the court, has a high inferential value. Provided witness testimony is not in itself hearsay, it may be admissible in legal proceedings (Anderson & Twining, 1991; Silverstone & Sheetz, 2007).

By its nature, digital evidence is not direct evidence but circumstantial evidence, and may be considered hearsay evidence, that may only be admitted in legal proceedings under established procedures (Anderson & Twining, 1991). Based on the inferences of some inanimate object that indirectly proves the ultimate fact, circumstantial evidence is often used to build up inferences to prove some fact in issue, such as a knife found at a murder scene, whose blade matches the stab wound and on whose handle the fingerprints are those of the assailant. By linking the body to the knife, and in turn the knife to the assailant, links are formed in the chain of evidence (Anderson & Twining; Silverstone & Sheetz, 2007; Tapper, 2004; Walton, 2000).

Circumstantial evidence is probabilistic in nature and often challenging when attempting to determine the truth of an issue because the examination processes used are poorly defined (Fiske, 1991; Nisbett & Ross, 1980; Nisbett, Krantz, Jepson & Kunda, 1983). Digital evidence is analogous to the more conventional forms of circumstantial evidence, most notably documentary evidence, and both forms are subject to the same degree of legal scrutiny afforded to direct evidence tendered by a human witness who has, for example, observed directly the events of a document forgery (Caloyannides, 2001; Tapper, 2004). Digital evidence is mute and cross-examination of the evidence is not possible, unlike a human witness who is able to offer explanation and comment to the court.

The common law and legislation in various jurisdictions accept that the contents of a document need not be treated as a separate item of judicial evidence, although in many jurisdictions, legal convention makes it expedient to do this because the admission of documents is governed by special rules (Tapper, 2004). A court would accept as real evidence a document tendered in evidence as a chattel which, according to Tapper, could occur in the case of a document, that has been allegedly stolen, being tendered as an exhibit during a trial. However, if tendered as a statement, the evidence would be circumstantial, as occurs when tendering documents during legal title challenges. These precedents and legal rules have implication for the admissibility of digital evidence.

Normally, computer-based crime consists of human witness-based evidence and physical exhibits, such as fingerprints lifted from a computer keyboard; however, much of the evidence is digital in form and circumstantial in nature (Stephenson, 2000). Although, each piece of circumstantial evidence may not always hold sufficient weight to prove a case in its own right, its worth becomes apparent when it can be used with other evidence to form part of a compelling legal case (Stephenson, 2000).

Physical documents are commonly used as exhibits in a trial and are treated usually as supporting evidence in tandem with other evidence that forms the combined testimony for the presenting party; because of some perceived similarity with physical documents, digital evidence is treated the same in the courts (Tapper, 2004). It is common that a documentary exhibit is not submitted as evidence in isolation, but is supported by other related evidence that enhances its admissibility and reliability (Tapper, 2004). For example, a drug sample may require some independent proof of its seizure, analysis and safe-keeping measures, to ensure that there is less chance of its validity being damaged by a challenge from the opposing party. This may include the evidence of expert witnesses, a register of case exhibits, a photograph, some other visual record, or a witness statement (Tapper, 2004).

The same expectation of supporting evidence is true when digital evidence used in a testimony requires some explanation from system administrators and information managers. For example, in the process of linking a suspect, believed to have sent a threatening email to another person, a witness observed the suspect typing at the computer terminal used to send the threatening email at that exact time of the offence. Presented with this prima facie evidence, the investigator would attempt to link the properties of the computer operating system, such as date and time stamps, and the email containing the threat, to the direct evidence from the human witness that confirms the suspect was using the computer at the exact time the email was dispatched to the victim.

Even in what looks like a straightforward reconstruction of the case, the case would fail if the digital evidence was inadmissible, or its evidentiary weight weakened because of anomalies or uncertainty about the computer operating system and application software (Sommer, 2000). Now the investigator may seek explanation from knowledgeable personnel in the organization about the computer network, its operating and application programs, user access controls, system security, and so forth. This corporate knowledge could well form part of the legal case and require the organization's personnel to testify and provide explanation about the computer network and attest to the efficacy of its security.

Hearsay Evidence

Another commonly accepted form of evidence is hearsay evidence, and digital evidence may take the form of indirect evidence, or hearsay, depending on the context in which it is used (Casey, 2004). Hearsay evidence is any matter that a witness does not have direct experience of - something the witness has not observed through the five senses. For example, if John tells Ann about some event he witnessed but Ann did not witness the event, Ann cannot use that evidence, as she has no firsthand knowledge of what John observed. All Ann possesses is hearsay from John (Stephenson, 2000). Courts look to establish the credibility of the witness based on the perception of the witness, their memory and ability to recount their observation of relevant matter; hearsay evidence does not provide such credibility and the court cannot cross-examine a witness to satisfy itself of the credibility of the witness (Kenneally, 2004).

Hearsay evidence is usually inadmissible in common law jurisdictions, such as in Australia, the USA, the United Kingdom, and a number of other countries because its truthfulness cannot be verified; digital evidence falls within this convention (Casey, 2004; Kenneally, 2004). However, in these countries, because of special statutes, digital evidence is commonly admissible in civil proceedings and may be admitted as a matter of discretion in criminal cases, but this does raise claims that such leniency runs contrary to the interests of justice (Tapper, 2004). For example, business records, including electronic records, are admissible in evidence as an exception to the hearsay rule but are subject to certain requirements, such as would be maintained in normal business activities and assurances that reasonable measures were taken to protect the authenticity and accuracy of the records (Chaikin, 2006). It is common in cases, where this evidence is presented that the custodian of the records, or other qualified witness, is asked to provide some evidence that the records are trustworthy (Chaikin, 2006).

For private organizations, where the requirements for maintaining business records are less stringent than for a government organization, the courts may expect some additional evidence to attest to the trustworthiness of the computer system holding the records and the personnel managing the system. This could include testimony about the security and integrity of the system, and the existence of quality checks to verify the accuracy and authenticity of records (Marcella, 2002).

In terms of digital evidence, such as database records and audit logs, it has been argued that they are often automatically computer-generated and do not contain a statement of declaration from a human witness (Chaikin, 2006). Successful argument during some trials has allowed the admission of such records, but such admission is contingent on the reliability and accuracy of the computer software applications that create and record the evidence, and provided that they are created as part of the normal course of business (Chaikin,2006).

Hearsay challenges have been avoided in trials by successful argument that digital evidence constitutes an outcome of a pre-programmed computer function, such as the processing of admissible data, like the automatic recording and processing of data by a radar gun recording the speed of passing vehicle[25] (Kenneally, 2004).

Expert Evidence

Opinion of witnesses is not admissible in court hearings and witnesses are not permitted to present their own inferences and interpretation of their observations. The court would direct them to confine their evidence to recounting events they have directly observed. The rule is relaxed for expert and scientific witnesses, who may be allowed to provide their opinion that falls within their range of expertise (Tapper, 1999).

Other issues arise concerning the reliability of expert witnesses testifying in cases relying on digital evidence. For example, in courts in the United States of America, the Daubert standard requires that the expert witness must satisfy strict criteria including a requirement for them to establish their personal standing in the relevant discipline, such as in publication and teaching (Brodsky, 2000). Furthermore, an expert witness must also satisfy the court that methods and techniques used to form the expert's opinion require empirical testing, that methodologies and techniques were subject to peer review, publication and were accepted in the corresponding scientific community, and that there should be known error rates for methodology and techniques.

The use of standards and controls in the course of cyber forensic analysis would assist courts in determining the credibility of the expert witness (Barbara, 2008). However, at the time of writing, there are no generally accepted tests for cyber forensics; such tests would need to describe the theory and methods used to explain the intricacies of how computers work (Mohay, 2003). The difficulties in providing meaningful tests or templates are overwhelming, as every test carried out individually would only reflect the interaction of the event of evidentiary interest with the entire system. As no two sequences of events would be identical, it may be difficult to explain the technical processes involved to the courts. Consequently, Mohay believes that a special case could be made for digital evidence to have its own standard, independent of the Daubert standard.

While enhanced information security reduces the risk of vexatious investigations and legal remedies, an analysis of what resources are at risk from a multitude of threats must be professionally analyzed.

CONCLUSION

This chapter has provided statistics and comments associated with real threats to business from security breaches and attacks on information resources and has also described the nature of digital evidence increasingly relied upon to support criminal, civil, and internal disciplinary proceedings. The chapter has also provided a basic overview of the security problem from a management of Information technology resources point of view, through interviews with IT personnel in a small Australian University, and from a mid-sized Australian wide retail organization. Both the statistics reported and insights of the IT professionals, whilst illustrative, are likely to be reflected in many other organizations in many other countries. The risks to businesses and to customers have also been addressed, with risks to businesses being identified not only in stock market fluctuations, but also in terms of brand reputation.

From the interviews, two approaches to security emerged; one of intensive lock down using third party propriety software tools, usually in some kind of outsource arrangement; and a more liberal view taking into account specific needs of employees. An alternative school of thought is also acknowledged in the literature, specifically of Workman et al. (2008); one that highlights the human behavioral aspects, and suggests that employees should be made more aware of the vulnerability of the organization to security breaches and how serious the implications may be for them. This is recommended as an educational program with follow up training to ensure that employees treat the security issue seriously. The philosophy of this approach is based on studies that indicate that employees are lax about security and lack motivation to use existing security features, resulting in some cases of breaches in security from "even modest and uninspired security attacks" (Workman, et al., p. 2813). Future predictions consistently indicate that cybercrime will increase and that organizations need to be aware of potential threats. Whilst technical solutions, policies and continuity planning all continue to be relevant responses, awareness by employees of the real threats and an understanding of the importance of security measures, both internally and externally, appears to be the best defense against a catastrophic security breach event.

ACKNOWLEDGMENT

The authors would like to thank all respondents, including Ms. Maureen Klinkert (Director, ITS - Information Technology Service of the University of the Sunshine Coast), Mr. Barry Mahoney (Manager, ITS - Information Technology Service) and Mr. Barry Pollard (ICT Infrastructure Team Leader - Information Technology

Service University of the Sunshine Coast) for their insights into the problem from an educational industry perspective.

REFERENCES

Akester, P. (2004). Internet law: authenticity of works: authorship and authenticity in cyberspace. *Computer Law & Security Report, 20*(6), 436–444. doi:10.1016/S0267-3649(04)00088-3

Anderson, T., & Twining, W. (1991). *Analysis of evidence: How to do things with facts based on Wigmore's Science of Judicial Proof.* Evanston, IL: Northwestern University Press.

Ashcroft, J. (2001). *Electronic crime scene investigation: A guide for first responders.* Washington, U.S.: Department of Justice.

Association of Chief Police Officers (ACPO) (1999). *Association of Chief Police Officers: Good practice guide for computer based evidence.* National Hi-tech Crime Unit.

Australian Security and Investments Commission. (ASIC, 2007). *Scams target you! Protect your money.* Retrieved October 28, 2008, from http://www.fido.gov.au/asic/asic.nsf/byheadline/07-51+Scams+target+you!+Protect+your+money?op enDocument.

Bajari, P & Hortaçsu, A. (2004). *Economic insights from Internet auctions Economic Literature, 42*(2), 457-486.

Barbara, J. J. (2008). Appropriate standards and controls in computer forensics. *Forensic Magazine* (December 2007/January 2008).

Bassett, R., Bass, L., & O'Brien, P. (2006). Computer forensics: An essential ingredient for cyber security. *Journal of Science and Technology, 3*(1), 26–30.

Berwick, D. R., & Thompson, D. E. (1998). *Minimum provisions for the investigation of computer based offences (No. 1320-5579).* Payneham, South Australia: National Police Research Unit.

Birdi, T., & Jansen, K. (2006). *Network Intrusion Detection: Know What You Do (Not).* Need.

Brodsky, S. L. (2000). The expert witness: More maxims and guidelines for testifying in court. *The Journal of Psychiatry & Law, 28*(2), 289–292.

Business Enterprise and Regulatory Reform. (BERR, 2008). *Information Security Breaches Survey.* Retrieved January 31, 2009, from http://www.pwc.co.uk/pdf/BERR_2008_Executive_summary.pdf

Caloyannides, M. A. (2001). *Computer forensics and privacy.* Norwood, MN: Artech House.

Carrier, B., & Spafford, E. H. (2003). Getting physical with the digital investigation process. *International Journal of Digital Evidence, 2*(2), 1–20.

Carrier, B. D., & Spafford, E. H. (2004). Defining event reconstruction of a digital crime scene. *Journal of Forensic Sciences, 49*(6). doi:10.1520/JFS2004127

Carrier, B. D., & Spafford, E. H. (2005). *Automated digital evidence target definition using outlier analysis and existing evidence.* Paper presented at the 2005 Digital Forensic Research Workshop (DFRWS) New Orleans, LA. Retrieved 5 September 2008 from: http://www.dfrws.org/2005/proceedings/carrier_targetdefn.pdf

Carrier, B. D. S. Eugene. H. (2004). *An event-based digital forensic investigation framework.* Paper presented at the fourth annual Digital Forensics Research Workshop Baltimore, Maryland. Retrieved 12 October 2009 from http://www.dfrws.org/2004/index.shtml

Carter, D. L. (1995). Computer crime categories: how techno-criminals operate. *FBI Law Enforcement Bulletin,* (18, May, 2005, pp.21-26).

Casey, E. (2000). *Digital evidence and computer crime: Forensic science, computers and the Internet.* London: Academic Press.

Casey, E. (2004). *Digital evidence and computer crime: Forensic science, computers and the Internet* (2nd ed.). London: Academic Press.

Chaikin, D. (2006). Network investigations of cyber attacks: The limits of digital evidence. *Crime, Law, and Social Change, 46,* 239–256. doi:10.1007/s10611-007-9058-4

Chang, I. C., Hwang, H. G., Yen, D. C., & Huang, H. Y. (2006). An empirical study of the factors affecting Internet security for the financial industry in Taiwan. *Telematics and Informatics, 23,* 343–364. doi:10.1016/j.tele.2005.11.001

Edwards, K. (2005). Ten things about DNA contamination that lawyers should know. *Criminal Law Journal, 29*(2), 71–93.

Enfinger, F., Nelson, B., Phillips, A., & Steuart, C. (2006). *Guide to computer forensics and investigations* (2nd ed.). Boston, Massachusetts: Course Technology.

Etter, B. (2001a, 21-22 June 2001). *Computer crime*. Paper presented at the 4th National Outlook Symposium on Crime in Australia - New Crimes or New Responses, Canberra.

Etter, B. (2001b). The forensic challenges of e-crime. *Australasian Centre for Policing Research*, *3*(10), 1–8.

Fiske, S. T., & Taylor, S. E. (1991). *Social cognition* (2nd ed.). New York: McGraw-Hill.

Flusche, K. J. (2001). Computer forensic case study: Espionage, Part 1 Just finding the file is not enough! *Information Security Journal*, *10*(1), 1–10. doi:10.1201/108 6/43313.10.1.20010304/31394.6

Fraud Watch, I. (2007). Internet Fraud Watch and the Internet Crime Complaint Centre. Retrieved February 28, 2009, from http://www.crime-research.org/news/20.04.2007/2627/

Garg, A., Curtis, J., & Halper, H. (2003). Quantifying the financial impact of IT security breaches. *Information Management & Computer Security*, *11*(2), 74–83. doi:10.1108/09685220310468646

Gold, S. (2008). A newsworthy year. *Infosecurity*, *6*(1), 24–28. doi:10.1016/S1754-4548(09)70008-7

Ho, H. L. (1999). A theory of hearsay. *Oxford Journal of Legal Studies*, *19*(3), 403–420. doi:10.1093/ojls/19.3.403

Janes, S. (2000). The role of technology in computer forensic investigations. *Information Security Technical Report*, *5*(2), 43–50. doi:10.1016/S1363-4127(00)02006-9

Jordan, E., & Silcock, L. (2005). *Beating IT risks*. Chichester: John Wiley & Sons Ltd.

Journal, I. S. A. C. A. *1*. Retrieved November 26th 2009 from http://www.isaca.org/Template.cfm?Section=Home&CONTENTID=52143&TEMPLATE=/Content-Management/ContentDisplay.cfm

Kenneally, E. E. (2004). Digital logs—proof matters. *Digital Investigation*, *1*(2), 94–101. doi:10.1016/j.diin.2004.01.006

Losavio, M., Adams, J., & Rogers, M. (2006). Gap Analysis: Judicial experience and perception of electronic evidence. *Journal of Digital Forensic Practice*, *1*, 13–17. doi:10.1080/15567280500541462

Marcella, A. J., & Greenfield, R. S. (Eds.). (2002). *Cyber forensics: A field manual for collecting, examining and preserving evidence of computer crimes*. Boca Raton, Florida: CRC Press Ltd.doi:10.1201/9781420000115

Mattord, H. J., & Whitman, M. E. (2003). *Principles of information security: preparing tomorrow's information security professionals*. Boston, Massachusetts: Thomson Learning, Inc.

Mattord, H. J., & Whitman, M. E. (2004). *Management of information security*. Boston: Thomson Learning.

Mayfield, R., & Cvitanic, J. (2001) Mathematical Proofs of Mayfield's Paradox: A Fundamental Principle of Information Security. *Information Systems Control Journal, 2*. Retrieved from http://www.isaca.org/Template.cfm?Section=Home& CONTENTID=17181&TEMPLATE=/ContentManagement/ContentDisplay.cfm

Mercuri, R. (2005). Challenges in forensic computing. *Communications of the ACM, 48*(12), 17–21. doi:10.1145/1101779.1101796

Mohay, G. M. (2003). *Computer and intrusion forensics*. Boston: Artech House Inc.

Nikishin, A. (2004). Malicious software – past, present and future. *Information Security Technical Report, 9*(2). doi:10.1016/S1363-4127(04)00020-2

Nisbett, R. E., Krantz, D. H., Jepson, C., & Kunda, Z. (1983). The use of statistical heuristics in everyday inductive reasoning. *Psychological Review, 90*, 339–363. doi:10.1037/0033-295X.90.4.339

Nisbett, R. E., & Ross, L. (1980). *Human inference: Strategies and shortcomings of social judgment*. Englewood Cliffs, NJ: Prentice Hall.

Palmer, G. L. (2001). *A road map for digital forensic research*. Paper presented at the First Digital Forensic Research Workshop (DFRWS), Air Force Research Laboratory, Rome Research Site.

Pollitt, M. M. (2001, 16-19 October 2001). *Report on digital evidence*. Paper presented at the 13th INTERPOL Forensic Science Symposium, Lyon, France.

Saferstein, R. (1998). *Criminalistics: An introduction to forensic science* (6th ed.). Upper Saddle Rive, NJ: Prentice Hall.

Schneier, B. (2000). *Secrets and lies: digital security in a networked world*. New York: Wiley Computer Publishing.

Silverstone, H., & Sheetz, M. (2007). *Forensic accounting and fraud investigation for non-experts*. New Jersey: John Wiley & Sons, Inc.

Sommer, P. (1998). *Intrusion detection systems as evidence: Recent advances in intrusion detection.* London: Computer Security Research Centre, London School of Economics & Political Science. Retrieved February 28, 2009, from http://www.raidsymposium.org/raid98/Prog_RAID98/Full_Papers/Sommer_text.pdf

Sommer, P. (2000). Digital footprints: Accessing computer evidence. [Special Edition]. *Criminal Law Review (London, England),* 61–78.

Stephenson, P. (2000). *Investigating computer-related crime.* Boca Raton, Florida: CRC Press.

Tapper, C. (1999). *Cross and Tapper on evidence* (9th ed.). London: LexisNexis Butterworths.

Tapper, C. (2004). *Cross & Tapper on evidence* (10 ed.). London: LexisNexis Butterworths.

Thompson, D. E., & Berwick, D. R. (1998). *Minimum provisions for the investigation of computer based offences.* Payneham, South Australia: National Police Research Unit.

Unnamed. (2003). *Guidelines for the management of IT evidence: A handbook (HB171).* Sydney: Standards Australia International Ltd.

US Federal Trade Commission. (2007). *Consumer fraud and identity theft complaint data for 2006,* data accessed from Consumer Sentinel and Identity Theft Clearinghouse. Retrieved March 20, 2008, from http://www.tamingthebeast.net/blog/ecommerce/internet-fraud-statistics-0207.htm.

Wall, C., & Paroff, J. (2004). Cracking the computer forensics mystery. *UtahBar Journal, 17*(7).

Walton, D. N. (2000). Argumentation and theory of evidence . In *New trends in criminal investigation and evidence* (*Vol. 2,* pp. 711–732). Antwerp: Intersentia.

West-Brown, M. J., Stikvoort, D., Kossakowski, K.-P., Killcrece, G., Ruefle, R., & Zajicek, M. (2003). *Handbook of Computer Security Incident Response Teams (CSIRTs)* (2nd ed.). Pittsburgh, PA, USA: CMU/SEI.

Whitman, M. E., & Mattord, H. J. (2009). *Principles of Information Security* (3rd ed.). Thomson Course Technology.

Workman, M., Bommer, W. H., & Straub, D. (2008). Security Lapses and the omission of information security measures: A threat control model and empirical test. *Computers in Human Behavior, 24,* 2799–2816. doi:10.1016/j.chb.2008.04.005

Yasinsac, A., Erbacher, R. F., Marks, D. G., Pollitt, M. M., & Sommer, P. M. (2003). Computer forensics education. *IEEE Security & Privacy, 1*(4), 15–23. doi:10.1109/MSECP.2003.1219052

Young, J. R. (2006). Security lapses common at colleges. *The Chronicle of Higher Education, 53*(10).

ENDNOTES

[1]   A Botnet is a term used to describe software robots or bots (usually malicious) that automatically run through a computer network and are controlled remotely

[2]   Three Ways Internet Crime Has Changed. Retrieved November 26th 2009 from http://www.cio.com.au/index.php/id;1872516899

[3]   For more information on the technical issues, readers are advised to refer to specialist publications that address this area in more detail. In addition, the rapidly changing environment of the internet, in particular, Web 2.0 technology makes a complete and up to date analysis of all aspects impossible.

[4]   The interviews of managers aspect of this study was approved by the ethics committee of the University of the Sunshine Coast and managers participated on the basis of informed consent

[5]   A denial-of-service attack (DoS attack) or distributed denial-of-service attack (DDoS attack) is designed to make a website unavailable to customers. This is usually done through generating external requests for services that are not legitimate, thereby slowing down genuine requests.

[6]   Personal and corporate identity theft Retrieved November 26th 2009 from http://www.businesslink.gov.uk/bdotg/action/detail?type=RESOURCES&itemId=1075422219

[8]   The protocol used to define the specifications for an information security management system

[10]   Cloud computing is computer technology that allows services to be provided over the Internet in such a way that the end user does not need to have any expertise or knowledge of the technology.

[13]   GXS provides Global Electronic Data Interchange and business to business e-Commerce & Data Synchronization Solutions

[14]   United States Department of Homeland Security National Cyber Security Division (DHS-NCSD) (2008) Information Technology (IT) Security Essential Body of Knowledge (EBK): A Competency and Functional Framework for IT Security Workforce Development

[15]   Byrum T (2003) The Impact of the Sarbanes Oxley Act on IT Security Retrieved November 26th 2009 from http://www.sans.org/reading_room/whitepapers/casestudies/1344.php

[16]   ACPO 2007 Good Practice Guide for computer based electronic evidence Retrieved November 26th 2009 from http://www.acpo.police.uk/asp/policies/Data/gpg_computer_based_evidence_v3.pdf

[17]   Larry R. Leibrock (2008) Duties, Support Functions, and Competencies: Digital Forensics Investigators From: Handbook of Digital and Multimedia Forensic Evidence
Edited by: J. J. Barbara © Humana Press Inc., Totowa, NJ Retrieved November 26th 2009 from
http://www.springerlink.com/content/xl25207356548416/fulltext.pdf?page=1

[18]   Retrieved November 26th 2009 from http://www.enisa.europa.eu/cert_guide/pages/01.htm

[19]   G. Killcrece, K.-P. Kossakowski, R. Ruefle, M. Zajicek, (2003) Organizational Models for Computer Security Incident Response Teams (CSIRTs), Technical Report CMU/SEI-2003-HB-001, Software Engineering Institute, Carnegie Mellon University, Pittsburgh.

[20]   Virus Attacks Named Leading Culprit of Financial Loss by U.S. Companies in 2006 CSI/FBI Computer Crime and Security Survey press release at http://www.gocsi.com/press/20060712.jhtml

[21]   Security Auditor's Research Assistant Retrieved November 26th 2009 from http://www-arc.com/sara/Updated 1 May 2009. SARA's final release was in 2009.

[22]   Although dated now, a still thrilling account of surveilling and tracking down a hacker is given in Stoll's (1990) book The cuckoo's egg (the Bodley Head, London)

[23]   Chapter three provides more details on how to address this situation, should a forensic investigation be required.

[24]   Cyber forensics is also known as computer forensics and digital forensics

[25]   For more enlightenment on the argument for and against the admission of hearsay evidence see: Ho, H.L., A theory of hearsay. Oxford Journal of Legal Studies, 1999. 19(3): pp. 403 - 420.

Chapter 2
Digital Evidence

Richard Boddington
Murdoch University, Australia

ABSTRACT

Digital evidence, now more commonly relied upon in legal cases, requires an understanding of the processes used in its identification, preservation, analysis and validation. Business managers relying on digital evidence in the corporate environment need a greater understanding of its true nature and difficulties affecting its usefulness in criminal, civil and disciplinary proceedings. This chapter describes digital evidence collection and analysis, and the implications of common challenges diminishing its admissibility. It looks at determining the evidentiary weight of digital evidence that can be perplexing and confusing because of the complexity of the technical domain. Digital evidence present on computer networks is easily replaced, altered, destroyed or concealed and requires special protection to preserve its evidentiary integrity. Consequently, business managers seeking the truth of a matter can find it a vexing experience, unless provided with a clear appraisal and interpretation of the relevant evidence. Validating evidence, that is often complex and incomplete, requires expert analysis to determine its value in legal cases to provide timely guidance to business managers and their legal advisers. While soundly configured security systems and procedures enhance data protection and recovery, they are often limited in the way they preserve digital evidence. Unprepared personnel can also contaminate evidence unless procedural guidelines and training

DOI: 10.4018/978-1-60566-806-2.ch002

are provided. The chapter looks at the benefits for prudent organisations, who may wish to include cyber forensic strategies as part of their security risk contingency, planning to minimise loss or degradation of digital evidence which, if overlooked, may have adverse legal repercussions.

INTRODUCTION: THE INVESTIGATION DOMAIN

Chapter two introduced the digital evidence domain and this chapter expands on this by providing details of how to handle digital evidence in order to preserve its integrity in court.

Forensic science adopts six stages in the investigation of forensic evidence that recognize, preserve the scene, classify, compare and individualize, and reconstruct the evidence (Crime Scene Investigation, 1994). Cyber forensics is still in its infancy and non-standardized processes are common in some civil and criminal investigation agencies, and standards, if they do exist, vary in different jurisdictions (Baryamu-reeba & Tushabe, 2006; Carrier & Spafford, 2003; Whitcomb, 2002). Courts expect computer forensic investigators and forensic auditors to have a sound understanding of computer technology for their testimony to have any credibility. This technical expertise is also important in civil actions and disciplinary proceedings, not intended to appear in court cases, to ensure that natural justice takes place (Mohay, 2003).

Several cyber forensic investigation models are in use emphasizing slightly different stages in the investigation process, and there is no universally agreed model used by investigators (Yasinsac, Erbacher, Marks, Pollitt, & Sommer, 2003). Figure 1 is a simple model highlighting the processing of digital evidence in the investigative and legal domains. The investigation domain consists of four stages taken by investigators in evidence preservation, location, selection and validation that precede the two stages in the legal domain involving legal practitioners constructing and then presenting legal arguments (Boddington, Hobbs, & Mann, 2008).

Preserving the Evidence

Preserving the evidence is the critical first stage in the investigative domain and may be overlooked by business managers, who fail to appreciate the fragility of digital evidence and take the correct steps to avoid contamination or loss of the evidence. Well-intentioned, but uninformed and improper handling and examination may fail to stabilize the evidence and may actually cause it to be altered, damaged, destroyed or contaminated (Ashcroft, 2001; Carrier, & Spafford, 2003). It is important to minimize overwriting digital evidence at the point of seizure and during the copying

Figure 1. Evidence processing stages in the investigative and legal domain. (Adapted from Boddington, Hobbs, & Mann, 2008).

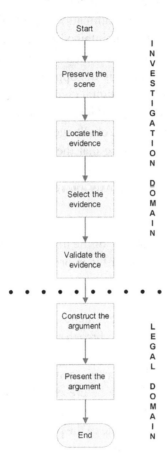

process, as it must be preserved in a pristine state for the examination and analysis stages of an investigation (Carrier, 2005).

When tendering evidence during legal proceedings, proof is required about the exhibit to verify it is the same as the exhibit seized at the crime scene. For a record to be admissible in legal hearings, a history of its condition, that is, an unbroken record of its state from creation to the time of its presentation as evidence is a legal requirement (Stephenson, 2000; Tapper, 2004). This condition is commonly referred to as the chain of custody and any break in the history of the chain potentially degrades its admissibility, as well as its evidentiary value (Stephenson, 2000; Association of Chief Police Officers, 1999; Whitcomb, 2002). In the case of a computer crime, such exhibits would include a hard drive, a storage device or a forensic image of a hard drive containing digital evidence obtained from a computer or storage device.

If the chain of custody is broken, the court can deny admissibility if the break is serious or, if not, can admit the evidence and let the jury decide whether it affects the weight of the evidence during examination (Marcella & Greenfield, 2002).

The chain of custody must be maintained to show that the evidence was preserved in its original state, and was uncontaminated; otherwise, the evidence may become inadmissible if challenged by the opposing party (Casey, 2000). It is difficult, but not impossible to collect digital evidence without altering it and various processes and forensic tools are used. Otherwise, any rigorous examination of the digital evidence could pose a serious challenge to its admissibility and evidentiary weight as courts do expect assurance that the chain of custody is intact (Tapper, 2004). In submitting digital evidence, challenges must be expected from the court and opposing legal teams, who will insist on verification of key issues (Whitcomb, 2002). These include:

- Guarantees about the reliability of the history of the custody of the exhibit
- Reasonable proof that the record is in pristine condition
- Proof of who created the record
- How the record was created
- Confirmation of the record's genuineness, completeness and accuracy
- Confirmation that there been no breach of confidentiality.

In the same way as a traditional crime scene is preserved, so must the physical crime scene holding digital evidence be preserved to prevent continued access to the potential evidence that may, for example, be stored in a computer or network server (Carrier & Spafford, 2003). One of the problems confronting investigators is the well-intentioned, but often disastrous, attempts by an organization's personnel, with little investigative training, to preserve the evidence for later analysis. Such actions often lead to evidence being lost or altered, sometimes rendering it inadmissible or lessening its evidentiary worth (Rogers & Seigfried, 2004; Stambaugh, Beaupre et al., 2000).

Because of the volatile and semi-volatile nature of data stored on a computer, it is inevitable that some evidence and corroborating data will be lost or modified when attempting to access and copy digital evidence. Volatile data requires a constant power supply to remain in the computer memory and is erased when the power is interrupted or shut down, unlike non-volatile memory or persistent data (Rowlingson, 2004). Consequently, shutting down the power to a computer can cause a loss of volatile memory in registries, random access memory, caches, network topologies and so forth.

Locating digital evidence may involve seizing all the hardware and software or locating the evidence and copying the relevant data. Seizing a stand-alone computer may inconvenience the individual suspect, but removing the entire hardware and software from an organization would be impractical and bring its operations to a standstill; therefore investigators would normally obtain a forensic image of the data (Casey, 2000, 2002).

Broadly speaking, because of the ephemeral nature of digital evidence, investigators must consider accessing the evidence through one of two processes: a live analysis and a dead analysis (and sometimes a combination of both). A live analysis occurs when the computer or network believed to hold digital evidence remains running and the investigator accesses the system to search and examine the evidence in a real-life setting (Carrier, 2005). There are disadvantages in using the live analysis approach, as it may result in data being overwritten or lost, and false information could be retrieved if some software programme has been set as a booby trap to conceal or destroy evidence (Carrier, 2005). A dead analysis occurs after the system has been shut down and trusted application tools are used to capture the evidence and may avoid the pitfalls of a booby-trapped system, but it is becoming impractical to seize anything more than actual terminals (Adelstein, 2006; Carrier).

In the past investigators have opted for dead analysis to capture and preserve digital evidence from fear of modifying it, yet the process of shutting down the computer modifies date and time stamps, and may permanently lock the investigator out of a password protected and encrypted hard drive (Casey, 2002). Passwords and knowledge of what was operating at the time the computer was shut down may also be lost (Casey). Evidence garnered during live analysis, however, provides evidence that would not be available from a forensic image of the system, thereby capturing a snapshot of the system that cannot be reproduced later (Adelstein, 2006). The courts have questioned the admissibility of digital evidence because of concerns of contamination during live analyses, even though it is evolving as the pragmatic means of collecting evidence from larger systems and datasets (Adelstein). However, provided any data loss is noted by the investigator, the courts may accept that the data loss does not detract from the remaining evidence presented, subject to explanation being provided by the investigator (Carrier, 2005).

Locating the Evidence

Once secured on the target computer system, the process of locating relevant evidence is undertaken. The location stage commences with an examination of the hardware devices suspected of storing the evidence and the data held on the devices. This stage includes filtering extraneous matter from that relevant to the investigation - a tedious task for trained investigators and more so for non-specialist personnel. The evidence may take the form of: electronic files; an email; user access logs; image files; traces of hacker intrusions, such as rootkit files; and records of unauthorized, or suspect access to information (Casey, 2000). Searching through the large amount of files stored on a computer or network makes this a challenging exercise when seeking important information about the suspected crime or event of interest, so that investigators may focus on obvious areas of interest within the system. Sufficient knowledge of criminal or civil case, investigative experience, and technical expertise is required to locate relevant digital evidence. Recognizing the evidence is a major obstacle because unlike a traditional crime scene, there is no body or smoking gun and very few clues to help the investigator; often there may be no obvious telltale signs at all (Caloyannides, 2003; Stephenson, 2000). Detecting fraud, for example, has always been problematic: even acknowledging fraud exists bewilders those not previously victim to it. Auditors, who tend to concentrate on finding and analysing large discrepancies, habitually fail to see a group of smaller anomalies that collectively could indicate fraud or some other illegal or improper activity (Silverstone & Sheetz, 2007). In seeking digital evidence, it is the small anomalies, or oddities, that are just as important as the large differences.

The primary role, when seeking the truth of a matter under investigation, includes locating evidence that supports the preliminary hypothesis, but just as important is locating evidence that refutes the hypothesis, also known as exculpatory evidence (Carrier & Spafford, 2003). Locating and identifying the digital evidence for the given class of crime or violation is required to support or refute hypotheses about the incident and an investigator uses various technical tools and investigative processes to accomplish this important task. Once preserved, the data on the computer or other device is examined to locate the evidence about the incident that has prompted the investigation (Carrier & Spafford). It may be discovery of evidence on a competitor's computer network that will clarify whether intellectual property has been misused in a civil action, or it may involve seeking evidence of downloading illegal and offensive images from the Internet in a crime investigation. If, for example, illegal images or stolen documents are being sought, then files with image and document extensions will be located and examined. In the event of a security breach, where unauthorized access was gained to protected records, then the user access logs would be a logical starting point to commence an investigation (Carrier & Spafford).

Investigators use a variety of forensic toolkits to help them search large datasets and complex, computer file structures to identify files of relevance to the case. These tools help filter and data mine large datasets and identify hidden or deleted evidence in obvious and more obscure locations, but for the main part, the experience of the investigator drives the examination of potential evidence, which is predominantly a mechanical process (Gong & Chan, 2005). During examination of the available information, the investigator discards what is considered irrelevant data and selects potential evidence, which is then refined through tedious, time-consuming and iterative processes in an attempt to recreate as much of the crime scene as possible (Gong & Chan).

It should be mentioned that not everybody wishes the evidence to be found or the crime to be investigated, and it is not uncommon for managers to conceal the misdemeanors of subordinates; sometimes to avoid bringing themselves into disrepute (Stephenson, 2000). Organizations are often inclined not to prosecute employees because of feared adverse publicity and are reluctant to seek assistance from law enforcement agencies. Many law enforcement agencies are under-resourced and have lengthy investigation waiting lists, further compounding this reluctance for organizations to seek redress through prosecution. Moreover, computer crime is sometimes considered less personal than a crime of violence or a burglary and it is not always possible to identify a victim. Investigating computer crimes involves costly, resource hungry investigations that are often protracted, seldom bringing culprits to justice, and so organizations are less inclined to resort to prosecution or litigation than in more traditional crimes, or at least in the case of smaller impact crimes.

Selecting the Evidence

The next stage in the investigation process is to select the evidence that will form part of a legal case. For those not familiar with investigations it is common to misread the readily available evidence and draw incorrect conclusions. Business managers attempting to analyze what they consider are the facts of a case would be wise to seek legal assistance in selecting and evaluating evidence on which they may wish to base a case. Selecting the evidence, sometimes referred to as the analysis stage, or event reconstruction stage, involves analysis of the located evidence to determine what events occurred in the system, their significance, and probative value to the case (Ashcroft, 2001; Carrier & Spafford, 2003). Using available evidence, including digital, physical and human evidence, a reconstruction of the crime, or events under investigation, provides a clearer understanding of what happened (Casey, 2002). Evidence that supports the initial crime hypothesis is collated along with exculpatory evidence that refutes the hypothesis for analysis (Carrier & Spafford). The outcome of this process will help refine or change hypotheses and should identify an alternative hypothesis. This is important because many jurisdictions require details of exculpatory evidence to be provided to the defending party to enable them to rebut the prosecution's case during later proceedings (Stephenson, 2000).

As in conventional crime investigations, investigators look for motive (why?), means (how?) and opportunity (when?) for suspects to commit the crime, but in cases dependant on digital evidence, it can be a vexatious process (Stephenson, 2000).

Motive

The motive of wrongdoers in cyber crime ranges from internal and external threats, such as mischief, fraud, theft and sabotage of information, extortion, threats of violence, and even business warfare.

Means

The means may vary and depend on the technical knowledge and skills of wrong-doers and their ability to access targeted systems. Reconstructing the events of the crime, by examining the computer system operating system and relevant files, can provide an insight into the means used to affect the crime or misdemeanor, but this requires considerable technical and investigative skills in more complex cases.

Opportunity

Opportunity can be difficult to verify as various issues can make it difficult or im-possible to link the time of the crime to the suspect's access to the computer system (Stephenson, 2000). Poorly configured system access security, the absence of audit journals, or malicious software events, for example, can obliterate, or make event records less than reliable, and create gaps in the chain of evidence needed for the crime reconstruction process. Audit logs are often relied upon heavily to link a sus-pect to an event but even logs can be falsified if they are not protected adequately from mischief-makers or system errors (Stephenson, 2000).

False evidence too can be generated upon which unreliable arguments are pro-pounded by those unfamiliar with the true nature of the digital domain (Diaconis & Mosteller, 1989; Koehler & Thompson, 2006). Koehler and Thompson advise caution when attempting to select circumstantial evidence that seems to support reasonable and compelling argument, but which may well be unreliable because it is are purely coincidental and nothing more. Moreover, investigators may miss evidence or worse still, resort to cherry-picking when choosing or omitting evidence to gain legal advantage.

Presupposing guilt or innocence of a suspect may be based on the absence of evidence. For example, a suspect may claim use of a different computer than the terminal used to commit some illegality, but the evidence to support the alibi may not be recorded in the network logs. Consequently, an absence of evidence does not necessarily show evidence of absence of some important event that did occur, but which can no longer be proven, which is a common phenomenon of the digital domain (Berk, 1983; Flusche, 2001; Koehler & Thompson, 2006).

Therefore, it should always be at the forefront of the business manager's mind that computers behave unpredictably and that they would unwise to accept any digital evidence at face value. Users can alter digital evidence intentionally or unintentionally, thereby obfuscating the chain of key events. The behavior of the computer operating system and software applications may not have been analyzed thoroughly, thereby prompting premature and unsafe conclusions. Validating the evidence, therefore, is a key stage in preparing the digital evidence for a legal case.

Validating the Evidence

During the validation stage the evidence is tested to determine its validity, namely if the assertion drawn from the digital evidence can be verified. For example, the assertion that an email message was deleted would require confirmation of the existence of the deleted file; that it was deleted at a specific time; that this information was not altered by system processes; and so forth. Whatever security measures exist on the host computer, they are not always helpful to the investigator as they are more often intended for auditing and monitoring the overall integrity of records, rather than for specifically validating digital evidence (Carrier, 2005). During the validation stage, the investigator may revisit the location and selection stages to seek verification of validity issues and to develop new lines of investigation as circumstances dictate (Carrier & Spafford, 2003).

Figure 2 shows a simple chain of evidence based on apparent or available evidence consisting of unprocessed facts from which a tentative hypothesis can be constructed. In this case, reconstruction of evidence based on human, physical, and digital evidence, suggests that the suspect accessed a computer with the intent to download illegal content from the Internet.

Figure 3 outlines a proposed validation interrogation process where exhibit F, taken from the chain of evidence example in Figure 2, requires validation (Boddington et al., 2008). A series of prompts determines if the evidence is valid. Each exhibit needs validating, and if we take Exhibit "F" for example, there is a presumption that the suspect used the peer-to-peer application Limewire to access illegal images on the Internet. Questions that should be asked include, the ability to link the suspect to the computer and the opening of the software, and that the date and times of these events can be verified. If these questions are not corroborated or are inconclusive, then this will have an adverse effect on the case. Additional evidence may be required, or other legal strategies considered, using the best evidence available.

Failure to locate all available digital evidence occurs because the location of relevant evidence is not always evident to the untrained enquirer, who may be relying solely on intuition (Cohen, 2006). While a technically astute and assiduous investigator can identify and analyze much relevant evidence, time constraints and

Figure 2. Chain of Evidence before validation of the evidence

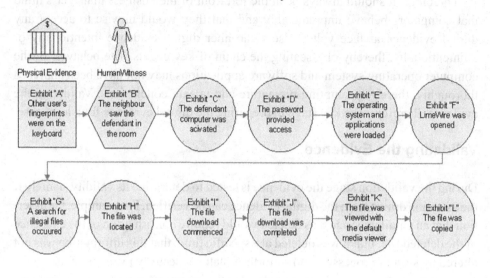

Figure 3. Chain of Evidence: Showing the validation process of digital evidence exhibit F. (Adapted from Boddington, Hobbs, & Mann, 2008).

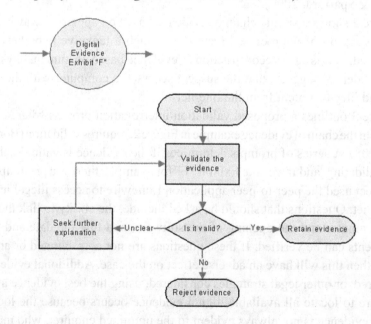

the uniqueness of the crime scene may, nevertheless, produce incomplete identification of all that should be located, consequently denying examination and analysis of crucial facts (Australasian Centre for Policing Research, 2000). Incomplete scrutiny of the available evidence during the validation stage of the investigative process and failure to validate the evidence at that point is where the investigation can fail (Cohen). The complexity of the digital domain compounds the problem and prosecution cases often fail during trials where the incompetence of the investigation is apparent and where validation issues arise.

There is error in every analysis method and the reliability of any particular test remains an issue for forensic investigators (Cohen, 2006; Palmer, 2002). A range of different factors can affect the validity of the evidence, including collection tools missing critical evidence, failure of the prosecution or a plaintiff to report exculpatory data, evidence taken out of context and misinterpreted, misleading or false evidence, failure to identify relevant evidence, system and application processing errors, and so forth (Cohen; Palmer). When presenting a legal case based on what appears to be convincing digital evidence, the case can collapse if the defense can show that the security or integrity of the network is defective and shows contamination or alteration of the digital evidence it is supposed to protect (Akester, 2004; Mattord & Whitman, 2004; Schneier, 2000). Conversely, if the validity of the evidence can be established, its weight in legal argument is enhanced.

Caloyannides (2003) asserts that because the legal fraternity understands little about computer science, the potential for miscarriages of justice are great, adding that the cyber forensics community exploits this situation and obfuscates the environment by focusing on issues such as preserving, collecting, and presenting digital evidence. Caloyannides warns that evidence found on computer systems can be contaminated intentionally or unintentionally through a range of factors, and it may not always be possible to determine the truth of a matter; yet faulty evidence continues to be accepted by the courts without proper validation. The evidence collated and processed during the investigative stages is then presented to the legal practitioner, who must test each piece of evidence to determine its weight in the legal argument and its suitability for use to prove or disprove the case.

Presenting Digital Evidence in Legal Cases

Having located and selected digital evidence and incorporated it in legal argument in a case that results in some legal adjudication, the next hurdle a business manager must tackle is having the evidence admitted to proceedings. Before digital evidence may be admitted in court proceedings, it may be required to meet additional conditions imposed by legislation and court conventions (Caloyannides, 2001; Tapper, 2004). The first condition is acceptance by the examining body, such as a court, to grant admission of the material tendered as evidence suitable for later examination and rebuttal by the opposing party (Tapper). Failure to have the evidence admitted precludes its use in the subsequent legal processes. The second condition subjects the evidence to rigorous, judicial examination of its evidentiary worth or weight. There is not as yet any formal accord on the admissibility and weight of digital evidence (Mohay, 2003). The following sections look at how jurisdictions treat these two conditions.

Admissibility of Evidence

Clearly, evidence that is denied admission in court proceedings becomes irrelevant to the case and detrimental to one of the contending parties (Tapper, 2004). Irrespective of whether tendered evidence is direct, circumstantial or hearsay, for it to be admissible in court proceedings, the court must be satisfied that it is authentic and unmodified. In the case of digital evidence, some forensic expertise may be required to ensure that the evidence is trustworthy (Casey, 2000).

Physical documents are tangible objects that require traditional storage and management processes to ensure, that when tendered in evidence, they comply with evidentiary requirements of the courts. Prior to the 1990s, documentary evidence was mostly on paper, with digital evidence usually taking the form of printed pages (Caloyannides, 2001). Subsequently, organizations have relied increasingly on computerized functions to manage their activities and for storing and maintaining their information records, which means the majority of documentary exhibits are digital or created from digitized information (Akester, 2004).

An organization's viability, and sometimes its continued existence, hinges on its ability to protect important information records adequately from a range of threats. The ability to preserve important digital records of potential evidentiary value is also of great importance to an organization (Baraani-Dastjerdi, Pieprzyk, & Satavi-Naini, 1996). Failure to protect digital evidence can result in it being discredited and its admissibility barred by the courts. The admissibility of documents tendered in legal proceedings is subject to legislation, case law, precedent, and the legal conventions of different jurisdictions (Caloyannides, 2001). Not surprisingly, the laws and rules governing evidence present a diversity of conditions that evidence tendered must meet before it may be admitted in court proceedings (Tapper, 2004). Evidence is often used to prove facts in issue, or facts from which facts in issue may properly be inferred; comprising the testimony of witnesses, hearsay, documents, and other physical objects. In using documents as evidence in legal processes, the contents of a document may be incorporated in the sworn evidence of a witness.

Courts have agonized over the admissibility of digital evidence, as legal anomalies may arise that hinder their presentation as evidence (Mattord & Whitman, 2004;

Schneier, 2000). Courts continue to debate the admissibility and reliability of DNA evidence used in trials, which shows some parallel issues over the admissibility and weight of digital evidence used in court proceedings (Myers, Reinstein, & Grille, 1999). These anomalies may occur because of the scientific complexities of DNA evidence, and in the case of digital evidence, complex technical issues relating to its special properties and environment, which often makes it hard for lawyers and courts to understand the nature and value of the evidence presented (Myers et al., 1999).

In 1979, the United States Department of Justice (Computer Crime, Criminal Justice Resource Manual, 1979) partitioned computer crime into three categories: computer abuse, computer crime, and computer-related crime. These definitions were blurred by the vast proliferation of computers and computer related products during the 1980s, and some technical and legal observers believed that any significant advances in computer technology should be mirrored by parallel changes in computer law (Morris, 1990).

In 1986, information technology security consultants were critical of legal practitioners, judges and legislators for failing to come to terms with technical advances in computer development that impact on the admissibility of digital evidence (Luddy Jr., 1986). This apparent failure to update legislation to enhance the admissibility of digital evidence was still not resolved when, even in 1990, a lack of universal agreement on what constitutes a computer crime, in the legal community, in the United States, was identified; such inertia being attributed in part to the rapid changes in computer technology and communications (Morris, 1990).

Some observers contend that well-defined legal definitions of computer crime are overdue and should be constructed to capture all acts which are criminal and involve computers (Morris, 1990). While acknowledging that the completeness of a definition seems problematic, some commentators believed it feasible by using technical, computer security concepts to examine a legal concept from a technical perspective that may yield insights into its strengths and weaknesses and even suggest avenues for legislative improvement (Morris). However, nothing significant has been tabled at the time of writing this chapter, in early 2009.

When admitted as evidence, difficulties remain when attempting to authenticate the authorship and antecedents of digital records - more so than in the past when paper document forgeries were common but required a high degree of technical expertise to make them convincing and avoid scrutiny (Akester, 2004). Digital forgeries are so much easier to carry out and it is not always possible to detect sufficient evidence to prove a forgery took place. Consequently, a legal precedent was set, jurisdictions were reasonably comfortable with the authenticity of paper documents, and documents presented in digital evidence form seem to have been awarded the same treatment. According to Akester, authenticity requires validation that the record is what it purports to be, whether its author is the real author, whether it is the genuine record or a substitute, and so forth.

In the United States of America, Rule 1003 (Admissibility of Duplicates) of the Federal Rules of Evidence, indicates that a copy of a document is equally admissible as evidence as the original provided the copy is produced by a process that ensures its accuracy and genuineness (Mercuri, 2005). Many state legal codes are based on Rule 1003 and this legislation was anticipated to be the focus for lawyers to raise questions about the validity of digital evidence.

Security researchers are increasingly concerned that digital evidence held in networked computers is not protected adequately to preserve its admissibility and, ultimately, its evidentiary weight (Akester, 2004; Halleck, 1996; Schneier, 2000). As mentioned previously, digital evidence is vulnerable to a variety of threats, both intentional and unintentional, as well as technical and non-technical attacks. Technical attacks may compromise the security of a controlled system, whereas a non-technical attack may consist of natural events or insider attacks by humans (Mattord & Whitman, 2004). Cognizant of these threats to computer networks, Australian courts have expressed doubts about the reliability of digital evidence recognizing its vulnerability to a range of threats. Although not clearly defined, the courts' concern over reliability appear to focus on authenticity and integrity of digital evidence, but again provides no helpful definition and explanation of these terms in the context of a wide range of legal cases.

Concerns raised by Australian judges over Section 155 of the Evidence Act 1995 (Commonwealth of Australia) was a departure from the earlier trend towards formulating a unilateral reliability of digital evidence. This section of the legislation asserts proof of authenticity and integrity of Australian Commonwealth departmental records, or public records of a state or territory, by allowing the production of a document purporting to be such a record if signed by the relevant minister. These ministerial certificates allow the printed copies of digital records to be admitted as documentary evidence (Nezovic v Minister of Immigration and Multicultural and Indigenous Affairs, 2003). In 2003, legal challenges to the interpretation of the ministerial certificates issued under the provisions of the Migration Act 1958, resulted in two court rulings about the admissibility of digital evidence used to produce the certificates. The appeal judges ruled that while section 155 of the Act facilitated the admissibility of records that might otherwise be inadmissible, section 155 did not negate the admissibility of digital evidence. However, the judges ruled that although section 155 did provide the convenience of certifying the production of computer-generated information held by the department, if subsequently challenged, then the truth of the contents of the digital information tendered as evidence would still need to be established by the department.

The various Evidence Acts of Australia contain a number of provisions facilitating proof of digital evidence. In November 2004, the Australian Law Reform Commission (ALRC) publicly requested commentary from interested parties on the viability of the uniform Evidence Acts of Australia. Of particular interest to the ALRC was comment it sought on the impact of computer-produced evidence on court proceedings, under section 48 that permits the tendering of such documents (Review of the Evidence Act 1995, 2004). Sections 146 and 147 of the Act were intended to facilitate the admissibility of evidence produced by processes, machines and other devices. In 2005, the Commission decided that a major overhaul of the legislation was unwarranted and not desirable as there was little evidence of problems arising from the operations of sections 146 and 147 and little empirical evidence that a more rigorous test was justified (Australian Law Reform Commission, 2005a).

Australian courts will admit certificates provided by prosecutors, certifying, for instance, that a speed camera has been prepared in accordance with the appropriate legislation (Warren, 1997). The admissibility of this evidence, that the reading in the device is proof of the speed, is based on digital records; such evidence may be challenged, but defense lawyers claim that speed camera legislation is biased to the prosecution (Warren, 1997). This de facto "proof of innocence" burden (Section 5.2) contrasts markedly with most other criminal cases, where the onus is with the prosecution to prove a charge beyond reasonable doubt. Speed camera, radar device legislation reverses the onus to a defendant but this may be seen as inequitable as most defendants' ability to mount a spirited and compelling defense is restricted by high costs, including payment for technical witnesses to challenge the digital evidence (Warren, 1997).

Very few speed camera cases are challenged and most that are, rarely have a positive outcome for the defendant. However, in August 2005 the Hornsby Local Court in New South Wales dismissed a motor vehicle speeding case after the New South Wales Road Traffic Authority (RTA) failed to produce an expert witness to prove a speed camera image had not been doctored, thereby reversing the onus back on to the prosecution (Schneier, 2004). When challenged by the defense, the RTA was unable to prove the authenticity of MD5 encryption algorithms used to protect the integrity of each picture stored in the police database. The MD5 algorithm, developed in 1992, was used as a security measure to prove the pictures have not been altered after they were taken (*The Age*, 2005; Schneier, 2004). Consequently, the motorist escaped a conviction by claiming that data was vulnerable to hackers after mathematicians in China decrypted the MD5 algorithm, and the motorist's lawyer argued successfully that the algorithm was discredited technology. It is debatable that the algorithm is unreliable, as it is still in common use.

Not all evidence found may be used if it is subject to court rules of exclusion concerning evidence improperly or illegally obtained, usually relevant only to criminal cases requiring a search warrant to locate and seize evidence. However, in corporate cases, the defendant may claim a breach of privacy in an attempt to prevent admissibility of digital evidence (Stephenson, 2000). It should be noted that although admissibility may not be an issue for digital evidence used in disciplinary proceedings, it would be prudent for an organization to ensure that the evidence has been processed, and thoroughly validated, to whether the ordeals of a potential legal suit from employees (Mohay, 2003).

Weight of Evidence

Once admitted, the evidence itself is subject to further scrutiny by the jury, or in the absence of the jury, the judge, magistrate or adjudicator, who will look at the evidentiary worth or weight of evidence of the tendered exhibits. Consequently, the legal practitioner must examine each piece of evidence to determine its weight in the legal arguments, and its suitability, whether the evidence supports or disproves the case. This analysis relies on identifying logical threads of inferences, linking one piece of evidence to another, with the strength of each inference used to determine the overall weight of a case (Silverstone & Sheetz, 2007). The persuasiveness that flows from the combined evidence presented in a legal case is used by adjudicators and juries to ascertain the guilt or innocence of the accused party or, in civil cases, the liability of a contesting party (Silverstone & Sheetz; Tillers, 2005).

A collation of evidence is tendered as part of the legal argument in an attempt to persuade the court of the probability of some truth or other matter. For example, in the case of a negligence suit, the court must be persuaded that the defendant did not exercise due care (Demougin & Fluet, 2006). In a civil case, it is important to establish a preponderance of evidence to show that something is more likely to have occurred, than otherwise (Devitt & Blackman, 1977). In the USA, the United Kingdom and Australian, for example, civil courts generally accept that the degree of certainty is above 50%. In other countries, including Germany and France, a preponderance of evidence in civil cases is often insufficient and requires a higher burden of proof; this is similar to criminal cases in Australia where proof beyond reasonable doubt is required (Demougin & Fluet, 2006).

In the past, courts may have been inclined to accept the weight of digital evidence based on expediency and intuition, or, if confused by technical issues, have dismissed cases out of hand. However, there is the likelihood of increased legal challenges that cast doubt on the weight of the evidence in the future (Ahmad, 2002; Pospesel et al, 1997; Schneier, 2000; Tapper, 2004; Whitcomb, 2002; Whitman & Mattord, 2005). This is evident by the growth in computer-based crime and greater reliance on digital evidence, both as partial evidence in otherwise conventional legal cases, or where the evidence exists entirely in digital form (Cohen, 2006; Etter, 2001; Palmer, 2001; Thompson & Berwick, 1998).

Information held in computers may be presented to courts as a printed document; the computer having in effect served as an electronic filing cabinet that stores information in much the same ways as a traditional filing cabinet (Stephenson, 2000). Courts will admit such documents but genuineness, completeness, and accuracy may be questioned because of the properties of the electronic filing cabinet that holds the history of the document in digital form (Stephenson). It is not the printed or monitor-viewed form of the digital evidence that is of concern, but the need for some assurance that it is the genuine article; the evidence must be validated before the weight of evidence can be considered.

In the case of a Multanova vehicle speed detectors used in Australian jurisdictions, the photograph of the speeding vehicle's number plates suggests that a vehicle registered to the owner was exceeding the speed limit at a confirmed location, date, and time. Unless there is other evidence to link the owner to the vehicle, such as a photograph of the driver, there is no proof the owner was driving the vehicle at the time of the offence; additional evidence is required to link the owner to the vehicle at the relevant time. Constructing legal argument is the next stage in progressing a case through the legal system.

Constructing Legal Argument

Legal argument relies on evidence that proves or disproves a case; based on the available evidence, the defendant is guilty or innocent of a crime. Legal practitioners use logical chains of inferences, linking one piece of evidence to another with the strength of each inference used to determine the weight of a case. The persuasiveness that flows from the combined evidence presented in a legal case is used to enable adjudicators and juries establish proof of guilt or innocence of the accused party (Silverstone & Sheetz, 2007). Legal arguments are based on logical probabilities that collectively prove the case and are constructed from the simplest logic possible. They may be mapped, for example, by a timeline of reconstructed events, or through inferential analysis processes. The weight of the evidence depends on the various relationships between key evidence, as well as the reliability of the supporting evidence (Silverstone & Sheetz).

It is unusual for legal cases to rely solely on circumstantial evidence, including digital evidence. Direct evidence, such as witness testimony, may be required to corroborate or, from the defense perspective, refute the digital evidence that asserts that the defendant accessed the computer at the time of an offence. Locating this supplementary evidence, often intuition-based, helps develop argument and strengthen the overall weight of available evidence. The example shown previously in Figure 2 of a simple chain of evidence was based on apparent or available evidence consisting of unprocessed facts from which tentative legal argument can be constructed. This amount of preliminary evidence is readily comprehensible to legal practitioners but is most likely incomplete, as digital evidence is complex and events are related to and dependant on a range of systems and application programs.

While experienced investigators may identify the less than obvious leads, or seek expert advice where their technical expertise fails, explaining the complexity of the digital evidence located to the legal practitioner may be difficult (Yasinsac et al., 2003). If the investigator is diligent, has sufficient technical and investigative expertise and skills, and is dedicated to seeking all relevant evidence, then the legal practitioner would be well served. Nevertheless, and it should not be understated, the legal practitioner must be able to determine whether enough evidence has been located and whether the validity of the digital evidence has been satisfactorily described and determined. The interface between the investigator, or auditor, and the legal practitioner is where organizations should ensure they obtain full information about the case in question, to ensure they have a sound understanding about the accuracy, nature, and relevance of the digital evidences.

Difficulties Using Digital Evidence in Legal Cases

Large, complex data sets and computer systems and networks can make evidence interpretation problematic and time-consuming. Sometimes there are too many potential suspects to investigate leading to protracted investigations (Mohay, 2003). Unlike traditional offences that are relatively easy to reconstruct, where evidence is tangible and with a narrower range of suspects, digital-based crime, especially if it involves networked computers and the Internet, has the problem of a larger number of potential suspects to investigate (Mohay). There is the common difficulty of determining whether a crime has actually occurred, for example in network computer crime, the nature of the event is often less obvious and immediate and victims may be unaware of a crime until well after it has taken place. Most notable attacks of this category are identity thefts (Hoar, 2001; Mohay). Moreover, there is often too much potential evidence to process, and when located, the evidence may easily be contaminated and ruin other digital evidence (Mohay). The increased storage size of computer hard drives and servers allows datasets to be stored that contain many terabytes of data, thereby making it difficult for investigators to determine how much of the dataset is evidence before commencing examination.

Another problem is the relative ease with which digital evidence can be contaminated when compared to evidence taken from a traditional crime scene that uses a series of separate analysis and preservation techniques (Mohay, 2003). The handling of digital evidence retrieved from a crime scene requires great care and expertise to avoid contamination, as the digital files are susceptible to corruption during the copying process. It is not uncommon that forensic copying techniques may inadvertently contaminate or destroy the evidence. Furthermore, contamination of some evidence may ruin all the other evidence used in a case. Unlike physical evidence, which may be a single component without which the case may still succeed, digital evidence is highly interconnected and its loss at any point in the chain of evidence may destroy the entire case.

Digital evidence may be modified without leaving any obvious trace of the commission of a crime or misdemeanor and although its previous existence is suspected, it is irretrievable; to reiterate, absence of evidence does not necessarily show evidence of absence of a relevant occurrence (Koehler, 2006). Considerable effort and expertise by an investigator would be required to seek corroboration to show that evidence existed but was later obliterated (Stephenson, 2000). For example, an illegal image may have been deleted and attempts made to erase links that show it existed; however, closer examination of the computer may not recover the deleted file name or its contents but may locate some metadata that shows proof of the file's existence (Carrier, 2005). Such occurrences are not unusual, and if overlooked by an investigator, it is unlikely that the business manager would understand their significance.

Other legal loopholes in the technical domain exist. Consider a hacker trespassing into a computer network for some illegal or improper reason, or perhaps out of idle curiosity. Some jurisdictions may require compelling evidence to prove some illegal action by an attacker that violated the data held on a proprietary network of an organization (Stephenson, 2000). Furthermore, it has been argued that if a network was within or adjacent to the public domain (Internet) and that even if unauthorized access was denied, the hacker should be warned that contrived access would be in breach of the proprietary rights of the organization, otherwise any legal reprisal against the hacker would be ineffectual.

These are just a few common problems, but there may well be others yet to emerge as lawyers gain a better insight into the network systems that host digital evidence. An experienced investigator, for example, may produce compelling digital evidence, only to lose the case because the integrity of the network security is questionable. Even if the network security does have a high level of integrity, the jury may not understand the expert opinion supporting this contention and reject the evidence out of hand.

It seems that the primary evidence, for example, a threatening email sent by a suspect, and corroborating evidence, such as computer logs linking the email to the suspect, can be undermined if the network security is unable to provide accurate records that cannot be validated. Similarly, it is improbable that a jury would have much confidence in evidence at a homicide trial, if claims that the murder weapon exactly matched the stab wound in the corpse were undermined by the effects of mutilation of the wound by maggots or wild animals. The environment was not conducive to preserving the crime scene in the natural world anymore than on a computer network. So for digital evidence to be of any use it must have validity and that can only be guaranteed if the environment is well protected.

How well does Computer Security Protect Digital Evidence?

This section looks at computer security and its ability to protect digital evidence. Digital evidence is fungible and when held on a storage device, such as a hard drive, or as a forensic image copied on to a storage disc, it can be easily replaced, altered, and destroyed; hence, the need for robust protection (Stephenson, 2000). During legal proceedings, examination of a record by opposing parties wishing to challenge its authenticity frequently occur (Tapper, 2004). Similarly, if the chain of custody is broken, or its robustness placed in doubt the opposing party may argue that the evidence has been contaminated or falsified and prevent its admission in legal proceedings. The chain of custody is important, and so is the need to validate the evidence itself and this begs the question as to the efficacy of conventional security measures protecting the operational and functional integrity of digital records (Caloyannides, 2003). Spenceley (2003) advocates that systems should provide a verifiable history of a record from its dates of creation to the date it is required as evidence in legal processes, thereby assisting the courts to determine the authenticity of digital evidence. An organization that owns a record may be less fastidious in accepting and accommodating gaps in the record's history but the same expediency is unlikely to occur during legal processes; greater scrutiny of records is necessary during legal proceedings (Tapper, 2004).

Inaccuracies in attribution of authorship and the content of digital evidence, for example, are common occurrences affecting legal argument as to the completeness, correctness, authenticity, and faithfulness to an original source; thereby, raising doubts as to the worth of the evidence (Akester, 2004; Mocas, 2004). More disturbing is that even in the absence of any obvious irregularity of the software platforms housing the evidence, examination of any material of evidentiary value does not in itself attest to the accuracy or integrity of the evidence (Spenceley, 2003). The more pessimistic argue that it is imprudent to assume that there is a low risk of inaccuracy in computer output due to application failures. However, this raises the question as to whether the courts are fully aware of the problems these issues can create as courts in various jurisdictions do not seem to be overly concerned about such serious deficiencies in system security (Spenceley).

Computer security includes such diverse counter-measures as cryptography, controlling authorized computer access, managing computer accounts and user privileges, copy protection, malicious code protection, database security, and protection for network connections against such threats as, password keystroke loggers, malware, and hackers (Schneier, 2000). Security analysts question how an organization can maintain a large database and communication networks where many users have different access privileges, and yet maintain sufficient operational functionality and security protection, thereby raising the specter of the reliability of the environment holding digital records that may later be used in evidence.

Some organizations have adopted a piecemeal approach to information security management, commonly assessing strategic risks at the time new technology is initiated, but subsequently do not always monitor their information systems to ensure they are configured securely (Jordan & Silcock, 2005). Even organizations, that have well configured and maintained systems, seldom prepare for events that require the use of potential digital evidence at some later time (Ghosh, 2004). Those responsible for information security within organizations may give scant regard to protecting and preserving digital evidence, yet a greater awareness and understanding of the importance of digital evidence is imperative.

However, if there has been such an abject failure of technical solutions to solve technical problems affecting computer database security, other non-technical countermeasures and intervention strategies, such as physical access controls and barriers, audits, biometric devices, and monitoring or surveillance, do not seem to have enjoyed more than partial success (Schneier, 2000). Notwithstanding the implementation of these and other security processes, there are additional factors that may impact negatively on their efficacy (Leiwo, 1999; Schneier, 1996). These include:

- A lack of mechanisms for evaluating security
- A gap between management and enforcement of information security
- Conflicts with top-down system design principles
- Lack of support for information security in non-traditional organizations
- Lack of consensus of definitions of concepts involved
- Scientific difficulties in information systems security research.

The United Kingdom's Computer Misuse Act of 1990 attempted to check the threats posed to network security by unauthorized activities (Coleman & Sapte, 2003). It created three specific offences of:

- Unauthorized access to computer material;
- Unauthorized access with intent to commit or facilitate commission of further offences; and
- Unauthorized modification of computer material.

However, the legislation was criticized by industry as having little deterrent value and, furthermore, the United Kingdom's Home Office figures revealed only thirty-three prosecutions for offences under the Computer Misuse Act in 1999 and 2000 (Coleman & Sapte, 2003). It would seem that the legislation was not a successful deterrent, with few successful prosecutions and lenient sentences handed out during the period. Coleman & Sapte quote the United Kingdom Home Office as explaining that while the number of successful prosecutions is low because of the difficulties of meeting the requirement to prove intent on the offender's part, another explanation is an apparent inadequacy in training the police and judiciary to understand and deal with cyber crime.

Networked computer and information security consist of procedures and processes designed to protect the reliability of an organization's information records from intentional and accidental threats. Such measures are intended to preserve the validity of records for operational and functional purposes of organizations rather than any planned concerns over digital evidence retrieval and preservation (Bettino, Jojodia, & Samarati, 1993; Castano, Fugini, Martella, & Samarat, 1995). By implementing various security measures, it is possible to prevent or minimize the corruption and degradation of the records from a range of threats. However, whatever security measures are used, they are more often used to assist in the auditing and monitoring of the overall integrity of records, rather than directly evaluating the evidentiary integrity of digital information (Carrier, 2005).

Data audits do not prevent attacks (although they may have some deterrent effect on would be attackers and are useful in analyzing attacks after the event) but they do play an important role in collecting digital evidence (Schneier, 2000). Database auditing, for example, is based on conventional standards and regulations for the documentation of an organization's financial transactions (Afyouni, 2006). In terms of information management, as in the case of a database audit, the auditor looks specifically at the information in the database and recognizes that security measures in place are inseparable from the auditing activity (Afyouni). If these security measures are weak, or the audit process inappropriate because of large datasets or both exist, then presumably it becomes unsafe to assume that all potential digital evidence in a database is valid.

This raises concerns for business managers about accepting digital evidence at face value, and whether there should be a rigorous examination of the evidence irrespective of the cost, resources, and time involved. The next section looks at these issues.

Proof of Innocence

In Australia, the Office of the Director of Public Prosecutions of New South Wales in a submission to the Australian Law Reform Commission (ALRC) was dismissive of a call for a higher threshold for admissibility of digital evidence for reasons summarized below. This was despite some scientific solutions put before the ALRC (Director of Public Prosecutions (NSW), 2005b). The submission stated that:

- A more rigorous testing is unjustified because of the absence of solid evidence to support the need for the provision and no cases are evident of wrongful conviction from computer-generated error;
- Litigation in Australia depends on an adversarial system and the burden of proof that rests on the prosecuting party, or plaintiff, ensures proper testing of evidence of this sort;
- It would impose a higher threshold than for other machine produced evidence;
- Data manipulation occurs with any machine-generated information, such as photos, tapes, and videos;
- The party challenging the accuracy of the evidence would have to be given the opportunity to inspect the relevant computer and perform their own tests, which is a costly and time-consuming exercise.

The New South Wales Director of Public Prosecution's stance could be seen by some observers as expedient and denying parties wishing to challenge the accuracy of the evidence to find some legislative remedy. The Australian Government Attorney-General's Department's response to the ALRC (Attorney-General's Department, 2005) was equally dismissive of the need for higher standards of admissibility of digital evidence, asserting that in criminal cases, the prosecution were hamstrung over the type of documentary material available in prosecuting cases. The department argued that it was not in the interest of justice to require a court to reject what appeared to be logical and reliable evidence, that may be corroborated by other material because preconditions of admissibility were not satisfied (Attorney-General's Department, 2005). However, such rulings may be potentially unjust to defendants, even if the potential numbers of cases where the evidence is challenged are numerically small.

Accepting digital evidence at face value may be imprudent, with adverse consequences for those most affected by its inappropriate use in trials. Consider the case of Aaron Caffrey, who in 2003 was acquitted of an offence under the United Kingdom's Computer Misuse Act 1990 offence of causing unauthorized modification of computer material by sending a flood of data from his computer that shut down the computer server operating the Port of Houston, in Texas, United States of America (George, 2004). Caffrey claimed that unknown hackers gained control of his computer and launched programs to hack into the Port of Houston computer to incriminate him. The prosecution's technical expert could find no evidence of a Trojan virus on Caffrey's computer. Caffrey claimed it was impossible to test every file on the computer, suggesting that a Trojan virus could have deleted itself leaving no trace – a claim strongly contested by the prosecution (George). This was one of a few cases where a Trojan virus defense was accepted by the court without any proof of the virus being found on the computer, although it is unlikely to set any legal precedent (George).

The prosecution of Julie Amero, a former Connecticut substitute schoolteacher, whose classroom computer displayed pornographic advertisements to her students, was dismissed in 2007 after legal experts and security professionals assisted her by providing a forensics report exonerating her after the prosecution failed to investigate all of the evidence (Lemos, 2008). Amero's support group, who criticized prosecutors for failing to exercise care before charging suspects with possession of child pornography, claimed that laws were poorly framed, and investigators and crazed fellow citizens were too quick to claim that mere possession of unlawful images establishes guilt (Lemos). Another child pornography case was thrown out of court in Massachusetts in 2008 involving a sacked government servant, Michael Fiola, who was able to hire a forensic investigator to show that a virus on his work computer terminal was responsible for downloading the illegal images (Lemos).

Conversely, parties appearing before the court have attempted to create fraudulent information and have benefited from the inability of forensic analysis to identify associated digital evidence to strengthen the claim against them. In a civil suit between Kucala Enterprises and Auto Wax Company, over a patent infringement and counter suit, it was claimed that Kucala had installed the software programme Evidence Eliminator for the purpose of destroying evidence (Meyers & Rogers, 2004). Although computer forensic analysis demonstrated that the software was installed, it could not provide evidence about the extent to which the programme was used. While Kucala paid court costs, the suit against the company was dismissed because of a lack of evidence (Meyers & Rogers).

It should be recalled that previous strength of DNA evidence was challenged in the OJ Simpson case when his defense team had unlimited access to funds, scientific and legal expertise, and photographic and video footage of the actual crime scene investigation, normally denied a defense team (Edwards, 2005). Consequently, Simpson was acquitted of the homicide charge, and although his guilt remains a matter of much public debate, errors in handling the DNA exhibits in the laboratory was unprofessional and contamination of the evidence was proven (Edwards, 2005). Could the same not occur with digital evidence in the investigator's laboratory?

Why a Sound Understanding of Digital Evidence is Essential

Current laws may be considered incapable of dealing with many of the current information and communication technologies as there are gaps, or deficiencies, in process procedures that require amendment, or the introduction of new laws (Berwick & Thompson, 1998). Spenceley (2003) looked at the gaps in the legal procedures vis-à-vis networked computers, asserting that computer software application failures may produce outputs that appear correct, but which incorporate some information that is inaccurate. These cases of latent inaccuracy pose serious challenges to legal fact finding, and while not deliberate, such inaccuracy has the potential to invite malicious exploitation.

Spenceley (2003) warned against preferential evidentiary treatment by the courts and legislators of computer output, which he believes is not always justified, and calls for a more rational foundation for asserting that a source of information will enable the courts to identify the reliability of the evidence presented. He suggested that the argument, that evidentiary treatment of digital evidence should be undertaken according to different standards, is imprecise in what it seeks and is concerned that such an argument does not define the boundaries beyond which different standards should not be applied. Spenceley feared that the complexity of digital evidence may encourage the legislators and courts to be injudiciously expedient with determining the reliability of the evidence, in respect of which various dispensations of proof might be superficially attractive.

To mitigate the unreliability of networked computers, Spenceley (2003) advocated a redundant mechanism approach rather than increasing the functional capacity of the computer system. The redundant mechanism uses a separate computer with identical input and processing to that of the processing computer, to compare both outcomes and to detect an otherwise unnoticeable change in outcomes. Section 59B of the South Australian Evidence Act of 1929 recognized the value of a redundant mechanism to validate the reliability of a computer system, but the Australian Law Reform Commission viewed the legislation with some reservation, believing it failed to provide a sufficiently reliable measurement of testing the reliability of evidence ALRC Discussion Paper 69, 2005.

Judges and juries attempt to determine the probability of the guilt (or liability in civil cases) or the innocence of the person or parties appearing before them and are partially influenced by the behavior and conduct of defendants, or contesting parties (Rubinfeld & Sappington, 1987). A greater effort in preparing a robust legal argument, and a more comprehensive collation of evidence, will influence judges and juries in estimating the probability of innocence (Rubinfeld & Sappington). The court is required to choose the standard of proof of innocence, and if the party does not meet the standard, then the court awards the appropriate penalty. Furthermore, courts are expected to minimize the social consequences of convicting the innocent and acquitting the guilty, all within the spirit of fairness, equity, and of course, deterrence.

There is some ongoing legal debate calling for a replacement of conventional forensic identification science that relies on untested assumptions and intuition, including cyber forensics, with sounder scientific analysis (Mohay, 2003; Saks & Koehler, 2005; Tobin & Thompson, 2006). Most writings on the examination and analysis of digital evidence focus on the preservation of evidence and the chain of evidence, with scant mention of the properties of the evidence itself, which may reflect the comparatively recent emergence of digital evidence and cyber forensics (Mohay; Slade, 2004). Irrespective of different legal views and understanding of digital evidence, some scientific research would no doubt be of value to business managers, as well as to the courts, lawyers, and investigators, especially if some standard definitions were established. For example, defining what is required to validate digital evidence in a broad range of legal settings. The terms accuracy, certainty, authenticity, integrity, in terms of the chain of custody, are mentioned in some literature but are not comprehensively defined in any standards (Mocas, 2004).

What of digital evidence itself? For example, the primary evidence may be a threatening email sent by a suspect or other digital evidence, such as a user access entry logs, links the suspect to the computer at the critical time. However, this evidence does not exist in isolation as there is associative information that may corroborate or refute the primary evidence (Mocas, 2004). The access logs do not prove the suspect was using the computer at a specific time any more than fingerprint or DNA conclusively links the suspect to the computer keyboard at a particular time; other corroboration is required to confirm or refute the assertion.

Casey (2007) warns against focusing too much on digital evidence being altered per se, as this obfuscates the worth of the evidence in the event that even if there had been some alteration, it does not necessarily negate the reliability or authenticity of the evidence. Casey stresses the importance of a sound forensic approach in analyzing digital evidence against using unrealistic standards that further confuse and obfuscate the truth of the evidence. However, the absence of standards and robust guidelines is unhelpful to investigators and legal practitioners and by association, the management of organizations.

Implications for Business Managers

This section looks at the implications of digital evidence for business managers. Fundamentally, poor perception of cyber crime and the impact of illegal actions themselves on a business are most likely to be problems, rather than apathy on the part of business managers, who take their responsibility for protecting information assets as seriously as their other responsibilities. Protective security of vital assets is obviously important but this needs to be considered in broader terms than is commonly considered as best-practice. For example, a major change in thinking by organizations is needed to see if security can be enhanced in advance of a crime, rather than treated as an after-thought in routine security strategies or as an ineffective, reactive remedy after a disaster (Williams, 2002). Certainly, complementary to computer and information security, cyber forensic planning should form a key part of an organization's risk management strategy.

While the relevance of computer forensics to information security is gaining recognition in IT circles, due to its technical nature, it is often misunderstood and undervalued by organizations (Quinn, 2005; Volonino, 2003). According to Quinn and Rowlingson (2004), an enhanced understanding by business managers of some of the common difficulties in preserving, locating, selecting, and validating digital evidence, can help organizations significantly enhance the worth of digital evidence in legal cases and employee disciplinary hearings. Moreover, recognition and tightening of poorly configured computer and network security reduces the likelihood that the value of digital evidence will be diminished, thereby minimizing potentially undesirable consequences (Quinn).

There does appear to be some awareness by more prudent organizations that they will benefit from some forensic strategies included in their security risk contingency planning. Well-conceived strategies recognize the potential value of digital evidence to an organization and ensure that it is gathered and secured at the time of a crime or when a security breach occurs. Such foresight must benefit an organization by better preserving potential evidence, whilst minimizing the costs of future investigations and the likelihood of more favorable outcomes for an organization (Rowlingson, 2004). Questions also arise over whether straightforward means exist to validate how effectively built-in security processes preserve evidence. It would be advantageous to be able to tender digital evidence with reliable knowledge of how well the measures in place do, in fact, preserve its admissibility and evidentiary weight. But how well do organizations understand the effectiveness of their own security measures for that purpose?

As Ghosh (2004) points out, cyber forensic specialists serve the law and technology, and while management of digital evidence is a cross-disciplinary practice, there are some common principles that can help business managers deal with digital evidence. Firstly, there is an obligation to provide records that:

- Understand regulatory, administrative and best-practice obligations to produce, retain, and provide records
- Understand the steps that can be taken to maximize the evidentiary weighting of records and the implications of not doing so

- Understand regulatory constraints to the retention and provision of records.

Secondly, Ghosh suggests that computer systems, procedures and documentation must be capable of establishing:

- The authenticity and alteration of electronic records
- The reliability of computer programs generating such records
- The time and date of creation or alteration
- The identity of the author of an electronic record
- The safe custody and handling of records.

Great difficulties confront organizations that are unprepared for the eventuality that their information holdings and computer networks may be accessed by external authorities to retrieve digital evidence. Rowlingson (2004) attempts to address this in a ten-step forensics readiness programme, which are:

- Define the scenarios that require digital evidence
- Identify available sources and different types of potential evidence
- Determine the evidence requirement
- Establish a capability for securely gathering legally admissible evidence to meet the requirement
- Establish a policy for secure storage and handling of potential evidence
- Ensure monitoring is targeted to detect and deter major incidents
- Specify circumstances when escalation to a full formal investigation should be launched
- Train staff in incident awareness
- Document an evidence-based case describing the incident and its impact.
- Ensure legal review to facilitate action in response to the incident.

Organisations should also consider the need for forensic readiness within the contemporary security culture and budgetary climate (Rowlingson, 2004). Using existing risk assessment standards, such as ISO17799, can form a base for implementing a forensic contingency strategy but do not cover many areas of cyber forensics where digital evidence may be required. Even when responding to discovery in civil litigation cases in something ostensibly straightforward as a litigant's request for an internal email can be a time consuming and costly exercise (Volonino, 2003). Searching for an email may be a relatively simple and quick process, or it may require exhaustive searches through large datasets that may need culling of confidential and non-relevant material (Sleek, 2000). In the Monica Lewinsky case, the cost of undertaking a search of relevant email files cost in excess of US$17 million (Streza, 2003).

Organisations might also consider employing the services of a Computer Incident Response Team (CIRT) in the event of an incident that requires a professional investigation and response under pre-established practice and standards (Stephenson, 2000). A CIRT investigates computer security incidents, manages evidence collection, interviews witnesses, and stabilises the business operations, by providing some forensic contingency planning for an effective response when needed (Stephenson). However, not all organisations can afford the services of in-house or external teams of computer forensic investigators. Many of the business managers and IT personnel are unlikely to possess sufficient understanding, let alone experience of dealing with digital evidence. A few tertiary institutions offer cyber forensic courses but there is no consensus on curriculum requirements that meet industry expectations (Kruse & Heiser, 2002). University IT departments generally turn out graduates able to deal with incident response against activities, rather than skills suitable for forensic investigation, and not necessarily rounded IT security professionals with forensic understanding and useful skills. Perhaps computer application and systems designers, in tandem with academic researchers, could consider widening their research and incorporating some processes, such as suggested by Spenceley (2003) that would enhance the identification and preservation of digital evidence, so that validation is a less tortuous task.

CONCLUSION

This chapter has characterized digital evidence, outlined the investigative and legal processes used to prepare it for a legal case, and has described how digital evidence fits into the legal domain. The challenges to business managers in dealing with digital evidence are many, but these can be overcome. Difficulties confront business managers and non-specialists. They are often the unwitting custodians of digital information, with limited understanding of computer security and cyber forensic methods. They may be unaware that illegal or improper use of their information has taken place. Organizations need to be cognizant of the complexity and difficulty in locating and using digital evidence, and be well prepared that measures are in place to protect the validity and preservation of the evidence. Such unpreparedness makes it difficult to determine what needs preserving for later use, and how that can be achieved without contaminating and diminishing its admissibility and evidentiary weight.

In addition, businesses relying on the legal fraternity need to recognize that most courts and lawyers still have a limited understanding of these issues. This lack of understanding can be further compounded by courts, legislators, and governments that make bad legal decisions. Such outcomes perhaps erode natural justice with the attendant negative implications for organizations mounting or defending legal battles. Explaining to the courts the technical complexities of digital evidence used in a legal case, might very well result in bad decisions for an organization. Reliance on a costly technical team may be a burden to many organizations, and even if such expertise is available, the outcome of a case is far from assured. Tightly-configured security of computer networks is more likely to satisfy the courts that the storage of digital evidence is of a high standard and enhance the likelihood of evidence being admissible and retaining its weight. The process of validating the security configuration of systems, and the digital evidence itself, is a further highly desirable enhancement, worthy of endorsement by professional and cyber forensic investigators. An understanding of the nature and complexity of digital evidence will enable business managers to develop contingencies to meet these aims, or at least minimize any potentially adverse consequences.

ACKNOWLEDGMENT

I would like to acknowledge and extend my sincere gratitude to my colleagues Dr. Val Hobbs and Dr. Graham Mann who have supported me and guided me in preparing this chapter, and empowered me to undertake other challenging ventures in the field of digital evidence validation.

REFERENCES

Adelstein, F. (2006). Live forensics: Diagnosing your system without killing it first. *Communications of the ACM, 49*(2), 63–66. doi:10.1145/1113034.1113070

Afyouni, H. A. (2006). *Database security and auditing: protecting data integrity and accessibility*. Boston: Thomson Learning Inc.

Ahmad, A. (2002). The forensic chain of evidence model: Improving the process of evidence collection in incident handling procedures. *The 6th Pacific Asia Conference on Information Systems*.

Akester, P. (2004). Internet law: authenticity of works: authorship and authenticity in cyberspace. *Computer Law & Security Report, 20*(6), 436–444. doi:10.1016/S0267-3649(04)00088-3

Ashcroft, J. (2001). *Electronic crime scene investigation: A guide for first responders*. Washington: U.S. Department of Justice.

Australian Law Reform Commission. (2005). *ALRC Discussion Paper 69*. Canberra: Australian Law Reform Commission.

Baraani-Dastjerdi, A., Pieprzyk, J., & Satavi-Naini, R. (1996). *Security in databases: a survey study*. Wollongong: Unpublished Survey, University of Wollongong.

Baryamureeba, V., & Tushabe, F. (2006). The Enhanced Digital Investigation Process Model. *Asian Journal of Information Technology*, *5*(7), 790–794.

Berk, R. A. (1983). An introduction to sample selection bias in sociological data. *American Sociological Review*, *48*, 386–398. doi:10.2307/2095230

Bertino, W., Jojodia, S., & Samarati, P. (1993). Access controls in object-oriented database systems: some approaches and issues . In Bhargava, N. A. A. B. (Ed.), *Advanced Database Concepts and Research Issues* (*Vol. 759*). Springer-Verlag.

Berwick, D. R., & Thompson, D. E. (1998). *Minimum provisions for the investigation of computer based offences (No. 1320-5579)*. Payneham, South Australia: National Police Research Unit.

Boddington, R. G., Hobbs, V. J., & Mann, G. (2008). *Validating digital evidence for legal argument*. Paper presented at the SECAU Security Conferences: The 6th Australian Digital Forensics Conference, 1st - 3rd December 2008, Perth, WA.

Caloyannides, M. A. (2001). *Computer forensics and privacy*. Norwood, Minnesota: Artech House.

Caloyannides, M. A. (2003). Digital evidence and reasonable doubt. *IEEE Security and Privacy*, *1*(6), 89–91. doi:10.1109/MSECP.2003.1266366

Carrier, B. (2005). *File system forensic analysis*. Upper Saddle River, New Jersey: Addison-Wesley.

Carrier, B., & Spafford, E. H. (2003). Getting physical with the digital investigation process. *International Journal of Digital Evidence*.

Casey, E. (2000). *Digital evidence and computer crime: Forensic science, computers and the Internet*. London: Academic Press.

Casey, E. (Ed.). (2002). *Handbook of computer crime investigation: forensic tools and technology*. London: Elsevier Academic Press.

Casey, E. (2007). What does "forensically sound" really mean? *Digital Investigation*, *4*(2), 49–50. doi:10.1016/j.diin.2007.05.001

Castano, S., Fugini, M., Martella, G., & Samarati, P. (1995). *Database Security: Addison-Wesley*. ACM Press.

Cohen, F. (2006). Challenges to digital forensic evidence. Retrieved June 22, 2006, from http://all.net/Talks/CyberCrimeSummit06.pdf

Coleman, C., & Sapte, D. W. (2003). Cyberspace security: securing cyberspace: new laws and developing strategies. *Computer Law & Security Report*, *19*(2), 131–136. doi:10.1016/S0267-3649(03)00208-5

Computer Crime. (1979). *Criminal Justice Resource Manual*. United States: United States Department of Justice.

Demougin, D., & Fluet, C. (2006). Preponderance of evidence. *European Economic Review*, *50*(4), 963–976. doi:10.1016/j.euroecorev.2004.11.002

Devitt, E. J., & Blackman, C. B. (1977). *Federal Jury practice and instructions* (3rd ed.). St. Paul, Minnesota: West Publishing.

Diaconis, P., & Mosteller, F. (1989). Methods for studying coincidences. *Journal of the American Statistical Association*, *84*, 853–861. doi:10.2307/2290058

Edwards, K. (2005). Ten things about DNA contamination that lawyers should know. *Criminal Law Journal*, *29*(2), 71–93.

Etter, B. (2001, 21-22 June). *Computer crime*. Paper presented at the 4th National Outlook Symposium on Crime in Australia - New Crimes or New Responses, Canberra.

Flusche, K. J. (2001). Computer forensic case study: Espionage, Part 1 Just finding the file is not enough! *Information Security Journal*, *10*(1), 1–10. doi:10.1201/108 6/43313.10.1.20010304/31394.6

George, E. (2004). Trojan virus defence: Regina v Aaron Caffrey, Southwark Crown Court. *Digital Investigation*, *1*(2), 89. doi:10.1016/j.diin.2004.04.005

Ghosh, A. (2004). *Guidelines for the management of IT evidence*. Paper presented at the APEC Telecommunications and Information Working Group 29th Meeting. Retrieved 5 October 2009 from http://unpan1.un.org/intradoc/groups/public/documents/APCITY/UNPAN016411.pdf

Gong, R., & Chan, K. Y. (2005). Case-relevance information investigation: Binding computer intelligence to the current computer forensic framework. *International Journal of Digital Evidence*, *4*(1), 1–13.

Halleck, J. (1996). Administrator ethical dilemma. Retrieved 23 June 2005, from http://www.cc.utah.edu/%7Enahaj/ethics/administrator.html

Hoar, S. B. (2001). *Identity theft: The crime of the New Millennium* (Vol. 49).

Jordan, E., & Silcock, L. (2005). *Beating IT risks*. Chichester: John Wiley & Sons Ltd.

Koehler, J. J., & Thompson, W. C. (2006). *Mock jurors' reactions to selective presentation of evidence from multiple-opportunity searches*. American Psychology-Law Society: Division 41 of the American Psychological Association.

Kruse, W. H. J. (2002). *Computer forensics: Incident response essentials*. Indianapolis: Addison-Wesley.

Leiwo, J. (1999). *Observations on information security crisis*. Bangkok: King Mongkut's Institute of Technology.

Lemos, R. (2008). Lax security leads to child-porn charges [Electronic Version]. *Security Focus*. Retrieved 22 November 2008 from http://www.securityfocus.com/brief/756.

Luddy, W. J. Jr, & Wolk, S. R. (1986). *Legal aspects of computer use. Prentice Hall*. Prentice Hall.

Marcella, A. J., & Greenfield, R. S. (Eds.). (2002). *Cyber forensics: A field manual for collecting, examining and preserving evidence of computer crimes*. Boca Raton, Florida: CRC Press Ltd.doi:10.1201/9781420000115

Mattord, H. J., & Whitman, M. E. (2004). *Management of information security*. Boston: Thomson learning.

Mercuri, R. (2005). Challenges in forensic computing. *Communications of the ACM*, *48*(12), 17–21. doi:10.1145/1101779.1101796

Meyers, M., & Rogers, M. (2004). Computer forensics: The need for standardization and certificate. *International Journal of Digital Evidence*, *3*(2).

Mocas, S. (2004). Building theoretical underpinnings for digital forensics research. *Digital Investigation*, *1*(1), 61–68. doi:10.1016/j.diin.2003.12.004

Mohay, G. M. (2003). *Computer and intrusion forensics*. Boston: Artech House Inc.

Morris, G. (1990). *Computer security and the law*.

Myers, R. D., Reinstein, R. S., & Griller, G. M. (1999). Complex scientific evidence and the jury. *Judicature Genes and Justice: The Growing Impact of the New Genetics on the Courts, 83*(3).

Nezovic v Minister of Immigration and Multicultural and Indigenous Affairs (2003).

Palmer, G. L. (2001). *A road map for digital forensic research.* Paper presented at the First Digital Forensic Research Workshop (DFRWS), Air Force Research Laboratory, Rome Research Site.

Palmer, G. L. (2002). Forensic analysis in the digital world. *International Journal of Digital Evidence, 1*(1).

Pospesel, H., & Rodes (jnr), Robert. E. (1997). *Premises and conclusions: Symbolic logic for legal analysis.* New Jersey: Prentice-Hall, Inc.

Quinn, S. (2005). Examining the state of preparedness of information technology management in New Zealand for events that may require forensic analysis. *Digital Investigation, 2*(4), 276–280. doi:10.1016/j.diin.2005.10.005

Review of the Evidence Act 1995. (2004). Australian Law Reform Commission. Issues Paper 28. Retrieved 5 October 2009 from http://www.austlii.edu.au/au/other/alrc/publications/issues/28/

Rogers, M. K., & Seigfried, K. (2004). The future of computer forensics: A needs analysis survey. *Computers & Security, 23*(1), 12–16. doi:10.1016/j.cose.2004.01.003

Rowlingson, R. (2004). A ten step process for forensic readiness. *International Journal of Digital Evidence, 2*(3).

Rubinfeld, D. L., & Sappington, D. E. M. (1987). Efficient awards and standards of proof in judicial proceedings. *The Rand Journal of Economics, 18*(2), 308–315. doi:10.2307/2555555

Saks, M. J., & Koehler, J. J. (2005). The coming paradigm shift in forensic identification science. *Science, 309*(5736), 892–895. doi:10.1126/science.1111565

Schneier, B. (1996). *Applied cryptography: protocols, algorithms, and source code in C* (2nd ed.). New York: John Wiley Sons, Inc.

Schneier, B. (2000). *Secrets and lies: digital security in a networked world.* New York: Wiley Computer Publishing.

Schneier, B. (2004, August 19, 2004). Opinion: Cryptanalysis of MD5 and SHA: Time for a new standard: Crypto researchers report weaknesses in common hash functions. *Computerworld.*

Silverstone, H., & Sheetz, M. (2007). *Forensic accounting and fraud investigation for non-experts.* New Jersey: John Wiley & Sons, Inc.

Slade, R. (2004). *Software forensics: Collecting evidence from the scene of a digital crime*. New York: McGraw Hill.

Sleek, S. (2000). Good e-recordkeeping saves you money, protects you from liability. *Digital Discovery and e-Evidence, 1*(1), 4-5.

Spenceley, C. (2003). *Evidentiary treatment of computer-produced material: a reliability based evaluation*. Sydney: University of Sydney.

Stambaugh, H., Beaupre, D., Icove, D. J., Baker, R., Cassaday, W., & Williams, W. P. (2000). *State and local law enforcement needs to combat electronic crime*. Retrieved 22 November 2008 from http://www.ncjrs.gov/txtfiles1/nij/183451.txt

Stephenson, P. (2000). *Investigating computer-related crime*. Boca Raton, Florida: CRC Press.

Streza, R. (2003). Discovery unplugged: Should internal e-mails be privileged confidential communications? *Defense Counsel Journal, 70*(1), 36–41.

Tapper, C. (2004). *Cross & Tapper on evidence* (10th ed.). London: LexisNexis Butterworths.

TheAge. (2005). NSW speed cameras in doubt. August 10.

Thompson, D. E., & Berwick, D. R. (1998). *Minimum provisions for the investigation of computer based offences*. Payneham, South Australia: National Police Research Unit.

Tillers, P. (2005). Picturing factual inference in legal settings. In *Gerechtigkeitswissenschaft: Kolloquium aus Anlass des 70: Geburtstages von Lothar Philipps*. Berlin.

Tobin, W. A., & Thompson, W. C. (2006). Evaluating and challenging forensic identification evidence. *Champion Magazine* (July, p.12).

Unamed. (1994). (H. C. Lee Ed.). *Crime scene investigation*. Taoyuan: Central Police University Press.

Unamed. (1999). *Association of Chief Police Officers: Good practice guide for computer based evidence*. Retrieved 5 October 2009. from. http://www.7safe.com/electronic_evidence/ACPO_guidelines_computer_evidence_v4_web.pdf

Unamed. (2000). *The virtual horizon: meeting the law enforcement challenges: developing an Australasian law enforcement strategy for dealing with electronic crime: scoping paper*. Paper presented at the Police Commissioners' Conference - Electronic Crime Working Party 2000, Adelaide. Retrieved 5 October 2009 from http://www.acpr.gov.au/publications2.asp?Report_ID=102

Unamed. (2005b). Australian Law Reform Commission: Review of the Evidence Act 1995. Submission E 17. Retrieved 5 October 2009 from http://www.austlii.edu.au/au/other/alrc/publications/reports/102/

Volonino, L. (2003). Electronic evidence and computer records. *Communications of the Association for Information Systems, 12*, 457–468.

Warren, L. (1997). *Radio National Transcripts: Santa, smog, and speed! The Law Report*. Australia: Australian Broadcasting Corporation.

Whitcomb, C. M. (2002). An historical perspective of digital evidence: A forensic scientist's view. *International Journal of Digital Evidence, 1*(1).

Whitman, M. E., & Mattord, H. J. (2005). *Principles of information security* (2nd ed.). Boston, Massachusetts: Thomson Learning.

Williams, P. (2002). *Organized crime and cyber-crime: Implications for business*. Retrieved 9 February 2009, from http://www.cert.org/archive/pdf/cybercrime-business.pdf

Yasinsac, A., Erbacher, R. F., Marks, D. G., Pollitt, M. M., & Sommer, P. M. (2003). Computer forensics education. *IEEE Security & Privacy, 1*(4), 15–23. doi:10.1109/MSECP.2003.1219052

Chapter 3
Recent Developments in Simplified Sign-On

Kevin Curran
University of Ulster, UK

Jennifer Caldwell
University of Ulster, UK

Declan Walsh
University of Ulster, UK

Marcella Gallacher
University of Ulster, UK

ABSTRACT

Authentication is the process of determining whether a user is to be granted access and verifying that they are whom they claim to be. This is generally done via a login system; typically consisting of a user ID and a corresponding password. An intrinsic weakness of this system of authentication is that passwords are easily forgotten, accidentally revealed, can be second guessed, or even stolen. Users today have multiple email accounts; manage their financial affairs, buy, and even sell regularly online. Many sites offer the opportunity to sign up. This can be problematic for managing usernames and passwords and it encourages insecure practices, such as writing them down, storing them electronically, or reusing the same login data on multiple Web sites repeatedly. One of the most common online security issues faced today is that every Web site has its own diverse authentication system that significantly heightens the probability of online crime, such as fraud and identity theft and, furthermore, can compromise the privacy of the individual. A common network identity-verification method is Simplified Sign-On, which allows users to roam between sites without having to repeatedly enter identifying

DOI: 10.4018/978-1-60566-806-2.ch003

information. Privacy of user's information should be maintained, as only relevant details are passed on to other sites. A number of organizations are already taking Simplified Sign-On on board and have had successful outcomes using this type of system. Some companies, such as Microsoft Passport, have used a Single Sign-On password system but they have had security and privacy issues after the launch. The future for most, if not all, users may be a secure and private single logon to access different sites and accounts on the Internet via Simplified Sign-On. This paper discusses Simplified Sign-On in more detail.

INTRODUCTION

Plain old authentication can be defined in many ways but perhaps the simplest and most relevant definition to most computer users is a security measure for checking a network user's identity. Even in today's world of digital certificates and biometrics, authentication most typically takes the form of a username and password. Figure 1 shows a standard authentication process. Note that this is *Basic* authentication, wherein the Web server prompts for a username and password. Other common Web authentication types are *Anonymous* (no authentication required) and *Integrated* (currently logged in authentication details automatically checked to see if the user can access the resource). Simplified Sign-On is the concept of allowing users to move from one Web site to another on the Web without having to enter identifying information numerous times (see Figure 2). A person would enter, for example, a username and password, at the start of a network session, and this authentication information would be automatically passed to each Web site they visit thereafter. A network session might be when a user connects to the Internet or opens a Web browser. The rationale behind Simplified Sign-On is obvious; the growth of the Web has led to people having to manage a host of usernames and passwords for Web sites. An average Web user now shops online, pursues hobbies online, manages their bank accounts online, and communicates online using email, instant messaging and photo-sharing (Perry, 2006). The list is lengthy and almost all of these require authentication, usually in the form of a username and password. For many users, a *single sign-on* would be welcome. Listed below are some of the obvious benefits of Simplified Sign-On.

- More convenient for the user as they have to remember only one username and password.
- Security issues reduced as the user should not have to write down the one username/password.

Figure 1. Authentication on the web

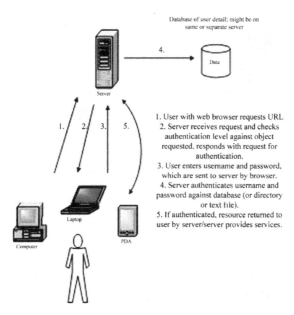

Database of user detail; might be on
same or separate server

1. User with web browser requests URL
2. Server receives request and checks
   authentication level against object
   requested. responds with request for
   authentication.
3. User enters username and password,
   which are sent to server by browser.
4. Server authenticates username and
   password against database (or directory
   or text file).
5. If authenticated, resource returned to
   user by server/server provides services.

- With only one authentication system, there is less chance of having the password stolen.
- As the user has to logon only once, there is faster access to different sites.
- There should be a continuous link to different sites.
- The system is managed centrally.

As well as speed and convenience, Simplified Sign-On also offers improved security. Web users no longer have to remember and manage countless logons (making them more vulnerable to fraud) and organizations have less responsibility for the security and privacy of peoples' authentication (and personal) information. The balkanization of today's online identity-verifying systems is a big part of the Internet's fraud and security crisis. Improving and maintaining people's trust in the internet is critical to its survival as a useful, thriving entity (Talbot, 2006). Also, if authentication is consolidated in one session or authority, Web users only need to share their personal information once instead of giving numerous copies of that information to multiple third parties. This means greater privacy for users and less risk of personal information being accessed. Many companies have already encountered these issues on an organizational scale; workers use numerous systems and have to manage authentication for each of them. This causes a lot of inconvenience to us-

Figure 2. Simplified sign-on on the web

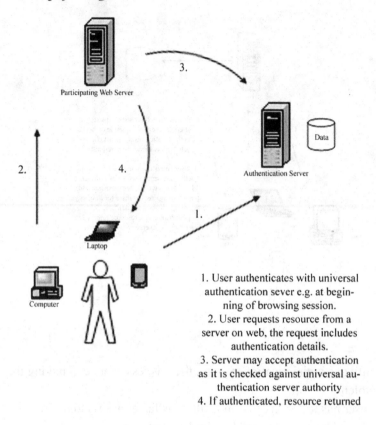

1. User authenticates with universal authentication sever e.g. at beginning of browsing session.
2. User requests resource from a server on web, the request includes authentication details.
3. Server may accept authentication as it is checked against universal authentication server authority
4. If authenticated, resource returned

ers, I.T. resources are wasted resetting passwords and administering user accounts, and security can be compromised by users writing down usernames and passwords because they cannot remember them. As a result, many organizations have implemented Simplified Sign-On that allows workers (or students, or customers) to log in once, in order to access all the systems they use. Scaling up this kind of solution to something as vast and heterogeneous as the Web is a challenge.

Simplified Sign-On Implementations

Most web surfers have encountered Simplified Sign-On, albeit on a relatively small scale at sites like MSN Hotmail and Windows Live Spaces. To date, there are a small number of players, which are discussed below.

Figure 3. Shibboleth. (Adapted from Talbot, 2006).

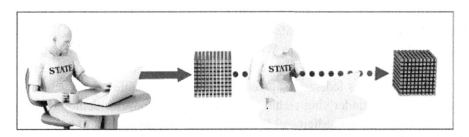

Shibboleth

Shibboleth is an open-standard authentication system, which allows users to "hop securely from one site to another after signing on just once" (Talbot, 2006, p1). Figure 3 shows Shibboleth being used to authenticate a university student when accessing another university's resources

Figure 4 illustrates a Shibboleth implementation for a project involving seven U.S. universities "to create cross-institutional authentication and authorization services on the Web" (Gettes, 1999, p2). Shibboleth is currently deployed at over 500 sites worldwide, predominately in educational institutions. The science and medical division of publishing conglomerate Reed Elsevier has allowed university-based subscribers to access its online resources using Shibboleth, and this progress into the private sector is apparently advancing with the Liberty Alliance. The Liberty Alliance is composed of companies such as America Online, France Telecom, Novell,

Figure 4. Shibboleth – Middleware Web Authentication Project. (Adapted from Gettes, 1999).

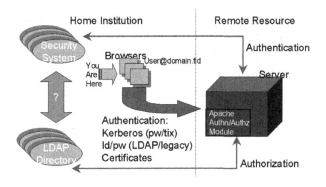

Sun Microsystems, Ericsson, Intel, Oracle Corporation, Hewlett Packard, NTT and Fidelity Investment. The design is based on the XML standard Security Assertion Markup Language (SAML) created by an industry group called OASIS. It is worth noting that other players, such as Window's Card Space, also use SAML.

Shibboleth is interoperable with Windows Active Directory Federation Services (ADFS). This allows federation agreements among companies and organizations regardless of the underlying technical solution they choose to deploy (Rotman, 2005). Such tie-ins with Microsoft could do Shibboleth no harm in its bid as a Web Simplified Sign-On standard. Microsoft may be cooperating with and publicly supporting systems like Shibboleth but there are two Microsoft systems addressing Simplified Sign-On. These are MS Passport.NET and Infocard/Windows Card Space, which are detailed next.

Microsoft Windows Live ID

Most users of Microsoft Web sites and services, like MSN, hotmail, and Windows Live Web Spaces, are likely to have encountered *Microsoft .NET Passport*, which has been renamed *Windows Live ID*. Under the umbrella of its .NET initiative, Microsoft launched a set of Web services; *.NET Passport* is a user authentication and single sign-in service. Users set up an email account, register with this email address and password for a.NET Passport, and have a .NET Passport profile created. They are then assigned a personal identification number, which is sent to the user's computer in the form of a cookie. The cookie allows users to visit participating Web sites without having to sign into each site. .NET Passport, and its SSI service, have been criticized for poor security and privacy, as its centralized nature makes it possible that other problems and security breaches will occur (Oppliger, 2003).

One similar system, in the form of a single sign-on, is the *Microsoft* Passport authentication service (see Figure 5). The Microsoft and Windows Live websites promote this service. Once signed in using an ID, which usually takes the form of a hotmail address, users can then interact between a number of different services, such as Windows Live accounts and Windows Live messenger. The single sign-on (SSO) works by directing users to a login screen, where they must supply correct credentials. Once they have been verified, the user is then sent back to the restricted page, along with an authenticated cookie which is proof that they have successfully logged in. When changing to a different site that has this system enabled, the user still has their authentication cookie, allowing them to browse these sites for the duration of the session.

Figure 5. Single Sign-On and Federations interactions

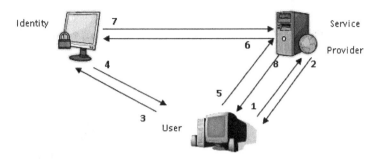

Microsoft Windows Card Space

Windows Card Space (originally named *Infocard*) was released as an Application Programming Interface (API) in .NET Framework Version 3.0. At the core of Windows Card Space lies the idea that users set up a set of digital identities, known as *information cards*, which they use for authentication or identification. Card Space has a user interface for managing these information cards. The system sits on top of security tokens (a security token could be a simple username, a digital certificate, SAML token etc.). This overcomes the security weakness of username/password authentication in Passport/Live ID, as illustrated in Figure 6.

In Figure 6, *Identity Provider* is the system which provides a digital identity. However, a provider could also be a credit card company, to make payments online, or an employer, when they supply a username and password to access systems. *Relying Parties* refers to online services, like shopping sites or online auctions, which use digital identities to authenticate a user (and often to authorize what a user has access to or can do). Windows Card Space can also be used to provide identities for Web sites and Web services applications, thereby tackling the other end of the identification and authentication conundrum of how to identify authentic Web sites to users and to prevent phishing (getting information fraudulently) using fake sites. In addition, as the identity metasystem underlying Card Space is based on open protocols, Card Space-compatible software for identity providers, relying parties, and other identity selectors can be built on any platform or device (Chappel, 2006).

Project Higgins

Project Higgins is an open source initiative, originating from the Berkman Centre for Internet & Society, a research programme based in the Law School of Harvard University in the U.S. It is being managed by the Eclipse Open Source Foundation

Figure 6. Interactions among the user, identity provider, and relying party roles. (Adapted from Chappel, 2006).

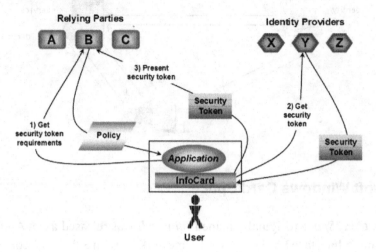

and in 2006 IBM, Novell and Parity Communications announced they were contributing code to spur swift adoption of Higgins by the broadest community of software developers. IBM plans to incorporate Higgins technology within its Tivoli identity management software, with added support by independent software vendors and IBM's consulting services division (Becker, 2006). Like Microsoft's Card Space, *user-centric* identity management is a central concept in its Project Higgins; it is intended that users manage their online personal information and decide what they want to share (by breaking their identity into pieces or *services*) with trusted Web sites that use the software. The developers believe it will support any technology platform and identity management system (Becker, 2006). The route Higgins is taking, that of using open and standard code or protocols (as are Shibboleth and Windows Card Space), works in its favor. Arguably, this is the only feasible way to go with a system aiming to be adopted by vast numbers of users and companies on the Internet.

Strong authentication is a must for the future but people may not feel as safe as many websites will already know various things about the user:

Essentially and eventually, authentication will result in the Web becoming one huge interconnected site where everyone who you want to do business with already knows who you are and what you like… It will be as if the Web was custom-designed just for you… Simplified Sign-On will only be widely used if people feel safe and feel they are getting fair value for giving up some privacy. (Delio, 2002, p. 1)

Simplified Sign-On Issues

Consolidating all, or at least a large segment, of authentication on the internet may reduce inconvenience to users but there is a worry that the single sign-on can become compromised. The question is whether concentrating everything in one authentication session becomes a massive security risk in itself. There is a responsibility for security on both the organization, which took on the considerable challenge of providing the authentication, and on the web users themselves. If Simplified Sign-On becomes a reality, this risk will have to be accepted, and as much done as possible to mitigate this risk. It seems inevitable that the standard username and password will be deemed too weak. Realistically biometrics, smartcards, digital certificates and the like will be necessary in an implementation of Simplified Sign-On. Simplified Sign-On systems operating at a business level already support multiple authentication methods, for example, ID's or passwords, dynamic passwords, certificates, biometrics, and security tokens. This entails some investment. In addition to these issues, the levels of agreement, cooperation, and standardization needed to achieve Simplified Sign-On, even among a section of organizations and companies on the web, are considerable. The disadvantages of Simplified Sign-On include:

- Potential security risk as a potential hacker has only one username and password to obtain.
- Potential hackers would have access to all users' accounts.
- Passwords can be forgotten by the user and they then do not have access to any of their accounts.
- Would have to include numerous layers of authentication between organizations.
- Systems will need more robust security and require powerful encryption.

CONCLUSION

Authentication is the procedure of deciding if a user or someone is, in fact who they are declaring they are. The internet and private computer networks mainly require authentication. This is normally done through the use of usernames and passwords. Business and personal transactions require a strict authentication process; therefore, a digital certificate verified by Certificate Authority (CA) is the standard way to perform authentication. Authentication precedes authorization, although they are commonly misguidedly considered to be the same. The commonly known problem that arises with authentication is that most users now have more than one username and password to use for work, the internet, university, e-mail and the bank. The proposed solution to this problem is Authentication Systems where each user enters their ID and password only once so that they can securely access other sites, thus speeding things up. Shibboleth is an open standard authentication system mainly used by universities with a high level of security and guarantee for each transaction. The system also provides a guard for privacy. For example, when a student logs on to the university's network, all their information is on their account and when they go to the library to request books, only the necessary information will be available to view by the librarian, as the librarian will not need to view the students test results. Microsoft also launched a similar system named Passport System, which allows Windows users to access specific Web sites with their hotmail address and password. If it is assumed that the development of Simplified Sign-On follows that of many technologies, it can be imagined that leaders will emerge and much Simplified Sign-On will converge on their standards, with the result of a level of homogeny. It is also likely that there may always be some scattering of technologies and companies who offer or manage Simplified Sign-On, with some resulting interoperability and incompatibility issues.

REFERENCES

Becker, J. (2006). Open Source Initiative to Give People More Control Over Their Personal Online Information. *IBM Press Release*. Retrieved August 17, 2009, from http://www-03.ibm.com/press/us/en/pressrelease/19280.wss

Chappel, D. (2006). Introducing Windows Card Space Online. *Windows Vista Technical Articles*. Retrieved August 17, 2009, from http://msdn2.microsoft.com/en-us/library/aa480189.aspx

Delio, M. (2002, February). Sun Shines Light on ID Alliance. *Wired Magazine*. Retrieved August 17, 2009, from http://www.wired.com/news/business/0,1367,53859,00.html

Gettes, M. R. (1999). *Shibboleth - Middleware Web Authentication Project*. Retrieved August 17, 2009, from http://shibboleth.internet2.edu/docs/shibboleth-project.html

Oppliger, R. (2003). Microsoft. NET Passport: A Security Analysis. *Computer, 36*(7), 29-35. Retrieved August 17, 2009, from http://csdl2.computer.org/persagen/DLAbsToc.jsp?resourcePath=/dl/mags/co/&toc=comp /mags/co/2003/07/r7toc.xml&DOI=10.1109/MC.2003.1212687

Perry, D. (2006, May 29). Can single sign-on be simple sign-on? *The Register*. Retrieved August 17, 2009, from http://www.theregister.co.uk/2006/05/29/simple_sso/

Rotman, L. (2005). Internet2 collaborates with Microsoft to Enable Interoperability of Federated Authentication Software. *I2 News Archive*. Retrieved August 17, 2009, from http://lists.aarnet.edu.au/pipermail/middle-l/2005-December/000074.html

Talbot, D. (2006). Simplified Sign-On. *MIT Technology Review*, March/April 2006. Retrieved August 17, 2009, from http://www.technologyreview.com/read_article. aspx?ch=specialsections&sc=emerging&id=16474

Chapter 4
The Effectiveness of Privacy Policy Statements

Roger Clarke
Xamax Consultancy Pty Ltd, Australia

ABSTRACT

An expectation exists in the U.S.A. that operators of business-to-consumer (B2C) Web sites will provide public notice of their privacy and security practices in relation to the personal data that they hold. Such documents are referred to in this paper as Privacy Policy Statements (PPS). The use of PPS has become mainstream in many other countries as well. Privacy and security of personal data are important elements in consumer trust, and hence in a consumer's decision to make purchases using Internet commerce services. PPS could therefore be expected to play an important role in overcoming the impediments to consumer purchases online. This paper adds to the growing research literature on PPS by developing a research design involving comparison of an organisation's PPS against a normative template developed on the basis of professional practice and laws, policies, practices, and public expectations around the world. A study of six B2C sites was undertaken, in order to assess the practicability of the design, and provide some initial substantive insight into the contributions that PPS currently make to consumer trust. It appears that many organisations' PPS may be seriously inadequate, and hence may be more of an impediment to trust than an enabler of Web-commerce adoption.

DOI: 10.4018/978-1-60566-806-2.ch004

INTRODUCTION

Consumers' perceptions of the security of corporate business systems are dependent on many factors. One important element is the understanding that consumers have of the organization's privacy practices. In order to communicate those practices, it has become common for operators of B2C eCommerce Web sites to explain their practices in relation to personal data in documents called by a variety of names, including *Privacy Policies, Privacy Statements, Privacy Notices*, and *Information Practice Statements*. This paper uses the term *Privacy Policy Statements* (PPS).

PPS emerged in the U.S.A. in the mid-to-late 1990s. The U.S. has no generic private sector privacy legislation, with successive Administrations and the heavy majority of Congress clinging to the beliefs that business should remain as unfettered as possible, and that self-regulation is an acceptable alternative to genuine regulation of business activities. PPS were intended to be an element in that framework. Their use has spread, however. They have come to be used in jurisdictions where data protection laws exist and the statement's impacts and purposes are rather different.

To date, a great deal of the literature on this topic has been conducted from the perspective of U.S. law, policy and practices, and most of the empirical studies have been undertaken in the U.S.A. Because U.S. law is so much more permissive than the laws of other economically advanced countries, the U.S. is emphatically not an appropriate context for works that are intended to have meaning for international audiences.

The research, on which this paper is based, adopts an approach different from most prior studies. Firstly, the purpose of the research is to consider the effectiveness of PPS from the perspective of the consumer. Secondly, the work began with a normative template that was previously developed on the basis of professional practice and the laws, policies, practices and public expectations around the world. This has taken into account OECD Guidelines, European Union Directives and laws in European countries, Canada, Australia, New Zealand and Hong Kong.

A study was undertaken to evaluate a number of PPS against that normative template, in order to assess the extent to which they were likely to represent effective protection for consumers' privacy. This is a further project, in a long-running research program undertaken by the author, in the general area of privacy and information technology, in the particular context of the Internet, and specifically in Business-to-Consumer (B2C) eCommerce. As a result, a substantial number of the c. 80 citations are to prior refereed papers by the author of this chapter. These provide fuller analyses and arguments supporting many of the points made, together with many further references to the relevant literature.

The paper commences by reviewing the role of privacy as a trust factor in Internet-based B2C eCommerce. This is followed by a consideration of the various means whereby privacy can be protected. The role and nature of PPS is delineated, existing conventions are identified, and an evaluation template is proposed. A research design is developed to investigate the effectiveness of PPS from the perspective of consumers. This includes attention to the population of B2C services, population segmentation, and sampling frames. A small sample is selected and a survey conducted. The results provide a basis for refinement of the research design, and lay the foundation for the conduct of more substantial surveys.

PRIVACY AS A TRUST FACTOR

According to the Theory of Reasoned Action (TRA) of Ajzen & Fishbein (1980), trust and risk are major determinants of attitude towards purchasing, and hence of intention to purchase. In the context of Internet-based B2C eCommerce, trust is usefully defined as confident reliance by one party about the behavior of other parties (Clarke, 2002a).

The concept of trust originates in familial and social settings, where parties have considerable mutual understanding, mutual interests, and mutual dependence. The strongest sources of trust arise from a pre-existing direct relationship between the parties, primarily through kinship and mateship, but also to some extent from such commercial forms as principal-agent relationships, contracts, and multiple prior transactions (Clarke, 2002a). A less strong source is direct experience, as arises from a prior transaction, or perhaps prior exposure to the organization concerned, for example, by watching a trusted friend conduct a transaction. Weaker again is referred trust, such as word-of-mouth and reputation. Still weaker are mere symbols of trust, which are often nothing more than contrived images, in the form of brands. The weakest form of all is *meta-brands*, such as accreditation and seals of approval, especially from industry associations that lack the power and/or the will to regulate even their members, let alone their non-members (Clarke 2001b). The strongest forms of trust are difficult to replicate in merely economic relationships. In B2C eCommerce, trust is in practice simply what the consumer is forced to depend on when no other form of risk amelioration strategy is available.

Trust is not easy to achieve in Internet contexts. The parties have little knowledge about one another and cannot depend on such confidence-engendering measures as physical proximity, handshakes, body language, a common legal jurisdiction, or even necessarily any definable jurisdiction (e.g. Lee & Turban, 2001; Clarke, 2001c). When business interests finally discovered the Internet in the mid-1990s, it was assumed that electronic commerce would explode. In fact, adoption was far slower than most Internet growth metrics because business failed to address the trust gap. This is examined in Clarke (1999b).

Trust issues are many and varied. Some are related to the terms and conditions under which consumers buy from business enterprises, especially their non-negotiability, their imbalance in favor of the vendor, the location of the contract in a jurisdiction that suits the vendor rather than the customer, and the lack of consumer protections that the consumer normally enjoys when purchasing goods and services in their home jurisdiction. Further concerns arise in relation to default by the vendor or by the carrier selected by the vendor. Yet many of these are security issues, relating to the consumer's identity and personal data, including the person's location, contact-points and credit-card details.

This paper is concerned with the particular cluster of impediments to the adoption of B2C eCommerce that are associated with privacy. Privacy is the interest that individuals have in sustaining a personal space, which is free from interference by other people and organizations (Clarke, 2006a). There are many dimensions of privacy. The one most relevant to the present context is personal data privacy. Key requirements include; the individual's ability to prevent data about themselves being available to other individuals and organizations; and, where data is available, the ability to control its quality, use and further disclosure.

The role that privacy plays in the achievement of trust has been examined by various researchers (e.g. Palmer, Bailey, & Faraj, 2000; Clarke, 2001c; Belanger, Hiller, & Smith, 2002, Xu, Tan, Hui, & Tang, 2003). The fundamental requirements are that the amount of personal data available to the marketer must be minimized, and such data that is available must be, and be perceived by consumers to be, protected against abuse by the marketer and others. This may be achieved through substantive measures combined with effective communication of their existence to consumers; or by effective communication based on as limited an actual set of constraints as the organization can get away with. There are significance cultural differences in the importance placed on privacy, and its role in trust (e.g. Dinev, et al. 2005; Kim, 2005).

PRIVACY PROTECTION MECHANISMS

Several different approaches are taken to privacy protection. This section briefly reviews ways in which online marketers can design their business processes to be privacy-sensitive and can use technology as an antidote, as well as a threat. This section culminates in a summary of the ways in which the law can be used to protect privacy. Together, these define key aspects of the various contexts within which PPS can be applied.

Business Process Protections

Until the early-to-mid twentieth century, most consumer transactions were conducted in physical marketplaces. Judgements were made based on the information available at the time the decision was made, and little data was stored. Progressively, as managerial rationalism took hold, as labor became more efficient through specialization, and as consumer marketing businesses became larger, more personal data came to be captured. During the second half of the twentieth century, enormous advances in information technology resulted in the capacity for marketers to depend more and more on data as a substitute for knowledge of their customers, and to become more and more remote from them. But businesses can choose the appropriate degree of dependence on intensive personal data. They can enable anonymous and pseudonymous purchasing, by denying themselves the opportunity to consolidate data about each customer, to use it, and to pass it on to others. Even where they transact with known identities, they can limit the data that they retain (as some vendors do, for example, by not retaining credit-card details, or not retaining some part of it, such as the last four digits). Businesses that hold identified data need to implement appropriate organizational security measures to protect it.

It is suggested in Clarke (1998) that direct marketing using electronic channels would be more successful if the following principles were applied:

- **Information** about the marketer's use of the technology, which is readily available to anyone who seeks it, and sufficient to enable people to understand how it works, and what it entails;

- **Choice**, such that each consumer can judge whether or not to engage in a relationship, or receive communications;

- **Consent**, by each consumer, to the establishment of a relationship, and the receipt of communications. Express consent is strongly preferable but implied consent may be appropriate in a few circumstances. Consent requires an *opt-in* arrangement, such that the person agrees in advance to the activity. *Opt-out* arrangements may be cheap, but they are not consumer-friendly, and require stringent justification of a kind that consumers will be comfortable with. This is discussed in greater detail in Clarke (2002b);

- **Fair Conditions**, such that each consumer has grounds for being confident in the nature of the commercial relationship;

- **Recourse**, such that marketer behavior, that does not comply with these norms, can be brought under control.

Technological Protections

Information technology has been primarily harmful to the privacy interest, resulting in increasingly widespread use of the term *Privacy-Invasive Technologies*, or *the PITs* (Clarke, 2001a). A movement has been in train for a decade now, intended to apply information technology in support of privacy rather than against it. This goes under the name *Privacy-Enhancing Technologies* (PETs), a term which appears to have originated in Information and Privacy Commissioner (IPCR, 1995). See also Electronic Privacy Information Center (EPIC) (1996) and Burkert (1997). Specialist PET Workshops have been held annually since 2001.

Clarke (2001a) distinguishes three broad kinds of PETs:

- **PIT countermeasures, or counter-PITs**, designed to defeat or neutralize Privacy-Invasive Technologies. Examples include SSL/TLS for channel encryption, cookie managers, anti-spam measures and personal firewalls;

- **savage PETs**. These deny identity and provide genuine, untraceable anonymity. Examples include, anonymous (Mixmaster) remailers and web-surfing schemes, and David Chaum's payer-anonymous Digicash; and

- **gentle PETs**. Accountability is undermined by savage PETs because retribution is difficult if the perpetrator cannot be identifed. Pseudonymity can provide a balance between the interests of privacy and accountability. But adoption is dependent on credibility, and pseudonymity is not credible if it can be readily circumvented by governments and corporations. Hence, as an alternative to Savage PETs, Gentle PETs are oriented towards protected pseudonymity.

Legal Protections

Several heads of law may provide privacy protections. In common law jurisdictions, the torts of breach of confidence and passing off may have some limited applicability. In addition, a tort of invasion of privacy has been very slowly emerging because of the failure of Parliaments to enact appropriate legislation. The legal measures of greatest relevance are explicit privacy laws, explicit data protection statutes, incidental privacy provisions within other statutes, contracts, and laws relating to misleading statements.

Comprehensive *privacy statutes*, which provide protections for all of the multiple dimensions of privacy (Clarke 2006a), are almost unheard of, although the human rights provisions in many countries' constitutions at least provide some basis for the development of case law. The first *data protection statute*, on the other hand, was passed in 1970 in the German state of Hesse. Since then, most advanced western nations have enacted such laws. These all reflect the *fair information practices* (FIPs) movement, which originated in U.S. business and government circles in the late 1960s, and flowered in Europe during the 1970s (Flaherty, 1989; Bennett, 1992). The FIPs notion was codified in the Organisation for Economic Cooperation and Development (OECD) Guidelines (1980).

The FIPs notion was intended to protect the interests of business and government, so it is no surprise that legislation based on it provides seriously inadequate privacy protection. FIPs-originated laws are of narrow scope, embody manifold exemptions and exceptions, and omit key control mechanisms (Clarke, 2000). Moreover, laws in most jurisdictions reflect the technology of the 1970s, rather than that of the new century. The FIPs notion has become so engrained, however, and the dominance of economic over social needs has become so strong, that privacy advocates have been at best only partly successful in their endeavors to shift the focus of public policy away from the nominal protection of data, back to the protection of people's privacy.

Almost alone among leading nations, the U.S. Congress has failed to enact comprehensive consumer privacy legislation. Many incoherent and narrowly sector-specific laws exist, however, due to flurries of public concern arising in such areas as health records, video rental records and the privacy of children. Provisions of this nature are largely redundant in most countries with comprehensive data protection laws, and they are not a primary focus of this paper.

In response to the demands of business lobbyists, the U.S. Federal Trade Commission (FTC) sought during the 1990s to roll back even the limited protections that had emerged from the FIPs movement. It issued its own and even more inadequate set of a mere four widely accepted fair information principles: notice, choice, access, and security, with a fifth principle added later, accountability (FTC, 2000). This brought the U.S. into conflict with the E.U. because many U.S. consumer marketing corporations are active there. After a period of uncertainty, the E.U. chose to ignore the concerns of its advisory group Art.29 (2000), and backed down on key requirements. It permitted the U.S. to devise a so-called *Safe Harbor* program (DOC 2000). This is an extension to the FTC's cut-down version of FIPs – with the original five principles supplemented by onward transfer, data integrity, and enforcement; however, despite the name of the final principle, the scheme is not subject to effective enforcement. More recently, the U.S. Administration, through the Department of Commerce, has sought to undermine the OECD Guidelines by exerting its influence on members of the Asia-Pacific Economic Cooperation

(APEC), in order to achieve publication of an alternative and much weaker set of principles (APEC, 2004).

Contract law may also provide a basis for privacy protections. Vendors may offer explicit terms that the courts will treat as part of the contract, binding vendor and consumer alike. Assurances about privacy protection may be embedded into those terms. Even where they are not, it is open to the courts, at least in common law jurisdictions, to find conditions to be implied in contracts. A PPS can form part of the terms of contract that the vendor and consumer enter into, either by the vendor's terms expressly reading in the PPS, or by the courts regarding the PPS as being an implied term of the contract. The effectiveness of contract as a privacy protection is very limited, however. There is often vast disparity between the resources and market power of the parties. In addition, and the jurisdiction in which an action must be brought is often distant from the consumer, and is usually incomprehensible to them and too expensive for them to utilize.

A further head of law of potential significance is provisions that make *misrepresentation* an illegal act. In common law countries, tort law may render misrepresentation a breach of the offended party's civil rights. Many countries have created statutory obligations of a similar nature, and some recognize criminal misrepresentation. Examples include, the U.K. Misrepresentation Act 1967, the Australian Trade Practices Act 1974 s.52, and Fair Trade Practices and Misrepresentation statutes in the various Australian States and Territories. If the PPS takes the form of an undertaking by the vendor (rather than just a vague description or inherently untrustworthy advertisement), then it may be feasible for it to serve as the basis for an action under such laws. In many cases, however, such actions may be brought only by a particular regulator, which fails to do so. As a result, the provision is nugatory that it to say, like most potentially privacy-protective laws, literally worthless.

The U.S. is a particularly important example, in this case, because of the absence of comprehensive privacy legislation. The Fair Trade Commission Act s.5(a) renders illegal an unfair or deceptive act or practice. This has been claimed to provide a sufficient restraint on privacy-abusive practices by American business (e.g. FTC 2005). But the FTC has serially failed its obligation to enforce those provisions, having pursued only 15 cases in 7 years in the world's largest and most dynamic economy. These claims are hollow. The FTC is consistent in its defense of business enterprises against privacy laws. It gutted the child protection law, by determining that Amazon.com's Toy Store web site is "not directed at children" (EPIC, 2004). Any organization can now unilaterally declare itself outside the scope of the Act simply by including a statement that it "does not sell products for purchase by children", despite the fact that children are highly unlikely to take any notice of such statements.

The U.S. self-regulatory Safe Harbor scheme has proven completely inadequate (Hoofnagle, 2005; Connolly, 2008) and is a much poorer deal for consumers than the inadequate FIPs-inspired laws in other countries. The longstanding calls for FIPs legislation in the U.S.A. (e.g. Clarke, 1999a), which were temporarily quietened in the years immediately following the terrorist strikes of September 2001, have resumed, with American business reported to be in support of regulation (e.g. Economist, 2005).

PRIVACY POLICY STATEMENTS

In the mid-to-late 1990s, it became fashionable in the U.S. for corporations to publish statements on their Web sites about their privacy practices (FTC, 1998a, 1998b; Hoffman, Novak, & Peralta, 1999). The notion has been adopted in other countries as well. In many countries it is primarily symbolic because a data protection statute that regulates the private sector is far more likely to be effective than a mere statement by the organization itself.

This paper adopts the view that, although a mere statement can only be a small part of a comprehensive approach to privacy protection, and hence consumer trust in B2C eCommerce, there is nonetheless potential value in PPS. The reasons are as follows:

• publishing a PPS can motivate corporations to reflect their declared corporate privacy undertakings in their business processes;

• in countries that have data protection laws, publishing a PPS involves the articulation of corporations' legal responsibilities. The existence of a PPS may simplify complaints-handling and actions in tribunals and courts; and

• in those countries without effective data protection laws, such as the U.S.A., the existence of a PPS may provide a basis for actions possibly in contract or under misrepresentation laws, as a limited substitute for explicit statutory protections.

A variety of researchers have examined various aspects of Web site privacy statements. Foundation works include Culnan (1993) and Smith, Milberg, and Burke (1996). Important among the analyses and empirical investigations have been Wang, Lee, and Wang (1998); Anton and Earp (2001); Earp, Anton, and Jarvinen (2002); Lichtenstein, Swatman, and Babu (2002); Milne and Culnan (2002); Earp and Baumer (2003); Lichtenstein Swatman, and Babu (2003); Culnan and Bies

(2003); Jensen and Potts (2004); Gauzente (2004); Kobsa and Teltzrow (2005); Milne, Culnan, and Green (2006); and Anton et al. (2007).

Some articles have focused on the benefits to business enterprises of a PPS. Meinert, Peterson, Criswell, and Crossland (2006) reported on a survey that showed that "the willingness [of graduate students] to provide information to Web merchants increased as the level of privacy guaranteed by the [privacy] statements increased" (p. 1). Hui, Teo, and Lee (2007) used a field experiment to show that "the existence of a privacy statement induced more subjects to disclose their personal information but that of a privacy seal did not" (p 19). Schwaig, Kane, and Storey (2004, 2006) and Hooper, Bunker, Rapson, Reynolds, and Vos (2007) noted the effectiveness of PPS for big businesses, despite the very limited protections they afford.

Other articles are more doubtful, variously about the quality and the value of PPS. Regan (2001) noted how infrequently they were accessed. Many authors have drawn attention to their complexity, notably FTC (2000) and Culnan and Milne 2001. Dubbeld (2006) concluded that "the underdeveloped state of online privacy notifications [on telecardiology Web sites] is disappointing". Markel (2008) found that "of 20 randomly selected US companies that claim to be in compliance [with the low-grade and unenforced U.S. 'safe harbor' norms] ..., 19 are not ..." (p. 1).

Kobsa & Teltzrow (2005) concluded that:

76% of users find privacy policies very important, and 55% stated that a privacy policy makes them more comfortable disclosing personal information. However, privacy statements today are usually written in a form that gives the impression that they are not really supposed to be read. And this is indeed not the case: whereas 73% of the respondents ... indicate having viewed web privacy statements in the past (and 26% of them claim to always read them), web site operators report that users hardly pay any attention to them (p. 1)

This conflict between the apparent importance of privacy and the limited use of privacy statements has been referred to as a "disconnect between public opinion and public behaviour" (Regan, 2003, p 12).

This disconnect reflects the highly situational nature of privacy. Most of the time, most consumers are only vaguely concerned about privacy, and lack the motivation to seek out and read carefully phrased, turgid *legalese*. But even vague concerns represent an impediment to the adoption of eCommerce. Moreover, once an individual consumer's concerns are triggered, the person may easily become an active avoider of Webcommerce. In response to the limited use of PPS by consumers, the concept of *layered notices* has been developed "to provide an easy to read one-page summary of a company's online privacy practices while conforming to all regulatory requirements and giving links to full legal statements and other relevant

Figure 1. Research model

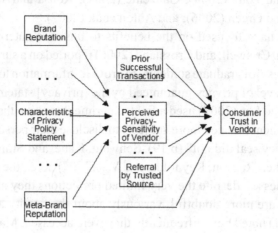

information" (Fleischer, 2005; Crompton 2004). It is unclear whether the initiative has delivered any value to consumers.

Only limited guidance is available in the literature as to what constitutes an appropriate form for a PPS. One important exception is the linked documents OECD (2000a, 2000b). The Committee of European Data Protection Commissioners, meeting as the EU's Article 29 Working Group on Data Protection, has been reported as having published guidelines on corporate privacy notices in late 2004 (e.g. Pruitt, 2005). But a search on the Article 29 Committee's Web site failed to provide access to a copy. A preliminary document is visible on the site of the German Federal Data Protection Commissioner (ICDCP, 2003).

The Web sites of the various privacy protection agencies provide almost no assistance, although a publication of the U.K. Commissioner is of some relevance (ICO, 2001). There are no guidelines apparent on the sites of the U.S. FTC, or even of the leading U.S. advocacy group EPIC, and the more business-aligned groups CDT and EFF. Some guidance is provide by TRUSTe (2004, 2005), the Better Business Bureau, and Freenetlaw.com (2008); however, these documents are seriously limited because they merely advise compliance with the FTC's minimalist FIPs model and a few U.S. sector-specific laws. Guidance intended for government agencies may also be of assistance, such as OFPC (2000), Australian Government Information Management Office (AGIMO, 2003), and TSB (2004).

As a prelude to the project reported on in this paper, this author drew on prior research, including the above sources, in order to compile a Privacy Statement Template. This is at Clarke (2005a), with accompanying comments in Clarke (2005b). The Template is normative, by which is meant that it is a compilation of the needs of consumers, and is not compromised by the exercise of market power by business enterprises, nor by the limited provisions of FIPs-based data protection laws. The Template stipulates requirements in the areas of data collection, data security, data use, data disclosure, data retention and destruction, access by data subjects to personal data, information about data handling practices, the handling of enquiries, general concerns and complaints, enforcement, and changes to privacy undertakings. The Template is applied in the research described below, as a basis for evaluating the PPS published by B2C vendors.

RESEARCH DESIGN

The general research question being pursued in this study is: How effective are Privacy Policy Statements in encouraging consumer trust of B2C vendors? The model that is assumed is depicted in Figure 1. Consumer trust is heavily dependent on the vendor's perceived privacy sensitivity. That perception is in turn heavily dependent on the characteristics of the vendor's privacy policy statement.

The purpose of this research is to consider the effectiveness of PPS from the perspective of the consumer. The research focuses on contexts in which vendors are seeking to implement substantive, rather than mere image-based, privacy protections. It also leaves to one side the need for effective marketing communications, to ensure that consumers understand that the protections are in place.

The operational interpretation of the research question is: Do the Privacy Policy Statements found on vendors web-sites measure up to the requirements expressed in the normative Privacy Statement Template? The vendor population is defined as those B2C services that are accessible on the World Wide Web. For simplicity, it does not encompass other forms of B2C eCommerce, such as emergent mobile services accessed through means other than web-browsers. This is, nonetheless, a highly diverse set of services. It is therefore important to analyze the population into meaningful segments, and probably important to over-sample from some of those segments. Figure 2 provides a two-dimensional segmentation model that appears to be appropriate for the research question. For each segment, a sampling frame is needed. Examples for Market Leaders include businesses that receive frequent mentions in the media in relation to their privacy statements and consumer terms. Aggressive Marketers could include organizations that have won awards for their B2C operations from such organizations as the (U.S.) Direct Marketing Association (DMA), or for whom Harvard case studies have been prepared. For Marketers of Sensitive Products, directories of on-line sex-shops and on-line gambling services could be consulted. Regional directories would provide links to marketers subject to the laws of particular jurisdictions. For Ethical Marketers, directories of not-for-profit B2C operations, including charities, could be consulted.

Figure 2. Population segmentation

Company-Type	Description	Justification
Dimension 1: The Company		Patterns in these two subcatagories may be materially different, because consumer trust is easier to achieve in an organization with physical presence.
A: "Pure Internet" B2C	Corporations that do not have a separate physical operation	
B: "Clicks and Mortar" B2C	Corporations that do have a separate physical operation	
Dimension 2: The Business		Patterns in these five sub-catagories may be materially different, due to various characteristics of the business and its content
A: Leaders	Businesses acknowledged as trend-setters in this field	It would be valuable to over-sample this category, because it offers an indication of future directions
B: Aggressive Marketers	Business recognized as being strong and direct in their approach to consumers	These businesses could be expected to be either distainful of privacy, or manipulative and image-concious
C: Marketers of Sensitive Products	Businesses that sell goods and services where purchasers are likely to be particularly concerned about privacy	These business could be expected to be highly subject to, and very well aware of, the need for effective privacy and visable privacy protections
D: Regional Marketers	Businesses primarily active in particular jurisdictions	Companies that are subject to data protection laws could be expected to adopt different approaches to those that are not subject to such laws
E: "Ethical" / Not for Profit Marketers	Businesses run by organizations that espouse strong values in relation to privacy	These operations could be expected to have adopted positive approaches to privacy protection

Audit of the organization's compliance with its PPS, and contact with the organisation to seek any clarifications, are highly desirable. Such procedures are highly resource-intensive, however, and long delays and refusals might be anticipated. It is therefore envisaged that all judgments will be based on the PPS review, supplemented by experiments with the relevant service.

The Survey

A survey was conducted. The primary purpose of this was to gain insight into the efficacy and practicability of the design, in preparation for its wider application. A secondary purpose was to gather information of relevance to policy discussions. The first assessments were performed in January 2006, with a follow-up in December 2008, to check the extent to which the content and presentation were stable or were in a state of flux.

The Sample

A small set of organizations was selected, in order to test the application of the Template to the PPS published by a manageably small list of organizations. These were selected in order to ensure some diversity and to provide the prospect of results with some policy value.

The organizations selected for evaluation are listed below. The two market-leaders are very apparent from media and popular discussions. The choice of a German company was based partly on the fact that the country has the longest history of data protection laws, and partly on the pragmatic grounds that German is the only language, other than English, that the author can read and the author has more familiarity with data protection laws in German-speaking countries than with those in other parts of Europe.

B2C Businesses Selected

- Leaders:
  - Amazon
  - Google
- Aggressive Marketers:
  - Sears, Roebuck and Co.
- Marketers of Sensitive Products:
  - Adultshop.com
- Regional Marketers:
  - Autoteile-Meile.de, an online supplier of tyres and automotive spare parts
- 'Ethical' Marketers:
  - National Geographic, which presents itself as "the largest nonprofit scientific and educational institution in the world"

Results

This section provides a brief summary of the outcomes. The detailed assessment sheets are available on the Web and the archived copies of the PPS, that were evaluated, are available from the author on request.

National Geographic and Google both implement the *layered notice* notion by offering a *highlights* page as well as a PPS. Google provides further PPS in respect of some of its services. The other organizations in the sample offer a single Web page, ranging from an equivalent of one to one-half pages of A4 (Adultshop.com) to four to six pages (Amazon, Autoteile-Meile.de and National Geographic).

Amazon declared for itself extraordinary latitude in its handling of personal data. The effect of the statements was essentially that it collects personal data from wherever it wants to, uses it however it wants to, and discloses it to whomever it wants to. It provided minimal information on data security, none on data retention and destruction, little on amendment, and none on deletion of personal data. In common with many other organizations, it provided no access to previous version of its PPS. Amazon had previously changed its PPS, reneging on previous undertakings, and providing itself with additional latitude (e.g. Rosencrance 2000a, 2000b). It has also been accused of breaches of the Children's Online Privacy Protection Act (EPIC 2003); although, the FTC found a way to ensure that the breach was only of the spirit rather than of the letter of the law (EPIC 2004). On re-visit, the date of latest change was visible, as was an explanation of what the changes had been. This represented a procedural improvement, but the mechanism remained deficient in that no chain was provided back to earlier versions. These changes in the PPS provided no substantive improvement, however, and Amazon remains privacy-hostile.

The analysis of the Google PPS was the subject of Clarke (2005c, 2006b). Serious shortfalls were identified in many areas. These included: the particular use of cookies; the vagueness of the statements about the purposes of the data Google collects; its transfer of personal data across borders; the absence of assurances about relevance and quality of personal data; its apparent attempt to obfuscate the meaning of *consent*; its failure to take any responsibility for personal data transferred to affiliates, or to any other organization; its failure to even address data retention and destruction issues; its failure to provide information about its data-handling processes, even on request; the general unenforceability of the assurances given; and the complete absence of protections in the event of merger, acquisition, or sale of assets. In short, the several positive aspects of Google's PPS were completely swamped by very serious deficiencies. On re-visit, a single further version had been added to the chain and all remained visible. However, no indication was provided of what change(s) had been made and the wide range of serious shortfalls remained. Some other changes of relevance had occurred, however. In mid-2008, Google at last adopted the widespread norm of having a link to the PPS from the home-page. Further, it responded to a few of the many criticisms leveled at it by privacy advocacy organizations by providing, *layered statements* (a short version, as well as the long one), links to the more specific PPS for particular services, and access to various videos it has published that are of relevance to privacy questions. However, no index exists of the video content and it is far from clear that such statements, as are made in them, are binding on the company. Google is a huge threat to the privacy, not only of its users, but also of people who correspond with gmail users.

Testing of the Sears site was made more difficult by its non-standard or bug-laden code, which caused malfunctions of the mainstream Mac Mozilla 1.7.8 browser being used. The PPS was found to have a wide array of deficiencies, not unlike Google's, but is worse in some respects. For example, the concept of *voluntary provision* of personal data was used in relation to data whose provision appears to be a condition of dealing; collection from, and disclosure to, third parties is undertaken on a non-consensual basis; the company appears to have no concept of data destruction on expiry of use; and no information is evident about any complaints process. This is consistent with a consumer-arrogant operation rather than a privacy-sensitive stance. On re-testing, the incompatibilities with mainstream browsers appeared to have been overcome. A date of last change was provided, but no indication was given of the changes made, and no chain was offered back to prior versions. There was considerable cosmetic change, but little in the way of substantive improvements appeared to have been made. Moreover, a catch-all disclaimer had been added: "While we work very hard to protect your privacy, we do not promise, and you should not expect, that your personal information will always remain private". In short, Sears' policies continue to be seriously privacy-hostile.

Adultshop.com is admittedly a very much smaller operation than the previous three, but its PPS is the antithesis of theirs. The PPS is expressly used as part of its positioning: "Our business success depends on our discretion and our understanding of the importance of your privacy. If you have suggestions for enhancing our privacy policy, please contact me directly...Malcolm Day, Managing Director". All statements are directly expressed, and all options taken are privacy-sensitive. It falls short of the Template's requirements on many details (for example, data retention, access by the data subject, changes to the PPS, and acquisition, merger and sale of business). But many of these weaknesses are far less important because of the business process design. It is possible that the site's privacy-sensitivity reflects the fact that the organization is subject to a data protection law (the Australian Privacy Act's private sector provisions, enacted in 2000). That is, however, a very weak implementation of the OECD's FIPs model, and it is reasonable to infer that the needs of the company's customers were a significant factor in determining its approach. No changes were apparent on re-visit in late 2008.

The German company, Autoteile-Meile, is subject to the German data protection law, the Bundesdatenschutzgesetz ss. 1-11 and 27-46. Remarkably, however, its PPS is largely a German translation of the current Amazon PPS (to the extent that it may be in breach of Amazon's copyright). Therefore, it inherits a large proportion of the weaknesses of that document. A number of modifications are apparent, to reflect the provisions of the German law. Others that might have been expected have not been made, however. Amazon has successfully opted out of the U.S. child privacy regulatory scheme merely by putting some well-chosen words on its Web site, but such corporation-friendly looseness is not a feature of European laws. It appeared that Autoteile-Meile's PPS might have been merely experimental because it would seem to have little, or no status, under German law. On re-visit, however, the PPS was still there, and the version was of a later date. Apart from some editing, the primary changes appeared to be the inclusion of a reference to a specific EU document, and a new section on Choice.

The PPS published by National Geographic was remarkable in two ways:

- it was brutally frank about the vast array of data collection, use and disclosure techniques it uses; and

- it featured a complete absence of choice, as indicated by the statement, "If you do not agree to this Privacy Policy, please do not use this Web site".

The privacy terms were arguably far worse even than those of Sears, Roebuck and Co. They failed dismally in relation to all of the following: data collection, security, use, disclosure, retention and destruction, personal access and complaints-handling. They imposed opt-out where consent (opt-in) is the norm. They provided no means to communicate complaints to the company. It appears that the PPS may have been designed by a very clever lawyer so that although it gave the appearance of compliance with the letter of the FTC's suggestions, it is non-compliant at the very least with the basic choice and access principles, and the additional onward transfer and enforcement principles. Perhaps large U.S. not-for-profit organizations have become imbued with the aggressive ethos of American corporations. National Geographic was included in the study as a member of the ethical segment, but its ethicality seemed to be limited to honesty about the organization's privacy-hostile stance. On re-visit, some uncertainty arose from date inconsistencies in the old and new pages. However, the PPS did not appear to be substantively different from that previously reviewed.

Observations arising from the evaluations are as follows:

- within large conglomerates, there is a vast amount of internal integration among business units, and many corporations are making the assumption that individuals, who transact with a business unit, thereby provide their data to the entire group;

- among nominally independent businesses (referred to by various terms, such as strategic partnering), the scale of inter-twining is enormous. Major consumer marketing corporations appear to regard personal data as being theirs to share with any company they do business with, as they see fit;

- the inclusion in a business group of a popular search-engine (as is the case with both Google and Amazon) delivers a great deal of additional consumer profile information, in the form of search-terms;

- there is a tendency towards tempting individuals to provide data about other people into corporate databases. This is most evident in social networking services, such as Google's Orkut, but also email services, such as Google's gmail. The prospect also exists of Amazon's Friends and Favorite People features being expanded;

- there is evidence that the self-permissive expressions used by American corporations (because of the substantial absence of a regulatory scheme there) are being adopted by companies elsewhere, even in circumstances in which they are subject to more stringent requirements.

One outcome of surprise was that it was not always as easy as it should be to discover the PPS. This identified the need to add an 'Accessibility requirement' into the Template. In most cases, the PPS was accessible from the home-page and from pages typically used during a consumer transaction. But Google did not have a link on its main pages at www.google.com, nor in country-specific services, such as www.google.com.au, nor even www.google.de, until mid-2008. It was necessary to follow the link to 'About Google' to find the link. All of the others offered the link in the page-footer, and some also draw attention to it at a relevant point in the purchasing process.

Other omissions from the template that became apparent during the course of the evaluations were:

- the need for the Data Security category to include a declaration that access control is imposed, and that accesses are limited to individuals and roles with a demonstrated 'need to know' about that particular information;

- the need for the Data Use category to include a requirement similar to that in the Data Disclosure category, to the effect that use is limited to those data-items necessary in the circumstances.

Some doubt was thrown on the segmentation used in the research design. In particular:

- there may be a need for a further dimension of corporation size or scale of operation. The patterns of use and abuse of personal data vary a great deal, and are apparently determined to a considerable extent by the size and complexity of business operations; and

- there may be a need for a further dimension of jurisdiction(s) in which the organization operates. The largely unfettered freedom in the U.S.A. is very distinct from the somewhat regulated environments in many other countries. A further consideration is that the virility of U.S. marketers is such that international consumer sales are showing a tendency towards globalism, and hence also towards the imposition of U.S. laissez faire on consumers everywhere, despite the protections they may enjoy in their own country.

CONCLUSION

In order to overcome consumer concerns about privacy-invasive practices in B2C eCommerce, there is no substitute for legal protection. Privacy policy statements originated within the U.S. self-regulatory context. They are, however, capable of playing a role within a statutory data protection framework, as well. A research design was prepared, to enable evaluation of privacy policy statements against a normative template. A survey applying the design to six organizations has established that the design required refinement, but was largely appropriate. To the extent that substantive conclusions can reasonably be drawn from the survey, it appears that major American corporations, and even not-for-profit corporations, fall far short of the privacy-sensitive norms that consumers would reasonably expect in relation to the handling of personal data. More consumer-friendly practices appear to be associated with two factors: a statutory framework for data protection, and vendors of especially sensitive goods and services. These tentative inferences of course need to be tested through the evaluation of a larger, and more representative, sample of privacy policy statements and extension beyond B2C eCommerce to Mobile Commerce. If the privacy-hostile positions adopted by this sample of organizations are reasonably common, then consumer distrust of corporations is both justified and inevitable. This has consequences for consumers' perception of the security of their dealings with companies, and hence for consumers' willingness to adopt and use Web-commerce. Complementary research is needed to address aspects of the research question that were intentionally left to one side. In particular, studies are needed of the extent to which consumers understand the degree of privacy-protectiveness that they do and do not enjoy when using different companies' services, and the extent to which their adoption and non-adoption decisions reflect that understanding. It is argued in Clarke (1996, 2006c) that consumer-facing corporations need to address privacy as a strategic factor. It appears that at least some companies have not yet adapted to the realities of the Internet era. The PPS template, that provided the basis for this study, can also be used as a checklist for organizations that are re-assessing the stances they adopt in dealings with their customers.

ACKNOWLEDGMENT

An early version of this paper was presented at the 19th Bled eCommerce Conf., Slovenia, 5-7 June 2006. This version reflects the comments of informal commentators, conference reviewers and delegates, and reviewers of the enhanced version submitted for this collection.

REFERENCES

Ajzen, I., & Fishbein, M. (1980). *Understanding Attitudes and Predicting Social Behavior*. Englewood Cliffs, NJ: Prentice Hall Inc.

Anton, A. I., Earp, J. B., Vail, M. W., Jain, N., Gheen, C. M., & Frink, J. M. (2007). HIPAA's Effect on Web Site Privacy Policies. *IEEE Security and Privacy*, *5*(1), 45–52. doi:10.1109/MSP.2007.7

Anton A. I., & Earp J. P. (2001). *A Taxonomy for Web Site Privacy Requirements*. NCSU Dept. of Comp Science Technical Report (TR-2001-14).

Art.29 (2000). Opinion 4/2000 on the level of protection provided by the 'Safe Harbor Principles'. *Article 29 Data Protection Working Party of the European Union*. Retrieved May 16, 2000, from http://europa.eu.int/comm/justice_home/fsj/privacy/docs/wpdocs/2000/wp32en.pdf, accessed 9 January 2006

Asia-Pacific Economic Council. (APEC, 2004). *APEC Privacy Framework*. Asia-Pacific Economic Council, November 2004. Retrieved December 16, 2008, from http://203.127.220.112/content/apec/news___media/2004_media_releases/201104_apecminsendorseprivacyfrmwk.downloadlinks.0001.LinkURL.Download.ver5.1.9

Australian Government Information Management Office. (AGIMO, 2003). *The Guide to Minimum Website Standards – Attachment C: Privacy Checklist*. Canberra: Australian Government Information Management Office. Retrieved December 16, 2008, from http://www.agimo.gov.au/practice/mws/attachments#C

BBB. (2003). *Sample Privacy Notice*. Better Business Bureau. Retrieved December 16, 2008, from https://www.bbbonline.org/privacy/sample_privacy.asp

Belanger, F., Hiller, J., & Smith, W. (2002). Trustworthiness in electronic commerce: The role of privacy, security, and site attributes. *The Journal of Strategic Information Systems*, *11*(3-4), 245–270. doi:10.1016/S0963-8687(02)00018-5

Bennett, C. (1992). *Regulating Privacy: Data Protection and Public Policy in Europe and the United States*. New York: Cornell University Press.

Burkert, H. (1997). Privacy-Enhancing Technologies: Typology, Critique, Vision . In Agre, P. E., & Rotenberg, M. (Eds.), *Technology and Privacy: The New Landscape*. Boston: MIT Press.

Clarke, R. (1996). Privacy, Dataveillance, Organisational Strategy. Keynote Address. In *Proceedings of the I.S. Audit & Control Association Conference; EDPAC, Perth, May 28, 1996*. Retrieved December 16, 2008, from http://www.rogerclarke.com/DV/PStrat.html

Clarke, R. (1998). *Direct Marketing and Privacy*. Xamax Consultancy Pty Ltd. Retrieved December 16, 2008, from http://www.rogerclarke.com/DV/DirectMkting.html

Clarke, R. (1999a). Internet Privacy Concerns Confirm the Case for Intervention. *Communications of the ACM, 42*(2) 60-67. Retrieved December 16, 2008, from http://www.rogerclarke.com/DV/CACM99.html

Clarke, R. (1999b). The Willingness of Net-Consumers to Pay: A Lack-of-Progress Report. In *Proceedings of the 12th International Bled Electronic Commerce Conference, Bled, Slovenia, June 7 - 9, 1999*. Retrieved December 16, 2008, from http://www.rogerclarke.com/EC/WillPay.html

Clarke, R. (2000). *Beyond the OECD Guidelines: Privacy Protection for the 21st Century*. Xamax Consultancy Pty Ltd. January 2000. Retrieved December 16, 2008, from http://www.rogerclarke.com/DV/PP21C.html

Clarke, R. (2001a). Introducing PITs and PETs: Technologies Affecting Privacy. *Privacy Law & Policy Reporter, 7*(9), 181-183. Retrieved December 16, 2008, from http://www.rogerclarke.com/DV/PITsPETs.html

Clarke, R. (2001b). Meta-Brands. *Privacy Law & Policy Reporter, 7*(11). Retrieved December 16, 2008, from http://www.rogerclarke.com/DV/MetaBrands.html

Clarke, R. (2001c). Privacy as a Means of Engendering Trust in Cyberspace. [from http://www.rogerclarke.com/DV/eTrust.html]. *The University of New South Wales Law Journal, 24*(1), 290–297. Retrieved December 16, 2008.

Clarke, R. (2002a). Trust in the Context of e-Business. *Internet Law Bulletin, 4*(5), 56-59. Retrieved December 16, 2008, from http://www.rogerclarke.com/EC/Trust.html

Clarke, R. (2002b). e-Consent: A Critical Element of Trust in e-Business. In *Proceedings of the 15th Bled Electronic Commerce Conference, Bled, Slovenia, 17-19 June 2002*. Retrieved December 16, 2008, from http://www.rogerclarke.com/EC/eConsent.html

Clarke, R. (2005a). *Privacy Statement Template*. Xamax Consultancy Pty Ltd., December 2005. Retrieved December 16, 2008, from http://www.rogerclarke.com/DV/PST.html

Clarke, R. (2005b). *About the Privacy Statement Template*. Xamax Consultancy Pty Ltd., December 2005, Retrieved December 16, 2008, from http://www.rogerclarke.com/DV/PSTAbt.html

Clarke, R. (2005c). *Evaluation of Google's Privacy Statement against the Privacy Statement Template of 19 December 2005*. Xamax Consultancy Pty Ltd., December 2005, Retrieved December 16, 2008, from http://www.rogerclarke.com/DV/PST-Google.html

Clarke, R. (2006a). *What's 'Privacy'?* Xamax Consultancy Pty Ltd., July 2006, Retrieved December 16, 2008, from http://www.rogerclarke.com/DV/Privacy.html

Clarke, R. (2006b). Google's Gauntlets. *Computer Law & Security Report, 22*(4), 287-297. Retrieved December 16, 2008, from http://www.rogerclarke.com/II/Gurgle0604.html

Clarke, R. (2006c). Make Privacy a Strategic Factor - The Why and the How. *Cutter IT Journal, 19*(11). Retrieved December 16, 2008, from http://www.rogerclarke.com/DV/APBD-0609.html

Connolly, C. (2008, December). The US Safe Harbor - Fact or Fiction? *Galexia Pty Ltd*. Retrieved December 16, 2008, from http://www.galexia.com/public/research/assets/safe_harbor_fact_or_fiction_2008/safe_harbor_fact_or_fiction.pdf

Crompton, M. (2004). Short Notices – why the Sydney resolution was adopted and progress in Australia since September 2003. In *Proceedings of the 26th International Conference on Privacy and Personal Data Protection, 14-16 September 2004, Wroclaw, Poland*. Retrieved December 16, 2008, from http://26konferencja.giodo.gov.pl/data/resources/CromptonM_paper.pdf

Culnan, M. (1993). How Did They Get My Name? An Exploratory Investigation of Consumer Attitudes Towards Secondary Information Use. *Management Information Systems Quarterly, 17*(3), 341. doi:10.2307/249775

Culnan, M. J., & Milne, G. R. (2001). The Culnan-Milne Survey on Consumers & Online Privacy Notices: Summary of Responses. *Federal Trade Commission.* Retrieved December 16, 2008, from http://www.ftc.gov/bcp/workshops/glb/supporting/culnan-milne.pdf, accessed 9 January 2006

Department of Commerce. (DOC, 2000). *Safe Harbor Overview*. U.S. Department of Commerce. Retrieved January 9, 2006, from http://www.export.gov/safeharbor/sh_overview.html, accessed 9 January 2006

Dinev, T., Bellotto, M., Hart, P., Colautti, C., Russo, V., & Serra, I. (2005). Internet Users, Privacy Concerns and Attitudes towards Government Surveillance - An Exploratory Study of Cross-Cultural Differences between Italy and the United States. In *Proceedings of the18th International eCommerce Conference, Bled, June 2005*. Retrieved January 9, 2006, from http://aisel.isworld.org/pdf.asp?Vpath=BLED&PDFpath=41Dinev.pdf

Dubbeld, L. (2006). Privacy and security disclosures on telecardiology Web sites. *First Monday, 11*(5).

Earp, J., Anton, A., & Jarvinen, O. (2002). A Social, Technical, and Legal Framework for Privacy Management and Policies. In *Proceedings of the Americas Conference on Information Systems 2002*. Retrieved January 9, 2006, from http://aisel.isworld.org/pdf.asp?Vpath=AMCIS/2002&PDFpath=021101.pdf, accessed 9 January 2006

Earp, J. B., & Baumer, D. (2003). Innovative Web Use To Learn About Consumer Behavior and Online Privacy. *Communications of the ACM, 46*(4), 81–83. doi:10.1145/641205.641209

Economist (2005, December 1). Demon in the machine: Privacy laws gain support in America, after a year of huge violations. *The Economist.* Retrieved January 9, 2006, from http://www.economist.com/business/displayStory.cfm?story_id=5259499&no_na_tran=1

Electronic Privacy Information Center. (1996). *EPIC Online Guide to Practical Privacy Tools*. Retrieved December 16, 2008, from http://www.epic.org/privacy/tools.html

Electronic Privacy Information Center. (2003). *EPIC Complaint and Request for Injunction, Investigation and for Other Relief In the Matter of Amazon.com, Inc.* Electronic Privacy Information Center. Retrieved April 22, 2003, fromhttp://www.epic.org/privacy/amazon/coppacomplaint.html

Electronic Privacy Information Center. (2004). FTC Fails To Enforce Children's Privacy Law Against Amazon.Com. *EPIC Alert,* 11(23). Retrieved December 8, 2004, from http://www.epic.org/alert/EPIC_Alert_11.23.html

Federal Trade Commission. (1998a). *Privacy Online: A Report to Congress'Federal Trade Commission.* Retrieved January 9, 2006 from http://www.ftc.gov/reports/privacy3/priv-23a.pdf

Federal Trade Commission. (1998b). *Self-Regulation Is The Preferred Method Of Protecting Consumers' Online Privacy.* Retrieved December 16, 2008, from http://www.ftc.gov/opa/1998/07/privacyh.htm, accessed 9 January 2006

Federal Trade Commission (1999). *Protecting Consumers Online: A Federal Trade Commission Report on the First Five Years of Its Internet Law Enforcement Program.*

Federal Trade Commission. (FTC, 2000). *Privacy Online: Fair Information Practices in the Electronic Marketplace: A Federal Trade Commission Report to Congress.* Retrieved January 9, 2006, from http://www.ftc.gov/reports/privacy2000/privacy2000.pdf

Federal Trade Commission. (FTC, 2005). *Enforcing Privacy Promises: Section 5 of the FTC Act.* Retrieved December 16, 2008, from http://www.ftc.gov/privacy/privacyinitiatives/promises.html, accessed 9 January 2006

Flaherty, D. H. (1989). *Protecting Privacy in Surveillance Societies.* University of North Carolina Press.

Fleischer, P. (2005, September 7). *Protecting Customer Data in an Evolving Technology Environment.* Microsoft. Retrieved from http://www.microsoft.com/emea/presscentre/peterfleischer.mspx

Freenetlaw.com. (2008). *Free privacy statement template.* Retrieved from http://www.freenetlaw.com/free-privacy-statement.php

Gauzente, C. (2004). Web Merchants' Privacy And Security Statements: How Reassuring Are They For Consumers? A Two-Sided Approach. *Journal of Electronic Commerce Research, 5*(3). Retrieved December 16, 2008, from http://www.csulb.edu/web/journals/jecr/issues/20043/Paper4.pdf

Hoffman, D. L., Novak, T. P., & Peralta, M. (1999). Building Consumer Trust Online. *Communications of the ACM, 42*(4), 80–85. doi:10.1145/299157.299175

Hoofnagle, C. J. (2005). Privacy Self Regulation: A Decade of Disappointment. *Electronic Privacy Information Center*. Retrieved March 4, 2005, from http://www.epic.org/reports/decadedisappoint.html

Hooper, A. S. C., Bunker, B., Rapson, A., Reynolds, A., & Vos, M. (2007). Evaluating Banking Websites Privacy Statements – A New Zealand Perspective on Ensuring Business Confidence. In *Proceedings of PACIS 2007, Paper 25*. Retrieved December 16, 2008, from http://aisel.aisnet.org/pacis2007/25

Hui, K., Teo, H. H., & Lee, S. (2007). The Value of Privacy Assurance: An Exploratory Field Experiment. *MIS Quartlery, 31*(3), 19–33.

Information and Privacy Commissioner. (IPCR,1995). Privacy-Enhancing Technologies: The Path to Anonymity. *Information and Privacy Commissioner* (Vol. 2). Retrieved January 9, 2006, from http://www.ipc.on.ca/web%5Fsite.eng/matters/sum%5Fpap/papers/anon%2De.htm

Information Commissioner's Office. (ICO, 2001). Compliance advice: Website Frequently asked questions. *Information Commissioner's Office*, Manchester, U.K. 26 June 2001, Retrieved January 9, 2006, from http://www.ico.gov.uk/documentUploads/Website%20FAQ.pdf

Jensen, C., & Potts, C. (2004). Privacy Polices as Decision-Making Tools: An Evaluation of Privacy Notices. In *Proceedings of CHI 2004, April 24-29, 2004, Vienna, Austria.*

Kim, D. (2005). Cognition-Based Versus Affect-Based Trust Determinants in E-Commerce: Cross-Cultural Comparison Study. In *Proceedings of International Conference on Information Systems*. Retrieved December 16, 2008, from http://aisel.isworld.org/pdf.asp?Vpath=ICIS/2005&PDFpath=WBISA03.pdf

Kobsa, A., & Teltzrow, M. (2005). Impacts of Contextualized Communication of Privacy Practices and Personalization Benefits on Purchase Behavior and Perceived Quality of Recommendation. In *Proceedings of Workshop: Beyond Personalization, IUI'05, January 9, 2005, San Diego, California, USA*. Retrieved January 9, 2006, from http://www.cs.umn.edu/Research/GroupLens/beyond2005

Lee, M. K. O., & Turban, E. (2001). A Trust Model for Consumer Internet Shopping. *International Journal of Electronic Commerce, 6*(1), 75–91.

Lichtenstein, S., Swatman, P. M. C., & Babu, K. (2002). Effective Online Privacy Policies. In *Information Systems: Enabling Organisations and Society: Proceedings of 13th Australasian Conference on Information Systems, Victoria University, Melbourne, Australia.*

Lichtenstein, S., Swatman, P. M. C., & Babu, K. (2003). *Narrowing the Gap Between Privacy Policy and Practice: Guidelines and Framework for Integrating Online Privacy Policy With Practic.* Working Paper 2003/05, School of Information Systems, Deakin University, Melbourne, Australia.

Markel, M. (2008). Safe harbor and privacy protection: a looming issue for IT professionals. *IEEE Transactions on Professional Communication, 49*(1), 1–11. doi:10.1109/TPC.2006.870462

Meinert, D. B., Peterson, D. K., Criswell, J. R., & Crossland, M. D. (2006). Privacy Policy Statements and Consumer Willingness to Provide Personal Information. *Journal of Electronic Commerce in Organizations, 4*(1), 1–17.

Milne, G. R., & Culnan, M. J. (2002). Using the content of online privacy notices to inform public policy: a longitudinal analysis of the 1998-2001 U.S. web surveys. *The Information Society, 18*(5), 345–359. doi:10.1080/01972240290108168

Milne, G. R., Culnan, M. J., & Green, H. (2006). A Longitudinal Assessment of Online Privacy Notice Readability. *Journal of Public Policy & Marketing, 25*(2), 238–249. doi:10.1509/jppm.25.2.238

Office of the Federal Privacy Commissioner. (2000). *Guidelines for Federal and ACT Government Websites.* Office of the Federal Privacy Commissioner, Sydney, Australia, Retrieved December 16, 2008, from http://www.privacy.gov.au/internet/web/index.html

Organisation for Economic Cooperation and Development. (1980). *OECD Guidelines on the Protection of Privacy and Transborder Flows of Personal Data.* Organisation for Economic Cooperation and Development, Paris. Retrieved December 16, 2008, from http://www.oecd.org/document/18/0,2340,en_2649_201185_1815186_1_1_1_1,00.html

Organisation for Economic Cooperation and Development. (2000a). *Developing a Privacy Policy and Statement.* Organisation for Economic Co-operation and Development, Paris, 2000. Retrieved December 16, 2008, from http://www.oecd.org/document/1/0,2340,en_2649_34255_28863233_1_1_1_1,00.html

Organisation for Economic Cooperation and Development. (2000b). *OECD Privacy Statement Generator*. Organisation for Economic Co-operation and Development, Paris, 2000, Retrieved December 16, 2008, from http://www.oecd.org/document/3 9/0,2340,en_2649_34255_28863271_1_1_1_1,00.html

Palmer, J. W., Bailey, J. P., & Faraj, S. (2000). The Role of Intermediaries in the Development of Trust in the WWW: The Use and Prominence of Trusted Third Parties and Privacy Statements. *Journal of Computer-Mediated Communication, 5*(3).

Pruitt, S. (2005, April 4). Europe takes lead on improving online privacy notices. *The Industry Standard*. Retrieved December 16, 2008, from http://www.thestandard.com/internetnews/002774.php

Regan, K. (2001, June 15). Does Anyone Read Online Privacy Policies? *E-Commerce Times*. Retrieved December 16, 2008, from http://www.ecommercetimes.com/story/11303.html

Regan, P. (2003). Privacy and Commercial Use of Personal Data: Policy Developments in the United States. *Journal of Contingencies and Crisis Management, 11*(1), 12–18. doi:10.1111/1468-5973.1101003

Rosencrance, L. (2000a, September 18). Amazon Loses 2 Partners Over Privacy Policy. *Computerworld*. Retrieved January 9, 2006, from http://www.computerworld.com/cwi/ story/0,1199,NAV47_STO50529,00.html

Rosencrance, L. (2000b, December 11). Amazon.com's Privacy Policies in Spotlight Again, U.S., U.K. Probes Urged. *Computerworld*. Retrieved January 9, 2006, from http://www.computerworld.com/cwi/story/ 0,1199,NAV47_STO54993,00.html

Schwaig, K. S., Kane, G., & Storey, V. C. (2004). Privacy, fair information practices and the fortune 500: the virtual reality of compliance. *Database, 36*(1), 49–63.

Schwaig, K. S., Kane, G., & Storey, V. C. (2006). Compliance to the fair information practices: How are the Fortune 500 handling online privacy disclosures? *Information & Management, 43*(7), 805–820. doi:10.1016/j.im.2006.07.003

Smith, H. J., Milberg, S. J., & Burke, S. J. (1996). Information Privacy: Measuring Individuals' Concerns About Organizational Practices. *Management Information Systems Quarterly, 20*(2). doi:10.2307/249477

25th International Conference Of Data Protection & Privacy Commissioners (ICDCP) (2003). Proposed Resolution on Improving the Communication of Data Protection and Privacy Information Practices. In *Proceedings of the 25th International Conference Of Data Protection & Privacy Commissioners, Sydney, 12 September 2003*. Retrieved accessed 9 January 2006, from http://www.bfdi.bund.de/cln_030/nn_535764/SharedDocs/Publikationen/EN/InternationalDS/ConferenceOfInternationalDataProtectionCommissioners2003ResolutionOnImprovingTheCommunicationOfDataProtectionAndPrivacyInformationPractices.html

Treasury Board of Canada Secretariat. (2004, November 5). *Directive on Government of Canada Web Site privacy policies*. Treasury Board of Canada Secretariat, Ottawa. Retrieved January 9, 2006, from http://www.tbs-sct.gc.ca/gos-sog/impl-rep/impl-rep2000/imp.report71/att-pj_e.htm

Truste (2004). Your Online Privacy Policy. *Truste*. Retrieved January 9, 2006, from http://www.truste.org/pdf/WriteAGreatPrivacyPolicy.pdf

Truste (2005, August). TRUSTe Guidance on Model Web Site Disclosures. *Truste*. Retrieved January 9, 2006, from http://www.truste.org/docs/Model_Privacy_Policy_Disclosures.doc

Wang, H., Lee, M. K. O., & Wang, C. (1998). Consumer privacy concerns about Internet marketing. *Communications of the ACM, 41*(3), 63–70. doi:10.1145/272287.272299

Xu, Y., Tan, B., Hui, K. L., & Tang, W. K. (2003). Consumer Trust and Online Information Privacy. In *Proceedings of the International Conference on Information Systems, 2003*. Retrieved January 9, 2006, from http://aisel.isworld.org/pdf.asp?Vpath=ICIS/2003&PDFpath=03CRP45.pdf

Chapter 5
An Evaluation of User Password Practice

John Campbell
University of Canberra, Australia

Kay Bryant
University of Canberra, Australia

ABSTRACT

Maintaining the security of information systems and associated data resources is vital if an organization is to minimize losses. Access controls are the first line of defense in this process. The primary function of authentication controls is to ensure that only authorized users have access to information systems and electronic resources. Password-based systems remain the predominant means of user authentication despite viable authentication alternatives. Research suggests that password-based systems are often compromised by poor user security practices. This chapter presents the results of a survey of 884 computer users that examines user practice in creating and reusing password keys, and reports the findings on user password composition and security practices for email accounts. Despite a greater awareness of security issues, the results show that many users still select and reuse weak passwords keys that are based on dictionary words and other meaningful information.

DOI: 10.4018/978-1-60566-806-2.ch005

INTRODUCTION

While there have been significant technological developments in online authentication methods especially in biometrics and graphics-based approaches (Ratha, Connell, & Bolle, 2001; Man Hong, Hayes, & Matthews, 2004; Jain, Ross, & Prabhakar, 2004; Wiedenbeck, Waters, Birget, Brodskiy, & Memon, 2005; de Paula et al., 2005), passwords remain the most common means of authenticating a user. Unfortunately, users can compromise password security by forgetting passwords, writing them down, sharing them with other people, and selecting easily guessed words (Spafford, 1992; Stanton, Stam, Mastrangelo, & Jolton, 2005; Trček, Trobec, Pavesić, & Tasič, 2007; Yan, Blackwell, Anderson, & Grant, 2004). These weaknesses are known to seriously undermine the efficacy of password access systems (Conklin, Dietrich, & Walz, 2004; Carstens, 2004). In particular, the issue of password reuse is an area that remains under researched and is, therefore, the major focus of this study. This chapter explores aspects of user password management practice within the context of email usage by profiling email account usage, password reuse, and user management practice.

PASSWORD SECURITY ISSUES

Password-based authentication remains the most common way to control access to computer-based resources. Passwords remain in widespread use because they are conceptually simple for both system designers and end users and provide cost effective protection for many systems if used correctly. Unfortunately, effective passwords are by nature complex and difficult to for users to remember (Ma, Campbell, Tran, & Kleeman, 2007). Prior research has shown that users are one of the main risks to the effectiveness of security measures (Rhodes, 2004). Organizations often rely on password composition policies to force users to create more secure passwords. These policies are usually implemented in such a way as to provide an explicit framework that constrains user choices during the password creation and replacement process. While this approach may help improve password security, these restrictions make the composition and memorizing of passwords complex and less intuitive (Campbell, Kleeman, & Ma, 2007).

Further, due to the predominance of password authentication systems, many users are required to remember passwords for a range of different systems and applications. As earlier research has demonstrated, the requirement to remember such a large number of passwords can cause a major problem for users (Yan et al., 2004; Zviran & Haga, 1999). Unfortunately, typical users are capable of managing a small number of unique passwords, generally less than five (Adams & Sasse, 1999). Also, remembered information can simply be forgotten, so users typically resort to using information that is easy to recall (Vu et al., 2007). One consequence of this is that while the information is easy to recall, it is also relatively easy to guess. Passwords that are more difficult to remember may be written down, thereby compromising password and system security (Stanton, et al., 2005).

A SURVEY OF EMAIL PASSWORD SECURITY

Remembering unique passwords for different systems and applications is difficult in practice and it is therefore no surprise that many users select dictionary words, personal names or other meaningful information as the basis for their passwords. For similar reasons users frequently select the same password for multiple accounts (Ives, Walsh, & Schneider., 2004). Password reuse can compromise the security of all of the password systems that a user might access. Cognitive limitations mean that many users will choose easy to remember passwords that are based on some meaningful combination of names and/or numbers (Brown, Bracken, Zoccoli, & Douglas, 2004). If the security of one system is breached, then all other password-based systems may become vulnerable.

Electronic mail is the most widely adopted password-protected application and affects the daily life of almost every working person in the industrialized world (Rudy, 1996; Bälter, 2000). Electronic mail systems provide a useful research context for studying the password behavior of users because of its widespread social and organizational impact. A preliminary study was undertaken to gain insight into password behaviors and to test our initial survey instrument (Campbell & Bryant, 2004). The pilot study involved 82 computer users and the results reaffirmed the importance of email as an ideal end-user application context for studying password management. Most respondents reported having several email accounts. As was anticipated, this multiplicity of accounts would create password management difficulties for users and encourages password reuse across different email accounts. In the pilot study, many users were found to be using insecure password management practices, including the use and reuse of passwords constructed from meaningful personal details.

Subsequently, changes were made to the initial survey instrument to elicit more detailed responses about the use and management of email passwords. The aim of this study is to assess the attitudes and awareness of users to password security issues, and to gain insight into password composition, reuse, and management practice. The study focused on the following issues:

- Profiling email account usage (purpose, number of accounts, frequency of access)
- Password practice (reuse, composition, management)

The first section of the questionnaire collected demographic data about the respondents and their computer and email usage. It also sought to ascertain the extent to which respondents shared passwords across applications and their awareness of password cracking techniques. The second section focused specifically on password composition and management practices.

Study Data

Undergraduate students from an Australian university business school were chosen to be the research participants. Although largely not organizational users of password-based systems, this sample can be considered indicative of the typical password security behavior that future recruits might bring with them into organizations. The survey was administered in late February 2005 across three campuses located in close proximity to one another (that is, no two campuses are more than 50 kilometers apart). The students surveyed were from the Business School and in their first semester of their first year of study. Participation in the survey was entirely voluntary. In all, 884 students volunteered to participate in this study.

Table 1 provides the demographic profile of the participants. There were slightly more males than females in the sample and the majority of the respondents were under 26 years of age (213 respondents were under 18 years of age and 584 between 18 and 25 years of age). The remaining 87 respondents were over 25 years of age. The majority of the respondents were enrolled at the University on a full time basis (811) and 59 were enrolled on a part-time basis. Thirteen participants did not respond to this question and one participant was auditing the course and therefore not formally enrolled. As a consequence, most of the respondents were either not employed (257) or employed on a part-time basis (533). Sixty-five respondents were full-time employees, while 29 participants did not respond to this question. The majority of respondents had used computers for more than 5 years (480 respondents had used computers between 6-10 years and 252 respondents for longer than 10 years). Only 25 respondents had used computers for less than 2 years, while 126 had used computers between 3 and 5 years. One participant did not respond to this question.

Table 1. Demographic details of participants

Variable	Category	Total	%*
Gender	Male	378	42.8%
	Female	505	57.1%
	No response	1	0.1%
Age	< 18 years	213	24.1%
	18 – 25 years	584	66.1%
	26 – 35 years	55	6.2%
	36 years +	32	3.6%
Enrolment	Full-time	811	91.7%
Status	Part-time	59	6.7%
	Not enrolled	1	0.1%
	No response	13	1.5%
Employment	Full-time	65	7.4%
Status	Part-time	533	60.3%
	Not employed	257	29.1%
	No response	29	3.3%
Computing	0 – 2 years	25	2.8%
Experience	3 – 5 years	126	14.3%
	6 – 10 years	480	54.3%
	> 10 years	252	28.5%
	No response	1	0.1%
	Total Participants:	884	100.0%

* Percentage totals may exceed 100% due to rounding.

Analysis

Participants were asked about their email and general computer usage. For each question, respondents were asked to select as many application options that were relevant to their personal usage. Tables 2a and 2b provide relevant details. The three columns on the left in both tables provide the overall totals and percentages for each option, while the remaining columns show the totals for each response combination. The options are numbered 1-6 in Table 2a and 1-4 in Table 2b. More than 83% of respondents indicated their main computer use was for Internet, email, and home use. Bank and work use formed a second grouping, between 47-50%, and other areas of use (e.g. study and research, entertainment including games, and online purchasing and selling) accounted for 15.0%. Personal email use was most prevalent (95.5%), followed by University use (84.7%) and work-related use (24.9%). As can be seen in

Table 2a. Participant computer usage and frequency of each response combination

Computer Use	Total	%*	Response	n	Response	n	Response	n	Response	n
1. Home	737	83.4	1	15	1, 2	3	1, 2, 3	2	1, 2, 3, 4	1
2. Work	422	47.7	2	4	1, 3	1	1, 2, 4	7	1, 2, 3, 5	1
3. Banking	444	50.2	3	0	1, 4	9	1, 2, 5	6	1, 2, 4, 5	123
4. Email	796	90.0	4	9	1, 5	15	1, 3, 4	4	1, 3, 4, 5	158
5. Internet access	821	92.9	5	29	2, 3	0	1, 3, 5	2	2, 3, 4, 5	11
6. Other	133	15.0			2, 4	0	1, 4, 5	148		
Did not respond	4	0.5			2, 5	4	2, 3, 4	0		
					3, 4	2	2, 3, 5	0	1, 2, 3, 4, 5	242
					3, 5	0	2, 4, 5	18		
					4, 5	44	3, 4, 5	20		

*Percentages have been calculated in terms of the total number of participants.

Table 2b, more than 95% of respondents reported that they used email for personal communication. This has serious implications for organizational security if users reuse passwords across email and other computer applications. When combined, password reuse and poor security practices increase the likelihood that a password might be deduced, thereby increasing the vulnerability of other systems where this password has been used. The analyses on the following pages provide details on participant responses to password composition and reuse.

Table 2b. Participant email usage and frequency of each response combination

Email Use	Total	%*	Response	n	Response	n
1. Personal	844	95.5	1	0	1, 2	30
2. Work	220	24.9	2	113	1, 3	14
3. University	749	84.7	3	2	2, 3	515
4. Other	24	2.7				
Did not respond	6	0.7			1, 2, 3	2

*Percentages have been calculated in terms of the total number of participants.

Password Composition

Participants were asked a number of questions concerning the composition and choice of passwords, see Tables 3a and 3b. Thirty-one respondents (3.5%) reported having passwords that consisted of five or fewer characters. The majority of respondents (84.7%) had chosen passwords of greater than 5 characters in length, while 11.9% did not respond to this question. The average length of passwords was 8.3 charac-ters, which exceeds the generally accepted standard of 8 characters (Yapp, 2001). Participants typically used 8 characters in their password (29.2%), 9 characters (11.8%), and 10 characters (7.7%), with 7.4% of respondents having passwords exceeding 11 characters. Approximately 39.4% used only alphabetic characters in their passwords, while 42.3% used alphanumeric characters. The remainder either used numerals only (6.4%), added symbols (4.1%), or did not respond to the question (7.5%). Typically, their choice of password contained some type of meaningful data (43.1%), such as a name, street, preferred word, nickname, and registration number. A few selected pronounceable words (5.2%). Almost 24% of respondents combined meaningful data items to make up their passwords. Only 10.7% choose a random combination of characters. Very few respondents had their passwords chosen for them (1.6%), while another 8% selected their password by some other means. Of concern, 61.9% of respondents reported that they never changed their password and a further 19.8% changed passwords no more than three times a year. Respondents were divided with respect to admitting whether they had forgotten their password, as 60.9% said they had not forgotten it compared to 30.4% who had; 8.7% chose not to answer this question. However, this finding is less than promising since most of those who stated they had never forgotten their password, never changed it (43.78%) or changed it less than once a year (7.92%). Further, even those who had admitted to forgetting their password, never changed their password (17.19%),or changed it less than once a year (5.32%).

Table 3b provides details of the results of the Analysis of Variance conducted on participant practices relating to password composition and management using gender, age and employment status as the independent variables. The results from the analysis on the number of characters in a password have not been reported, as there were no significant findings for any of the independent variables. However, there were significant differences in the type of characters used in the composi-tion of passwords for all independent variables, where employment status and age group was at the 1% level, while gender was significant at the 5% level. Females are more likely to choose alphabetic or numeric characters only, while males tended to choose character combinations, which included symbols. Full-time employees, and those who are unemployed, tend to use character combinations, while those who are employed on a part-time basis are more likely to choose alphabetic or

Table 3a. Participant practices relating to password composition and management

Variable	Categories	Total	%*
Password length	1-5 characters	31	3.5
	6 characters	126	14.3
	7 characters	93	10.5
	8 characters	258	29.2
	9 characters	104	11.8
	10 characters	68	7.7
	11 characters	34	3.8
	> 11 characters	65	7.4
	Did not respond	105	11.9
	Average	8.3	
	Minimum	1.0	
	Maximum	25.0	
Password composition	1. Alphabetic only	348	39.4
	2. Numeric only	57	6.4
	3. Alphanumeric	374	42.3
	4. Includes symbols	36	4.1
	5. Other	3	0.3
	Did not respond	66	7.5
Choice of password	1. Meaningful data	381	43.1
	2. Combo meaningful data	210	23.8
	3. Pronounceable word	46	5.2
	4. Random characters	95	10.7
	5. Not self-chosen	14	1.6
	6. Other	71	8.0
	Did not respond	67	7.6
Frequency of changing password	1. Never	547	61.9
	2. Less than once a year	119	13.5
	3. 1-3 times a year	56	6.3
	4. 4-6 times a year	79	8.9
	5. Once a month	10	1.1
	6. Several times a month	6	0.7
	Did not respond	67	13.5
Forgotten password	1. No	538	60.9
	2. Yes	269	30.4
	Did not respond	77	8.7

*Percentage totals may exceed 100% due to rounding.

Table 3b. Results of analyses of variance of password composition and management

Password composition					
	Groups	*Count*	*Average*	*SD*	*P-value*
Gender	Male	347	2.233	1.006	
	Female	471	2.055	1.054	0.015
Age Groups	Less than 18yrs	202	1.837	1.016	
	18-25yrs	541	2.172	1.046	
	26-35yrs	49	2.633	0.809	
	36 and over '	26	2.615	0.697	0.000
Employment	Full/Time	63	2.206	1.285	
	Part/Time	499	2.036	1.119	
	Not Employed	230	2.304	1.047	0.004
Choice of password					
	Groups	*Count*	*Average*	*SD*	*P-value*
Gender	Male	346	2.445	1.676	
	Female	471	2.057	1.480	0.000
Age Groups	Less than 18yrs	202	2.223	1.703	
	18-25yrs	541	2.231	1.561	
	26-35yrs	48	1.896	1.189	0.297
	36 and over	26	2.615	1.472	NS
Employment	Full/Time	62	2.161	1.549	
	Part/Time	497	2.282	1.632	0.366
	Not Employed	231	2.108	1.454	NS
Frequency of changing password					
	Groups	*Count*	*Average*	*SD*	*P-value*
Gender	Male	347	0.718	1.210	0.192
	Female	470	0.615	1.034	NS
Age Groups	Less than 18yrs	201	0.557	1.104	
	18-25yrs	541	0.660	1.103	
	26-35yrs	49	0.918	1.170	0.121
	36 and over	26	0.923	1.197	NS
Employment	Full/Time	62	0.952	1.311	
	Part/Time	497	0.620	1.097	0.085
	Not Employed	231	0.649	1.077	NS
Forgotten password					
	Groups	*Count*	*Average*	*SD*	*P-value*
Gender	Male	339	0.304	0.461	0.131
	Female	468	0.355	0.479	NS
Age Groups	Less than 18yrs	200	0.260	0.440	
	18-25yrs	534	0.333	0.472	
	26-35yrs	48	0.500	0.505	
	36 and over	25	0.600	0.500	0.000
Employment	Full/Time	61	0.311	0.467	
	Part/Time	492	0.321	0.467	0.384
	Not Employed	229	0.371	0.484	NS

NS = Not Significant $p < 0.01$

numeric characters only. With respect to age group, younger respondents (aged 25 years and under) are more likely to choose alphabetic or numeric characters only, while the older respondents tended to choose alphanumeric combinations that may also include symbols.

Females are also more likely to choose meaningful detail or some combination thereof, while males tend towards pronounceable passwords or a random combination of characters. The frequency of changing passwords was not significant for all three independent variables. There was a significant difference in whether the respondent had forgotten their passwords by age group. It appears that the older the participant, the more likely they are to have forgotten their password at some stage.

Email Access

Tables 4a and 4b show details of participant practices relating to email access. More than 75% of respondents had either two or three email accounts (49.4% had two accounts and 27.9% had three). The remaining respondents had either one account (11.7%), or had four or more email accounts (11.0%). Almost half of the respondents access their email at least once a day, with another 27.7% gaining access several times a week. Sixty-one respondents (almost 7% of the sample) did not answer this question.

The number of email accounts and frequency of access were further tested with an Analysis of Variance using gender, age group, and employment status as the independent variables. Table 4b reports the outcomes of the analyses conducted on participant practices related to email access. As can be seen from Table 4b, there is a significant difference in the number of email accounts due to employment status and age group, but not for gender. Participants aged between 26 and 35 have the most number of email accounts, while the older participants (36 years and over) have the least. Respondents who are employed on a part-time basis have the least number of accounts, while those employed on a full-time basis, or who are not employed, have the most. The frequency of checking emails was significant at the 1% level for all of the independent variables. Males tended to check their email accounts more frequently than females. Mature-aged respondents (26 and over) checked the most often, as do respondents who are either full-time employees or unemployed.

Password Reuse

Tables 5a and 5b provide relevant details about password reuse associated with email accounts and other computer applications. Over half of respondents reported that they used the same password (24.9%), or a slight variation of that password (31.2%), across email accounts. More than one-third used passwords that were

Table 4a. Participant practices related to email access

Variable	Categories	Total	%*
Number of email accounts	1 account	102	11.5
	2 accounts	437	49.4
	3 accounts	247	27.9
	> 4 accounts	98	11.1
Frequency of access	1. Several times a day	159	18.0
	2. Once a day	272	30.8
	3. Several times a week	245	27.7
	4. Once a week	103	11.7
	5. Several times a month	36	4.1
	5. Never check email	8	0.9
	Did not respond	61	6.9

*Percentages have been calculated in terms of the total number of participants.

Table 4b. Results of analyses of variance of number of email accounts and frequency of access

Number of email accounts					
	Groups	*Count*	*Average*	*SD*	*P-value*
Gender	Male	378	2.413	0.873	0.405
	Female	506	2.366	0.798	*NS*
Age Groups	Less than 18yrs	213	2.263	0.787	
	18-25yrs	584	2.421	0.820	
	26-35yrs	55	2.618	0.991	
	36 and over	32	2.156	0.884	0.006
Employment	Full/Time	65	2.569	0.809	
	Part/Time	533	2.323	0.821	
	Not Employed	257	2.490	0.853	0.006
Frequency of accessing email					
	Groups	*Count*	*Average*	*SD*	*P-value*
Gender	Male	348	2.356	1.087	
	Female	474	2.650	1.139	0.000
Age Groups	Less than 18yrs	202	2.728	1.070	
	18-25yrs	545	2.543	1.142	
	26-35yrs	49	1.878	0.927	
	36 and over	27	1.815	0.834	0.000
Employment	Full/Time	63	2.206	1.285	
	Part/Time	500	2.682	1.119	
	Not Employed	233	2.318	1.047	0.000

NS = Not Significant $p < 0.01$

Table 5a. Participant practices related to password reuse

Variable	Categories	Total	%*
Across email accounts	1. Same password	220	24.9
	2. Slightly different	276	31.2
	3. No similarities	321	36.3
	Did not respond	67	7.6
Across other applications	1. Same password	154	17.4
	2. Slightly different	178	20.1
	3. No similarities	194	21.9
	Did not respond	358	40.5

*Percentages have been calculated in terms of the total number of participants.

Table 5b. Results of analyses of variance of password reuse

Password reuse across email accounts					
	Groups	*Count*	*Average*	*SD*	*P-value*
Gender	Male	349	1.063	0.814	0.063
	Female	468	1.169	0.796	*NS*
Age Groups	Less than 18yrs	198	1.081	0.789	
	18-25yrs	541	1.135	0.813	
	26-35yrs	51	1.157	0.809	0.855
	36 and over	27	1.148	0.770	*NS*
Employment	Full/Time	61	1.393	0.714	
	Part/Time	490	1.147	0.793	
	Not Employed	238	1.021	0.829	0.004
Password reuse across other applications					
	Groups	*Count*	*Average*	*SD*	*P-value*
Gender	Male	227	1.057	0.821	0.644
	Female	299	1.090	0.804	*NS*
Age Groups	Less than 18yrs	116	0.983	0.823	
	18-25yrs	343	1.067	0.812	
	26-35yrs	44	1.205	0.734	0.066
	36 and over	23	1.435	0.788	*NS*
Employment	Full/Time	49	1.347	0.779	
	Part/Time	325	1.037	0.797	0.044
	Not Employed	152	1.072	0.839	*NS*

NS = Not Significant p < 0.01

very different (36.3%). Sixty-seven respondents (7.6%) did not answer this question. The participants were also asked whether they used other applications that required the use of passwords. Approximately 60% of respondents reported that they used passwords for other applications in three predominant application domains: banking; other University applications; and communication applications, such as chat rooms, messenger services, and forums. When asked whether they reused the same passwords across other applications, 37.5% reported using the same password (17.4%) or a slight variation (20.1%). Approximately 40% of respondents did not answer this question.

Password reuse was further tested using Analysis of Variance with gender, age group, and employment status, entered as independent variables. Table 5b shows that there is no significant difference in reuse that is associated with age, gender or employment status, for additional email accounts and other applications. However, it was noted that if a respondent used the same, or a slight variation in passwords across email accounts, they also used the same or a slight variation of their password across other computer applications. A similar outcome is apparent for respondents who did not share passwords across email account, or across other computer applications. However, this outcome is tenuous and further research is needed, as just over 40% of respondents did not respond to this question.

DISCUSSION

Not surprisingly, our survey has shown that email accounts are heavily used, with approximately 30% of respondents checking their email several times a week, and a further 50% who check one or more times a day (Table 4). While full-time employees have the most number of email accounts, they also check them least often. What is concerning, is the reuse of the exact or similar passwords for different email accounts and for other computer applications (Table 5). Of the participants responding to these two questions, almost 25% used the exact same password for other email accounts and 17.4% for other applications. Full-time employees are least likely to reuse passwords across email accounts and other computer-based applications. This is most likely due to organizational requirements for creation and management of passwords. However, a concern is raised with respect to respondents who are not employed. The question arises as to who is controlling the creation of these passwords and whether any guidance is provided to help users create passwords that are not easily guessed. Further, the issue as to whose responsibility it is to ensure secure practices for those who are not employed, is one that has not been adequately researched.

Less than half of the respondents indicated that their passwords contained a combination of alphabetic, numerical, and symbol characters. Such combinations of characters increase the level of difficulty in cracking the password, as well as the time taken to do so. However, females, unemployed, and younger respondents are more likely to choose passwords that consist of either alphabetic or numeric characters. An interesting point is that only 1.6% of participants had their passwords chosen by another entity, such as their email provider. All other passwords were self-selected, notwithstanding the 7.6% of participants who did not respond to the question.

With the exception of 3.5% of respondents, whose passwords were fewer than six characters long, password length ranged between six and twenty-five characters (Table 3). Further, 60% of respondents had passwords of eight or more characters in length. The average password length was eight characters, with no significant difference across the independent variables. While this result appears positive at first glance, the fact that almost three-quarters of the passwords contained meaningful detail, a combination of meaningful details or pronounceable words, is of some concern. Females tended to choose more meaningful or a combination of meaningful details while males selected pronounceable words. This outcome, coupled with the fact that over three-quarters of the respondents never changed their password or changed it no more than three times a year, indicates a serious lack of concern with password security.

Overall, respondents appear to be unconcerned about the risks associated with poor password composition. The issue is more relevant for those who are not employed, since organizations typically have a security policy, or at least minimum requirements for password management and security. However, full-time employment does not eliminate poor password behaviors, with the full-time employees in our sample changing their password less frequently. Further research is required to determine the impact of organizational policies and procedures on password management.

CONCLUSION

Although authentication technologies are constantly evolving, it appears that password-based access systems will remain the predominate means of user authentication for some time to come. This study has explored aspects of user password management practice within the context of email usage and has provided important insight into user behaviors in relation to the creation and management of passwords. The survey results support our initial focus on email account management as an important end-user application context. Email usage was very high with more than 75% of respondents using two or more email accounts. As anticipated, this situation creates password management difficulties for users and encourages password reuse, not only between different email accounts, but also across other computer-based applications. The use of weak password choices further complicates this situation, with the majority of respondents in our survey having chosen passwords that are based on meaningful information and/or personal detail that could be easily guessed by others. The survey results also show that most users still do not adopt secure password management practices, with many user selected passwords being at risk to dictionary style password attacks. Organizations might influence user practice by providing training and technical support to ensure that users are fully informed about the risks and benefits of adopting secure password management practices. However, further research is required to better understand how different password policy environments and user practice aids might improve password security by encouraging more secure user behaviors.

REFERENCES

Adams, A., & Sasse, M. A. (1999). Users Are Not the Enemy. *Communications of the ACM, 42*(12), 41–46. doi:10.1145/322796.322806

Bälter, O. (2000). How to Replace an Old Email System with a New. *Interacting with Computers, 12*(6), 601–614. doi:10.1016/S0953-5438(00)00020-5

Brown, A. S., Bracken, E., Zoccoli, S., & Douglas, K. (2004). Generating and Remembering Passwords. *Applied Cognitive Psychology, 18*, 641–651. doi:10.1002/acp.1014

Campbell, J., & Bryant, K. (2004). *Password composition and Security: An Exploratory Study of User Practice,* Paper presented at Australasian Conference on Information Systems, December 1-3, University of Tasmania, Hobart.

Campbell, J., Kleeman, D., & Ma, W. (2007). The Good and Not So Good of Enforcing Password Composition Rules. *Information Systems Security, 16*(1), 2–8. doi:10.1080/10658980601051375

Carstens, D. S., McCauley-Bell, P., Malone, L. C., & DeMara, R. F. (2004). Evaluation of the Human Impact of Password Authentication Practices on Information Security. *Informing Science Journal, 7*(1), 67–85.

Conklin, A., Dietrich, G., & Walz, D. (2004). *Password-Based Authentication: A System Perspective.* Paper presented at the 37th Hawaii International Conference on System Sciences, Hawaii.

de Paula, R., Ding, X., Dourish, P., Nies, K., Pillet, B., & Redmiles, D. F. (2005). In The Eye of The Beholder: A Visualization-Based Approach to Information System Security. *International Journal of Human-Computer Studies*, *63*, 5–24. doi:10.1016/j. ijhcs.2005.04.021

Ives, B., Walsh, K. R., & Schneider, H. (2004). The Domino Effect of Password Reuse. *Communications of the ACM*, *47*(4), 75–78. doi:10.1145/975817.975820

Jain, A. K., Ross, A., & Prabhakar, S. (2004). An introduction to biometric Recognition. *IEEE Transactions on Circuits and Systems for Video Technology*, *14*(1), 4–20. doi:10.1109/TCSVT.2003.818349

Ma, W., Campbell, J., Tran, D., & Kleeman, D. (2007). A Conceptual Framework for Assessing Password Quality. *International Journal of Computer Science and Network Security*, *7*(1), 179–185.

Man, S., Hong, D., Hayes, B., & Matthews, M. (2004). *A Password Scheme Strongly Resistant to Spyware* (pp. 94-100). Paper presented at the International Conference on Security and Management, Las Vegas, USA.

Ratha, N. K., Connell, J. H., & Bolle, R. M. (2001). Enhancing Security and Privacy in Biometrics-Based Authentication Systems. *IBM Systems Journal*, *40*(3), 614–634. doi:10.1147/sj.403.0614

Rhodes, K. (2004). Operations Security Awareness: The Mind Has No Firewall. *Computer Security Journal*, *16*(2), 27–36.

Rudy, I. A. (1996). A Critical Review on Research on Electronic Mail. *European Journal of Information Systems*, *4*, 198–213. doi:10.1057/ejis.1996.2

Spafford, E. H. (1992). Opus: Preventing Weak Password Choices. *Computers & Security*, *11*(3), 273–278. doi:10.1016/0167-4048(92)90207-8

Stanton, J. M., Stam, K. R., Mastrangelo, P., & Jolton, J. (2005). Analysis of End User Security Behaviours. *Computers & Security*, *24*(2), 124–133. doi:10.1016/j. cose.2004.07.001

Trček, D., & Trobec, R., Pavesić and Tasič, J. F. (2007). Information systems security and human behaviour. *Behaviour & Information Technology*, *26*(2), 113–118. doi:10.1080/01449290500330299

Vu, K. L., Proctor, R. W., Bhargav-Spantzel, A., Tai, B., Cook, J., & Schultz, E. E. (2007). Improving Password Security and Memorability to Protect Personal and Organizational Information. *International Journal of Human-Computer Studies*, *65*, 744–757. doi:10.1016/j.ijhcs.2007.03.007

Wiedenbeck, S., Waters, J., Birget, J. C., Brodskiy, A., & Memon, N. (2005). PassPoints: Design and longitudinal evaluation of a graphical password system. *International Journal of Human-Computer Studies*, *63*, 102–127. doi:10.1016/j. ijhcs.2005.04.010

Yan, J., Blackwell, A., Anderson, R., & Grant, A. (2004). Password Memorability and Security: Empirical Results. *IEEE Security & Privacy*, *2*(5), 25–31. doi:10.1109/ MSP.2004.81

Yapp, P. (2001). Passwords: Use and Abuse. *Computer Fraud & Security*, *9*(1), 14–16. doi:10.1016/S1361-3723(01)00916-2

Zviran, M., & Haga, W. J. (1999). Password Security: An Empirical Study. *Journal of Management Information Systems*, *15*(4), 161–185.

Chapter 6
Wireless handheld Device and LAN Security Issues:
A Case Study

Raj Gururajan
University of Southern Queensland, Australia

Abdul Hafeez-Baig
University of Southern Queensland, Australia

ABSTRACT

The application of WLAN (Wireless Local Area Network) technology in the health-care industry has gained increasing attention in recent years. It provides effective and efficient sharing of health information among healthcare professionals in timely treatment of patients (Collaborative Health Informatics Centre, 2000; Whetton, 2005a). However, there is still a concern among healthcare professionals whether health information is shared safely with WLAN technology. The primary aim of this study is to explore factors influencing healthcare professionals' adoption of WLAN security technology. This study was conducted in regional health settings in Queensland, Australia using a focus group discussion and a questionnaire survey in a mixed research methodology. The outcomes indicate that learning support, user technology awareness, readiness of existing system, and social influence, are four important factors in healthcare professionals' adoption of WLAN security technology. The findings suggest that healthcare professionals prefer to be more informed and prepared on knowledge of WLAN security technology before they decide to adopt it in their work environment. Therefore, their awareness of what the technology can do and cannot do for them, and the support they could get in learning to use the technology, play a crucial role. The healthcare professionals are concerned with how readily their existing system could support WLAN security technology and how

DOI: 10.4018/978-1-60566-806-2.ch006

people important to them would influence their decision in adopting WLAN security technology. Future research should extend the study in three areas. Firstly, future study should examine factors in this study with more regional areas of Australia. Secondly, future research should also examine the relationship between the factors and the demographic variables. Finally, there is also the possibility of examining the adoption factors with other security technology in healthcare, such as the pairing of WLAN technology and biometric security.

INTRODUCTION

Information and communication technologies (ICT) have been a key driving force in reshaping and improving our quality of life (Whetton, 2005b). ICT is perceived to have the potential of breaking down communication barriers across nations and geographical locations, and bringing about economic growth and prosperity (Burke & Weill, 2005; Whetton). The concept of information and communication technology could be explained as electronic devices that are used in the organization and management of data and information (Burke & Weill, 2005). The term *communication* is included in the concept because information by itself is of little use to people unless it is shared and utilized among people. Communication technologies refer to devices that are used in the exchange of information between two or more sources (Burke & Weill; Khan, 2005; Yang & Zahur, 2005).

Communication technologies are divided into wired and wireless technologies. Wired technologies consist of cables, twisted pairs and fiber optics, whereas wireless technologies consist of microwave, radio waves, infrared, and laser beam (Alesso & Smith, 2002; Burke & Weill, 2005; Jamalipour, 2003). Recently, radio wave technology, in particular, has received a great amount of attention and growth over the local area network deployment (Collins, 2005; Havenstein, 2005; Sciannamea, 2005). The same infrastructure can also be described as a wireless local area network (WLAN). This technology is known to promote mobility and reduce the deployment cost of physical equipment, in comparison to a wireless infrastructure (Aktar, 2005; Alesso & Smith; Kong, Gerla, Prabhu, & Gadh, 2005; Quaddus, Fink, Gururajan, & Vuori, 2005; Rehman, 2005; Wong, 2005).

Wireless devices have a lot to offer to for-profit and nonprofit organizations. For example, in the healthcare industry, it has the potential to offer many interesting possibilities to improve old legacy systems (Coakes, 2003; Coiera, 2004; Ilyas & Qazi, 2005; Whetton, 2005a; Whetton & Showell, 2005). The idea of sharing health information effectively and efficiently among healthcare professionals would enable timely and effective treatment of patients, better quality of care, error reduction, and improved resource management (Versel, 2008; Wu & Wu, 2007; Gururajan,

2007). However, there are still concerns and issues in the capability of WLAN to secure sensitive health information during the exchange of information (Baker, 2003; Coiera, 2004; Johnson, 2002; Oleshchuk, 2003; Stanford, 2001; Zeeshan, 2003; Hamalainen, Pirenen, & Shelby, 2007).

In a series of workshops with healthcare professionals in Queensland and Western Australia by one of the authors, it was discovered that the major barrier to the uptake of wireless technology appears to be user concerns over various security issues including physical, logical and data security (Gururajan, Rai, & Edward, 2003; Quaddus et al., 2005). This is further supported in studies by Misra, Wickramasinghe, and Goldberg (2003), Maine Medical Center (2002), and Stanford (2001).

Quaddus et al. (2005) conducted interviews in the 2004-2005 period with the Queensland Nursing Council staff, and these clearly demonstrated concerns about the loss of equipment in a wireless domain, the security of data due to unexpected breakage in wireless communication, and the privacy legislation when data are transmitted between various stakeholders. There were concerns that WLAN security breaches may prove demoralizing in terms of healthcare privacy issues, including wireless hacking and mobile phone viruses (Boston, 2005; Sinnot, 2004). Therefore, healthcare professionals would need to consider their desired WLAN security features when they select for a wireless healthcare environment. While current wireless technology addresses technical aspects associated with the complex healthcare environment, it appears that socio-technical issues specific to healthcare in Australia appear to have been neglected (Gururajan et al., 2003). Furthermore, informal models used in public healthcare, in terms of security, appear to have attached little importance to user behaviors and concerns (Baker, 2003; Oleshchuk, 2003; Zeeshan, 2003).

User behavior is a good indicator of how well a system would be accepted (Chismar & Wiley-Patton, 2006; Emanavin, 2004). The user in this study refers to the healthcare professional who uses the system. It is important to investigate user behavior in regards to the usage of WLAN security technology in the Australian healthcare setting. Recent solutions emerging in public health appear to have ignored this issue because the emphasis is strong on technical security concerns rather than user behaviors (Chau & Turner, 2004; Misra, Wickramasinghe, & Goldberg, 2003; Zeeshan, 2003). This has given impetus to this study.

LITERATURE

The measure of user perception and intention is a good prediction indicator for user acceptance of a technology (Emanavin, 2004; Venkatesh, Morris, Davis, & Davis, 2003). It is a measure of the socio-technical aspects of information technology usage. Coakes (2003) described socio-technical aspects as "the study of relationships between the social and technical part of any systems in helping organizations to explore and adjust to conflicts and complexity in the human, organizational and technical aspects of change" (p. 1). Nykanen (2006) also comments that the introduction of ICT in healthcare services is a reengineering of healthcare processes that takes the socio-technical aspect of design and development of application into consideration. In particular, these principles emphasize an ethical principle related to individual participation in decision making and control over their immediate working environment.

The implementation of WLAN technologies in a healthcare organization causes changes and would impact the design of its business processes, economic performance, and the working conditions of its members (Doherty & King, 2003). It could have either a positive or negative impact. It is important to investigate how information collection, storage, and dissemination strategies could affect people's attitudes, beliefs, and behaviors (Stanton, 2003). The measurement of healthcare professionals' perceptions of WLAN security technology concepts would be a good indicator of what constitutes a secure WLAN environment in Australia. Fisher (2003) describes several elements that contribute to a successful system from a user's perspective. They are: understanding user requirements and perspective, user and developer communication, effective user involvement, accessibility of quality user information, ease of use, and appropriateness of the design of user interface. Therefore, it is possible to measure healthcare professionals' perceptions on WLAN security by associating certain attributes to the technology.

There are many technology adoption models produced over the past years but the most recent model is the Unified Theory of Acceptance and Use of Technology (UTAUT) model, which unifies the strength of previous models into a single representative model (Emanavin, 2004; Venkatesh et al., 2003). The UTAUT model is a predictive model on user acceptance of technologies. It measures user intentions and predicts technology usage with four factors and four modifiers. The four factors are performance expectancy, effort expectancy, social influence, and facilitating conditions (Anderson & Schwager, 2004; Emanavin; Venkatesh et al.). The four modifiers are gender, age, experience, and voluntariness of use. Figure 1 illustrates the UTAUT model.

Performance expectancy is how the user perceives the technology to be useful for their tasks (Anderson & Schwager, 2004; Doktor, Bangert, & Valdez, 2005; Emanavin, 2004; Schaper & Pervan, 2004). The benefit of WLAN technology is most notable in telemedicine, where the sharing of medical information is crucial for more effective and responsive medical care (Ilyas & Qazi, 2005). The research report by the Project for Rural Health Communications and Information Technologies (1996) also comments that another significant potential for WLAN technology is

Figure 1. UTAUT model (Adapted from Venkatesh et al., 2003)

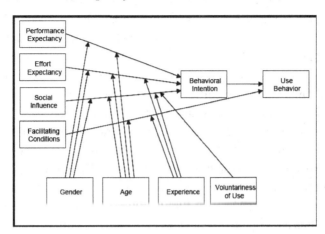

the broad range of online resources available worldwide. It brings health providers closer to the vast amount of information relevant to their work (Whetton, 2005a).

Performance expectancy in WLAN security technology would refer to the WLAN ability to make healthcare users feel safe in conducting their daily operations. This would mean the reliable protection of WLAN security. If a user feels safe in his or her working environment, it might bring about an increase in work performance (Emanavin, 2004; Khan, 2005; Project for Rural Health Communications and Information Technologies, 1996). When WLAN security technology increases work performance, the users would be more likely to accept the technology. Gritzalis and Lambrinoudakis (2005) also commented that the willingness of end users to conduct business and facilitate other activities in an advanced and wireless network environment, would be determined, not only by the performance, but also by the deployment of an integrated trust framework that surrounds such activities.

Effort expectancy is how much effort is needed to use the technology (Schaper & Pervan, 2004; Emanavin, 2004; Anderson & Schwager, 2004; Doktor et al., 2005). This would encompass ease of access, short learning curve, and the concept of smart security (Alesso & Smith, 2002; Kawaguchi et al., 2005, Project for Rural Health Communications and Information Technologies, 1996). It is important to provide patients and healthcare people with great flexibility, high accuracy, and strict accountability in the generation and management of patient information (Kawaguchi, Russell, Qian, Miyata, & Becerra, 2005). Here, user friendliness is very important when it comes to user acceptance (Whetton, 2005a). The complexity of WLAN security should be in the background, as authorized users should not have to feel the complex level of security mechanisms in the protecting of their data.

Effort expectancy also covers the issue of computer literacy. Computer literacy has been an issue in many industries, including healthcare (Walker & Whetton, 2005; Whetton, 2005a). The need for appropriate training, education and information on new technology has been a salient issue in this domain. If users perceive the learning curve of WLAN security to be steep, it would deter them from the course of its adoption. This would also cause an unwillingness to adapt to change (Project for Rural Health Communications and Information Technologies, 1996). There-fore, there is a need to understand how people interact with technologies in order to design a socio-technical WLAN system in health environments (Whetton). The concept of a *smart* wireless system is notable, especially in security management. It would be smart in enabling access to authorized people, and protecting resources from unauthorized people (Alesso & Smith, 2002, Salden et al., 2005). Alesso and Smith describe this as "connecting devices to people rather than people connecting to the devices" (p. 2).

Social influence is the measure of people support in adopting the technology (Anderson & Schwager, 2004, Doktor et al., 2005, Emanavin, 2004, Schaper & Pervan, 2004). Social influence covers credibility, organization culture, working relationships and management decisions (Burke & Weill, 2005; Coakes, 2003; Doherty & King, 2003; Fisher, 2003; Gritzalis & Lambrinoudakis, 2005; Whetton, 2005a; Whetton, 2005b). A person with a high social status and credibility may influence and persuade users in understanding and accepting new technology implementation (Emanavin). People tend to listen to persuasive people. If an authoritative figure, such as the head nurse, believes in the maturity of WLAN and starts persuading people, it would influence the subordinates to follow suit. This would also imply working relationships between people could influence the trust in WLAN security (Gritzalis & Lambrinoudakis).

The healthcare professionals would also be people at the management level. The healthcare managers, who see benefits in the system and endorse it, would have significant influence on the acceptance of the technology throughout the organi-zation (Project for Rural Health Communications and Information Technologies, 1996). This would also mean that a certain level of coercion is used in the adop-tion, especially trust in the management level (Doherty & King, 2003, Whetton, 2005a). There is also the influence of the organizational culture. If an organization is more open to new technologies, the adoption of WLAN security would have less resistance. If an organization is more conservative and cautious, then there would be more resistance, as well as frequent review of the technology (Burke & Weill, 2005; Whetton).

Facilitating condition is the organizational resource dedicated for supporting the adoption of new technology (Emanavin, 2004; Anderson & Schwager, 2004; Schaper & Pervan, 2004; Doktor et al., 2005). The resources would incorporate the training resources, supporting personnel, cost, and existing infrastructure (Burke & Weill, 2005; Coakes, 2003; Khan, 2005; Walker & Whetton, 2005; Whetton, 2005a). Training resources are very important as they improve the computer literacy of system users (Burke & Weill, 2005; Project for Rural Health Communications and Information Technologies, 1996). An inexperienced user would have a challenging task to appropriately use WLAN security to gain access to WLAN services (Ilyas & Qazi, 2005; Project for Rural Health Communications and Information Technologies). For example, if a security mechanism is designed to lock out a user after a few failed logon attempts, the user must be informed or they may not gain access to important medical information. Healthcare professionals may be more aware of the various strengths and limitations of WLAN security through these training sessions. Khan also comments that an informed user would accept new technology more readily than an uninformed user.

There is also the resource of supporting staff in WLAN operation. Healthcare professionals should have someone they could ask for assistance if they encounter a problem with the new technology (Project for Rural Health Communications and Information Technologies, 1996). Cost is also an important resource of any technology adoption (Johnson, 2004; Whetton, 2005a). Technology adoption would fail without proper investment in technology application and people would need to be employed to manage the complex and dynamic WLAN health environment. Healthcare professionals would need training equipment and instructors and infrastructure would need to be setup. These activities need cost evaluation and monetary support. The existing infrastructure would also need to support possible integration of wired and wireless technologies (Baase, 2003; Stanford, 2001; Turisco, 2000).

An examination of the four adoption factors in the UTAUT model has assisted in a preliminary understanding of how users perceive to use a technology in their environment. The four adoption factors are adapted as the initial theme in extracting factors influencing healthcare professionals' decision to adopt WLAN security technology.

RESEARCH METHODOLOGY

This study adopts a mix of qualitative and quantitative research method. The mixed method is implemented in the sequential exploratory style, as described by Creswell, Plano-Clark, Gutmann, and Hanson (2003). The study first executes a qualitative method to analyze the qualitative data gathered from the healthcare professionals. A quantitative approach will be used to analyze the data from survey questionnaires. This is because a qualitative research method helps to explore initial themes needed for the research objectives as the domain of the research is relatively new, and a quantitative research method is used to generalize the findings in the qualitative methods to a larger audience (Creswell et al., 2003; Zikmund, 2003). The exploratory theme for the qualitative research method is derived from the literature review. The findings of the qualitative research method are then used as the exploratory theme for the quantitative research method. A combination of both qualitative and quantitative approaches, as have been recommended in IS domain, provides strength to the research design in social science studies (Morse, 2003).

The mixed research method is conducted in two phases in this study. The first phase utilizes a focus group session to gather and explore the healthcare professionals' perceptions of WLAN security adoption factors in regional Queensland. The second phase uses questionnaire surveys to explore the focus group findings on a wider audience. As this study explores healthcare professionals' behavior and perception of WLAN security technology adoption factors in regional Queensland, the measurement is based on healthcare professionals' perceptions and opinions rather than measurement of the technology. It is possible to investigate healthcare professionals' behaviors and perceptions because there are common elements in the use of medical information among healthcare professionals, such as doctors, nurses, pharmacists, and pathologists. This study addresses this research question: What are Healthcare Professionals' adoption factors for WLAN security technology in regional Queensland, Australia?

This study looks into healthcare professionals' behaviors arising from their concerns for WLAN security in healthcare to obtain a general and early view for adopting WLAN security technology. It appears that these concerns are not yet answered by the current wireless solutions developed in Australian healthcare (Chau & Turner, 2004; Gururajan et al., 2003; Quaddus et al., 2005). In this study, wireless technology is limited to the wireless local area network technology. It is otherwise known as WLAN or IEEE 802.11 Standard, which employs radio wave technology. The transmission distances of the technology covers 100 meters, or within a confined building (Aktar, 2005; Dasgupta & Boyd, 2005; Gritzalis & Lambrinoudakis, 2005). WLAN technology has numerous applications in the healthcare industry. For this study, the application would be the exchange of information for administrative purposes and health records because this information would be the core element in providing efficient and effective healthcare activities (Suomi, 2006). This includes the access of health information from the exchange of information between computers, and the exchange of information between handheld devices and a central computer (Chau & Turner; Gritzalis & Lambrinoudakis; Suomi). Security refers to the resources put in place that ensure the smooth and protected operations of an organization.

Qualitative Study

The first stage of this research involved exploring the views and opinions of the healthcare professionals through focus group discussion sessions. The study adopted focus group techniques to identify an initial set of themes, which affect the security of wireless LAN in healthcare setting. For this purpose, 12 healthcare professionals were identified in the Queensland Health facilities. These healthcare professionals were grouped into two groups. Grouping was done on the basis of convenience and location. The focus group questions were derived from existing literature. The data collection concentrated on public and private hospitals with some form of wireless technology already in use. The participants were also chosen based on their wireless technology awareness or working experience. They were drawn from both private and government hospitals. The focus group sessions were conducted over a 60-75 minute period and recorded using a digital recorder.

Quantitative Study

The quantitative research method in this study entailed the use of a questionnaire survey. The survey questions were derived from the focus group study conducted in the qualitative data collection stage. The objectives of using the questionnaire survey were to quantify and reaffirm the findings of the focus group with a wider audience. This is because a focus group sample size is not large enough to represent an actual population. Questionnaire surveys are a quick, inexpensive and efficient way of gathering confirmation information from a large group of people (Czaja & Blair 1996; Zikmund 2003). However, the survey questions need to be carefully designed to collect accurate and reliable information. The limitation of a questionnaire survey is that it is often difficult to obtain a sufficient response rate from a distributed population, especially in the healthcare environment, because healthcare professionals often do not have the time to answer the survey (Pett, Lackey, & Sullivan, 2003). The quantitative data collection exercise was conducted in two phases. The first phase was a pilot study in a public hospital on a small group of nurses. The pilot study feedback was then used to revise and improve the questionnaire design and response rate. The second phase involved distribution of the revised questionnaires to healthcare professionals in a regional area of Queensland.

Table 1. NVIVO analysis of focus group keywords

Themes related to security of WLAN	
1. Benefits	14. Formal Systems Better than Technology
2. Time	15. Place with no technology
3. Mobility	16. Known Limitation
4. Reliability	17. No Negative Impact
5. Reliability	18. Education
6. Efficiency	19. Resources
7. Simple to Pick Up	20. Cost Effective
8. Familiarizes	21. Existing Systems
9. Computer Literacy	22. Total Commitment
10. Comfort	23. Culture
11. User Friendly	24. Group
12. Work Practices	25. Person's Credibility
13. Security Level	26. Management Decision

DATA ANALYSIS

Qualitative

The focus group secessions were recorded through digital voice recorders and data was transcript by professional transcribers into a word document. First, the word file was reviewed visually for errors and possible themes. A professional application of NVIVO was used to extract a number of keywords and identify specific patterns and themes in the statements. The keywords were identified via recurring comments, positive and negative connotations, or intense words. These patterns were classified to represent factors in WLAN security technology adoption. Table 1 illustrates the extracted keywords from the NVIVO analysis.

Quantitative

The survey instrument was then distributed to over 200 health professionals in the state of Queensland. Out of the 200 questionnaires, only 66 useable questionnaires were received, which was a response rate of 33%. Responses from the survey were transcribed into a spreadsheet file and a visual basic interface was used to generate the numerical code to analyze the data by SPSS. Initially data was reviewed for missing or incorrect values. Descriptive analysis techniques were also used to review the data using SPSS.

Table 2. Extracted factor matrix with varimax

Attributes	WLAN Security Factor			
	LS	UTA	RES	SI
Doesn't Take Long to Learn	.869			
User Friendliness	.784			
More Computer Literate	.719			
Formal System Better than Policy	.613			
See Quick Benefits		.854		
Clinical Data Higher Protection Priority		.694		
Adopting Right Practices		.587		
Know the limitation		560		
A Place With No Technology Welcomes		.539		
Education and Training Provided		.517		
Existing Infrastructure			.903	
No Negative Effect on Existing System			.695	
Enormous Supporting Resources			.668	
Cost Effectiveness in Supporting			.654	
Management Decisions				.866
People I work with				.737
Person's Credibility				.725

WLAN Security Technology Adoption Factors

These factors were extracted through a data reduction technique using Principal Component Analysis (PCA) extraction with Varimax rotation. The Varimax method assumes that the attributes are not correlated and independent of each other. Varimax is a direct and commonly used approach to rotate the extracted list of attributes into meaningful factors in healthcare research (Pett et al., 2003). The 17 attributes were categorized under four principal factors in the rotated factor matrix. Only attributes with factor loadings higher than 0.5 are displayed in the matrix in Table 2.

The first principal factor consisted of the attributes: "Doesn't Take Long to Learn", "User Friendliness", "More Computer Literate", "Formal System Better than Policy", and "Education and Training Provided". This factor was labeled Learning Support (LS). The second principal factor consisted of the attributes: "See Quick Benefits", "Clinical Data Higher Protection Priority", "Know the Limitation", "A Place with No Technology Welcomes", and "Adopting Right Practices". This factor was labeled User Technology Awareness (UTA). The third principal factor consisted of the attributes: "Existing Infrastructure", "Enormous Supporting Resources",

Figure 2. Healthcare professionals' adoption factors in WLAN security technology

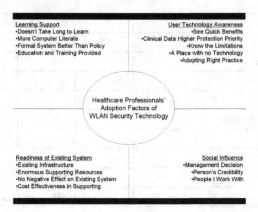

"No Negative Effect on Existing System", and "Cost Effectiveness in Supporting". This factor was labeled Readiness of Existing System (RES). The fourth principal factor consisted of the attributes: "Management Decision", "Person's Credibility", and "People I Work With". This factor was labeled Social Influence (SI). Figure 2 below illustrates the healthcare professionals' adoption factors of WLAN security technology.

DISCUSSION

Learning Support

Healthcare professionals believe that the ability to quickly learn to use WLAN security technology is an important element. Healthcare professionals would be resistant in adopting WLAN security technology if the technology itself takes a long and difficult time to learn because they often have very tight work schedules. Mann (2005) also comments that resistance to a technology would often be because the technology is difficult to use, the person does not know how to use the technology, or use of the technology requires assistance from another person. Also, being computer literate in WLAN security technology is one of the important elements. Healthcare computer literacy was established as an ongoing issue in the focus group discussion. Having some computing knowledge would also help speed up the learning process, as well as a better understanding of what the technology is about. Horan, Tulu and Hilton (2006) state that the more technology ready a healthcare professional's work practice, the more he or she is willing to adopt new technology.

The user friendliness of the WLAN security technology is another important element. This is also one of the important requirements, which was revealed in the focus group discussion. The WLAN security technology interface should be friendly for authorized people and possibly complex for unauthorized people. One of the focus group participants also suggested the pairing of biometric security technology and WLAN technology as a desirable solution (Crow, 2004; Holt, 2000; Kavanaugh, 2000). It is also noted that healthcare professionals believed that having a formal system in place is better than setting policy in providing learning support for adoption of new technology. In the focus group discussion, healthcare professionals perceived policy as boring information that takes too long to read. An automated system that governs the use of WLAN security technology would be a preferred option for healthcare professionals.

Healthcare professionals perceived education and training as part of the learning support factor because education and training could improve healthcare professionals' practice and knowledge in using WLAN security technology in their work setting. The Project for Rural Health Communications and Information Technologies (1996) reported that continuing education and training, both in terms of practice and in use of communication and information, are regarded throughout Australia as a major area of concern. This finding is further validated by Hegney et al. (2006). Khan (2005) also maintains that education about information of all goods and services, related to a secure wireless system, is essential before a community at large can adopt and benefit from the system. This learning support factor appears to be similar to the concept of effort expectancy in the UTAUT model (Emanavin, 2004; Venkatesh et al., 2003).

User Technology Awareness

The data analysis of the survey responses indicated that healthcare professionals would like to see quick benefits arising from the use of WLAN security technology. This is also evident in the focus group discussion. Although, 'see quick benefits' is similar to performance expectancy in the UTAUT model, it is part of a larger factor, which is the user technology awareness in this study. Hemsoth (2000) states that the lack of employee awareness is one of the biggest roadblocks to improving an organization's data security. This would encompass an awareness of the quick benefits that a technology could bring to the healthcare environment. Users would be reluctant to use a technology that is of no benefit to them, especially when it fails to minimize human errors in the healthcare operation (Borgner, 1994; Chismar & Wiley-Patton, 2006; Sheridan & Thompson, 1994). In addition, O'Moore (1995) comments that strong user needs usually govern the adoption of a technology.

Healthcare professionals, in both the questionnaire survey and the focus group discussion, believed that they should be informed of the WLAN security technology limitations. Any technology would have limitations. If a user is kept aware of its limitations, the user would be able to factor these limitations through non-technological solutions. One of the non-technological approaches might be to develop work practices on the device usages (Horan, Tulu, & Hilton, 2006). This might also bring opportunities to improve the technology.

The data analysis of the survey responses also showed that healthcare professionals believe in adopting the right practice for the use of WLAN security technology. Horan et al. (2006) discovered that work practice compatibility issues play a significant role in predicting behavioral intent. They comment that the more technologically ready a physician's work practice, the more likely the physician was to adopt the technology. The right practice of using WLAN security technology would determine users' awareness in using a technology correctly. This is essentially collaboration between humans and computers. Sheridan and Thompson (1994) claim that the a proper collaboration of humans and computers is expected to yield greater performance and reliability, as well as a reduction of errors in the healthcare system.

This study also revealed that healthcare professionals believed that a work environment without any technology would be open to the adoption of new technology. This was evident in the focus group discussion. One of the reasons for such behavior could be that the paper based and manual systems strain the healthcare professional's workload. Any awareness of new technology would help reduce the workload and human errors. Baase (2003) believes that the reduction of human errors would free healthcare professionals from tedious chores so that they could spend more time on patient care. Furthermore, a majority of the survey respondents believed that clinical data required a higher data protection priority than non-clinical data. This was also evident in the focus group discussion. This shows that healthcare professionals are aware of the data protection priorities in their healthcare environment.

Readiness of Existing System

Readiness of existing system factor is similar to the facilitating condition factor in the UTAUT model. Both of the factors take the technology users' environment into consideration. In this study, healthcare professionals believed that the cost effectiveness of supporting a secure WLAN environment is an important element of adoption factors. Healthcare users also believed that the resources involved are extensive. However, the challenge with resources is often that the research funding, for supporting WLAN technology, is limited (Ilyas & Qazi, 2005). This was evident in the focus group discussion and was also previously reported in the study by Collaborative Health Informatics Centre (2000). Any significant investment in a secured WLAN environment would need additional costs. Salden et al. (2005) also commented that the WLAN deployment cost is low, but the cost of creating and managing value-added mobile WLAN application services remains considerably high.

The impact, whether negative or positive, on existing systems is crucial in a healthcare setting (Sheridan & Thompson, 1994). Healthcare professionals would like to have a new system that is better than the old system. They would also expect the new system to perform significantly better. Mann (2005) stated two issues in the adoption of new technologies in regards to the readiness of an existing system. The first issue is that a device may not work equally well in all intended environments or situations, which may be due to compatibility problems. The Productivity Commission (2005) reported that many hospitals have primitive information and communication technology systems compared with other businesses of similar size. This would cause a complexity in compatibility and future upgrade of the Australian health system. The second issue is that a device could be dangerous in some situations (Mann, 2005). For example, the signal emitted from wireless security technology might disrupt medical equipment. This concern was also raised during the focus group discussion.

The cost effectiveness of managing a secure WLAN environment, the extensive resources, and the possible impact of the WLAN security technology, has contributed to the factor of readiness of an existing system. Horan, Tulu and Hilton (2006) comment that organizational and technical readiness plays a significant part in predicting healthcare professionals' behavioral intent. It would be a challenge to securely integrate the increasing number of small mobile devices into the existing network infrastructure (Alesso & Smith, 2002).

Social Influence

In the data analysis of the survey responses, the healthcare professionals believed that management decision, a person's credibility, and group influence, are important elements in deciding to adopt WLAN security technology. This factor is consistent with the social influence determinant in the UTAUT model (Venkatesh et al., 2003). Management is the top component of an organization pyramid. Management decides when to commit the organization's resources to implementing the technology. In the report by the Collaborative Health Informatics Centre (2000), it is suggested that IT executives should coordinate efforts to demonstrate the value of automating business processes to the health organization. If management decided to adopt the technology based on the demonstrated value, the healthcare professionals might agree with their decisions. This was also evident in the focus group discussion.

On the individual level, credibility is one of the critical elements in persuading people in favor of WLAN security technology adoption. This is consistent with the focus group discussion. A credible person's voice, such as the head nurse, has a significant impact, especially if the person is trusted by staff. Lu, Yu, Liu, & Yao (2003) describe trust as "a complex social phenomenon that reflects technological, behavioral, social, psychological, and organizational aspects of interactions among various human and non-human agents" (p. 216).

At the group level, it is usually the common interest that is being weighted (Lapointe et al., 2006). Venkatesh et al. (2003) states that "social influence is the degree to which an individual perceived that important others believe he or she should use the new system"(p. 451). Therefore, healthcare professionals in a group would have strong influence on each other. An individual might give up his or her personal interest for the common interest of the group. This would also influence the commitment of the group to use the technology and nurture a new culture for the new technology use.

CONCLUSION

Security is always an issue in information and communication technology. This is also valid for the application of WLAN technology in the healthcare environment and for the successful implementation of WLAN in the healthcare environment, where adoption factors, specific to WLAN security technology, need to be identified and addressed. The identification of adoption factors would help greatly in the design and implementation of suitable wireless security technology that would incur a high acceptance rate by the users. This exploratory study identified healthcare professionals' adoption factors of WLAN security technology in regional Queensland: as learning support, user technology awareness, readiness of existing infrastructure, and social influence. This study found that healthcare professionals place understanding and learning to use a new technology as important factors to adopt the technology. This would also suggest that healthcare professionals still prefer to be more informed and prepared on WLAN security technology before they decide to adopt it in their work environment. In a healthcare setting, socio-technical requirements are stronger than technical requirements. Healthcare professionals are more concerned with their interaction with WLAN security technology than the benefits it can bring to their work. These findings are especially important when the Australian government is promoting the use of an E-Health System to enhance their healthcare industry (Nykanen, 2006). The sharing of health information would certainly involve privacy issues and security protection. These adoption factors would greatly influence whether health professionals perceive wireless technology to be secure for their working environment.

ACKNOWLEDGMENT

The authors acknowledge the initial data collection exercises conducted by Mr. Tiong Ing Chee as part of his Master's work in developing this paper.

REFERENCES

Aktar, S. (2005). WLAN Performance . In Ahson, S., & Ilyas, M. (Eds.), *Handbook of Wireless Local Area Network: Applications, Technology, Security, and Standards*. Boca Raton: Taylor & Francis Group.

Alesso, H. P., & Smith, C. F. (2002). *The intelligent wireless Web*. Boston: Addison-Wesley.

Anderson, J. E., & Schwager, P. H. (2004). *SME adoption of Wireless LAN technology: Applying the UTAUT model*. Paper presented at the 7th Annual Conference of the Southern Association for Information Systems, Savannah, GE.

Baase, S. (2003). *A gift of fire: Social, legal, and ethical issues for computers and the Internet*. Upper Saddle River: Pearson Education Inc.

Baker, D. B. (2003). Wireless . In *Security for Healthcare*. San Diego: SAIC Enterprise and Health Solution.

Borgner, M. S. (1994). Introduction . In Borgner, M. S. (Ed.), *Human error in Medicine*. New Jersey: Lawrence Erlbaum Associates.

Boston, B. C. (March 2005). Phone viruses: How bad is it? *NewScientist Technology.*

Burke, L., & Weill, B. (2005). *Information Technology for the Health Professions*. New Jersey: Pearson Prentice Hall.

Chau, S., & Turner, P. (2004). *Implementing and evaluating a wireless handheld clinical care management system at an Australian aged care facility. HIC 2004*. Brisbane, Australia: HISA.

Chismar, W. R., & Wiley-Patton, S. (2006). Predicting Internet use: Applying the Extended Technology Acceptance Model to the healthcare environment . In Spil, T. A. M., & Schuring, R. W. (Eds.), *E-Health Systems diffusion and use: The Innovation, the user and the USE IT Model*. Hershey: Idea Group Publishing.

Coakes, E. (2003). Socio-technical thinking - A holistic viewpoint . In Clarke, S., Coakes, E., Hunter, M. G., & Wenn, A. (Eds.), *Socio-Technical and Human Cognition Elements of Information Systems*. Hershey: Information Science Publishing.

Coiera, E. (2004). Four rules for the reinvention of health care. *British Medical Journal, 328*, 1197–1199. doi:10.1136/bmj.328.7449.1197

Collaborative Health Informatics Centre. (2000). *E-health - An exploratory study of health IT in Australia and New Zealand*. Milton: Collaborative Health Informatics Centre.

Collins, G. (2005). Evolving architecture drives enterprise WLAN growth. *Business Communication Review*, 28-30.

Creswell, J. W., Plano-Clark, V. L., Gutmann, M. L., & Hanson, W. E. (2003). Advanced mixed methods research designs . In Tashakkori, A., & Teddle, C. (Eds.), *Handbook of Mixed Methods in Social & Behavioral Research*. Thousand Oaks: Sage Publications.

Crow, A. (2004). *Defining the balance for now and the future - Clinicians perspective of implementing a care coordination information systems management. HIC 2004*. Brisbane, Australia: HISA.

Dasgupta, P., & Boyd, T. (2005). Security in Wireless Networks . In Ahson, S., & Ilyas, M. (Eds.), *Handbook of Wireless Local Area Network: Applications, Technology, Security, and Standards*. Boca Raton: Taylor & Francis Group.

Doherty, N. F., & King, M. (2003). From technical change to socio-technical change: Towards a proactive approach to the treatment of organizational issues . In Clarke, S., Coakes, E., Hunter, M. G., & Wenn, A. (Eds.), *Socio-Technical and Human Cognition Elements of Information Systems*. Hershey: Information Science Publishing.

Doktor, R., Bangert, D., & Valdez, M. (2005). *Organizational learning and culture in the managerial implementation of clinical e-Health systems: An international perspective*. Paper presented at the 38th Hawaii International Conference on System Science, Hawaii, University of Hawaii.

Emanavin, C. C. (2004). *Testing Lessig: Applying user acceptance theory to Internet use and behavior for privacy and security applications. Faculty of the Graduate School of Arts and Science*. Washington: Georgetown University.

Fisher, J. (2003). Human factors and the Systems Development Process . In Clarke, S., Coakes, E., Hunter, M. G., & Wenn, A. (Eds.), *Socio-Technical and Human Cognition Elements of Information Systems*. Hershey: Information Science Publishing.

Gritzalis, S., & Lambrinoudakis, C. (2005). Security in IEEE 802.11 WLANs . In Ahson, S., & Ilyas, M. (Eds.), *Handbook of Wireless Local Area Network: Applications, Technology, Security, and Standards*. Boca Raton: Taylor & Francis Group.

Gururajan, R. (2007). Drivers of wireless technology in healthcare: an Indian Study. In *Proceedings of the 15th European Conference on Information Systems (ECIS 2007), University of St Gallen, Switerland*

Gururajan, R., Rai, S., & Edward, D. (2003). *The study in the use of hand held devices in an Emergency Department for a Hospital in Western Australia.* IEEE TENCON International Conference, Bangalore.

Hamalainen, M., Pirinen, P., & Shelby, Z. (2007). Advanced Wireless ICT healthcare research . In Pirinen, P. (Ed.), *Mobile and Wireless Communications Summit, 2007.*

Havenstein, H. (2005). *Industry Focus: Wireless in Healthcare.* Techworld.

Hegney, D., Eley, R., Bulkstra, E., Fallon, T., Soar, J., & Gilmore, V. (2006). Australian Nurses Access and Attitudes to Information Technology - A National Survey. In H. A. Park., P. Murray, & C. Delaney (Eds.), *The 9th International Congress on Nursing Informatics (NI2006),* Seoul, Korea.

Hemsoth, C. M. (2000). Security policies: The foundation for information protection. In P. L. Davison, (Ed.), *Healthcare Information Systems.* Boca Raton: Auerbach Publications.

Holt, P. J. (2000). Biometrics. In P. L. Davidson, (Ed.), *Healthcare Information Systems.* Boca Raton: Auerbach Publications.

Horan, T. A., Tulu, B., & Hilton, B. N. (2006). Understanding physician use of Online Systems: An empirical assessment of an Electronic Disability Evaluation System . In Spil, T. A. M., & Schring, R. W. (Eds.), *E-Health Systems Diffusion and Use: The Innovation, the User and the USE IT Model.* Hershey: Idea Group Publishing.

Ilyas, M., & Qazi, S. (2005). Applications of WLANs in Telemedicine . In Ahson, S., & Ilyas, M. (Eds.), *Handbook of Wireless Local Area Network: Applications, Technology, Security, and Standards.* Boca Raton: Taylor & Francis Group.

Jamalipour, A. (2003). *The Wireless Mobile Internet: Architectures, Protocols and Service.* West Sussex: John Wiley & Sons Ltd.

Johnson, B. C. (2002). *Wireless 802.11 LAN Security: Understanding the Key Issues.* Boston: Systems Expert Corporation.

Johnson, C. (2004). *Realising value from Health technology investments: Improving the selection and delivery of a portfolio of projects. HIC 2004.* Brisbane, Australia: HISA.

Kavanaugh, C. (2000). The future of automated patient identification, car coding, and smart cards. In P. L. Davidson, (Ed.). *Healthcare Information Systems.* Boca Raton: Auerbach Publications.

Kawaguchi, A., Russell, S., Qian, G., Miayata, C., & Becerra, J. (2005). Integrated WLAN Deployment: Implementation of a Mobile Wireless Diabetes Management System . In Ahson, S., & Ilyas, M. (Eds.), *Handbook of Wireless Local Area Network: Applications, Technology, Security, and Standards.* Boca Raton: Taylor & Francis Group.

Khan, M. F. (2005). WLAN Security: Issues and solution . In Ahson, S., & Ilyas, M. (Eds.), *Handbook of Wireless Local Area Network: Applications, Technology, Security, and Standards.* Boca Raton: Taylor & Francis Group.

Kong, J., Gerla, M., Prabhu, B. S., & Gadh, R. (2005). An overview of network security in WLANs . In Ahson, S., & Ilyas, M. (Eds.), *Handbook of Wireless Local Area Network: Applications, Technology, Security, and Standards.* Boca Raton: Taylor & Francis Group.

Lapointe, L., Lapointe, L., & Fortin, J. P. (2006). The Dynamics of IT Adoption in a Major Change Process in Healthcare Delivery . In Spil, T. A. M., & Schuring, R. W. (Eds.), *E-Health Systems Diffusion and Use: The Innovation, the User and the USE IT Model.* Hershey: Idea Group Publishing.

Lu, J., Yu, C. H., Liu, C., & Yao, J. E. (2003). Technology Acceptance Model for Wireless Internet. *Internet Research: Electronic Networking Applications and Policy.*

Maine Medical Center. (2002). *Wireless security and management in healthcare organization.* Portland: Maine Medical Center.

Mann, W. C. (2005). Aging, disability, and independence: Trends and perspectives . In Mann, W. C. (Ed.), *Smart Technology for Aging, Disability, and Independence.* New Jersey: John Wiley & Sons Incorporated Publication. doi:10.1002/0471743941.ch1

Misra, S. K., Wickramasinghe, N., & Goldberg, S. (2003). Security challenge in mobile healthcare setting. *Wireless I.T. Committee Meeting.* Cleveland: Information Technology Association of Canada.

Morse, J. M. (2003). Principles of mixed methods and multimethods research design . In Tashakkori, A., & Teddlie, C. (Eds.), *Handbook of Mixed Methods in Social & Behavioral Research.* Thousand Oaks: Sage Publications.

Nykanen, P. (2006). E-Health Systems: Their use and visions for the future . In Spil, T. A. M., & Schuring, R. W. (Eds.), *E-Health Systems Diffusion and Use: The innovation, the user and the USE IT Model*. Hershey: Idea Group Publishing.

O'Moore, R. (1995). The conception of a Medical Computer System . In Van Gennip, E. M. S. J., & Talmon, J. (Eds.), *Assessment and Evaluation of Information Technologies in Medicine*. Amsterdam: IOS Press.

Oleschuk, V. (2003). *Wireless Security and Health Care Information Systems*. Grimstad: Agder University College.

Pett, M. A., Lackey, N. R., & Sullivan, J. J. (2003). *Making sense of factor analysis: The use of factor analysis for instrument development in health care research*. Thousand Oaks: SAGE Publications.

Project For Rural Health Communications and Information Technologies (1996). Telehealth in rural and remote Australia. *Report of the Project for Rural Health Communications and Information Technologies*. Moe, Monash University: Australian Rural Health Research Institute.

Quaddus, M., Fink, D., Gururajan, R., & Vuori, T. (2005). *Driver and inhibitors of the adoption of wireless handheld technology in the healthcare industry: Views from selected WA stakeholders. HIC 2005*. Melbourne, Australia: HISA.

Salden, A. H., Hesselman, C., Van Eijik, R., Tokmakoff, A., Bargh, M., De Heer, J., & Benz, H. (2005). Mobile WLAN application services . In Ahson, S., & Ilyas, M. (Eds.), *Handbook of Wireless Local Area Network: Applications, Technology, Security, and Standards*. Boca Raton: Taylor & Francis Group.

Schaper, L., & Pervan, G. (2004). A model of information and communication technology acceptance and utilization by Occupational Therapists. *Decision Support in an Uncertain and Complex World: The IFIP TC8/WG8.3, International Conference 2004*, Curtin University of Technology.

Sciannamea, M. (2005). *Study says WLAN growth to triple within two years*. therfidwebblog.

Sheridan, T. B., & Thompson, J. M. (1994). People versus computers in medicine . In Bogner, M. S. (Ed.), *Human Error in Medicine*. New Jersey: Lawrence Erlbaum Associates.

Sinnot, D. (2004). *Wireless insecurity*. ProActive Network and Security.

Stanford, V. (2001). Pervasive Health Care Applications Face Tough Security Challenges. *Pervasive Computing. IEEE, 1*, 8–12. doi:10.1109/MPRV.2002.1012332

Stanton, J. M. (2003). Information Technology and privacy: A boundary management perspective . In Clarke, S., Coakes, E., Hunter, M. G., & Wenn, A. (Eds.), *Socio-Technical and Human Cognition Elements of Information Systems*. Hershey: Information Science Publishing.

Suomi, R. (2006). Introducing electronic patient records to hospitals: Innovation adoption paths . In Spil, T. A. M., & Schuring, R. W. (Eds.), *E-Health Systems Diffusion and Use: The Innovation, the User and the USE IT Model*. Hershey: Idea Group Publishing.

The Productivity Commission. (2005). *Impacts of advances in medical technology in Australia: Productivity Commission Research Report*. Melbourne.

Turisco, F. (2000). Mobile computing is the next technology frontier for Health Providers. *Healthcare Financial Management, 55*, 78–82.

Ur Rehman, T. (2005). IP Mobility . In Ahson, S., & Ilyas, M. (Eds.), *Handbook of Wireless Local Area Network: Applications, Technology, Security, and Standards*. Boca Raton: Taylor & Francis Group.

Venkatesh, V., Morris, M. G., Davis, G. B., & Davis, F. B. (2003). User acceptance of Information Technology: Towards a unified view. *Management Information Systems Quarterly, 27*, 425–478.

Versel, N. (2008). *Use of mobile and wireless technology jumps in hospitals*. Digital Health Care.

Walker, J., & Whetton, S. (2005). Health informatics in action: Rural and remote health . In Whetton, S. (Ed.), *Health Informatics: A Social-Technical Perspective*. Oxford: Oxford University Press.

Whetton, S. (2005a). The health care environment and Health Informatics . In Whetton, S. (Ed.), *Health Informatics: A Social-Technical Perspective*. Oxford: Oxford University Press.

Whetton, S. (2005b). What is Health Informatics? In Whetton, S. (Ed.), *Health Informatics: A Social-Technical Perspective*. Oxford: Oxford University Press.

Whetton, S., & Showell, C. (2005). Tools: Promises and Pitfalls . In Whetton, S. (Ed.), *Health Informatics: A Social-Technical Perspective*. Oxford: Oxford University Press.

Wong, K. D. (2005). *Wireless Internet Telecommunications*. London: Artech House.

Wu, K., & Wu, X. (2007). A wireless mobile monitoring system for home healthcare and community medical services. In X. Wu (Ed.), *Bioinformatics and Biomedical Engineering, 2007. ICBBE 2007. The 1st International Conference.*

Yang, T. A., & Zahur, Y. (2005). Security in WLANs. In Ahson, & M. Ilyas (Eds.), *Handbook of Wireless Local Area Network: Applications, Technology, Security, and Standards.* Boca Raton: Taylor & Francis Group.

Zeeshan, A. (2003). *Wireless security in health care.* SA, Australia: University of South Australia.

Zikmund, W. G. (2003). *Business Research Methods.* Ohio, Thomson: South Western.

Chapter 7
Web 2.0 Technologies for Business Solutions:
A Security Perspective

Shah Jahan Miah
Griffith University, Australia

ABSTRACT

Web 2.0 is a new way of using existing Web resources interactively, and has attracted growing interest from the Web community, and more recently from businesses. However, there are emerging issues associated with security with the use of Web 2.0. This chapter provides an overview of Web 2.0 and outlines the security issues with Mashups and other applications within the Web 2.0 environment.

INTRODUCTION

Web 2.0 is a new way of using existing Web resources interactively. This is achieved by using a programming technique called AJAX, which stands for Asynchronous JavaScript and XML. This technique helps make Web pages more interactive and enables collaboration from participants. It may also provide ways for hackers to hit a Web server and to exploit sites in attacks on visitors.

Recently, Web 2.0 technologies have been used for many business solutions, in terms of user enabled Web-services, and it has attracted growing interest from the Web community. For example, Digital library services (Curran, Murray, & Chris-

DOI: 10.4018/978-1-60566-806-2.ch007

tian, 2007; Pearce, 2006) can be viewed as a platform where Web 2.0 technologies have been used to enhance user participation. In addition, the growing number of social networking features in websites, such as myspace, facebook and blogger, has potentially become a useful tool for business in terms of market research and increased exposure of products on the market. In the past, business applications driven by users were not able to be developed easily using traditional requirement and build approaches, especially for Web based service development.

Business processes are rapidly changing, due to the potential for improved virtual operations, and Web developers have started using Web 2.0 technologies for Web based user interface design, service composition design, as well as social or community based features design, to create more interactive business applications. As conventional technologies for Web services suffer from weaknesses, such as dynamicity, scalability, and flexibility, the view of emerging technologies offers an innovation to businesses and online communities. However, the security concerns of such technologies are an emergent problem for business users. This chapter describes key aspects of the security issues of the Web 2.0 technologies.

Web 2.0 technologies, especially Mashups[1], help develop Web-based applications by gathering content from several online sources. The basic principle of the technologies is to reuse existing content or services developed by other parties. The end result of such services can provide enhanced support for business and end-users, and the use of Mashup technologies can provide Web browsers with an important role at the user side. For example, Hakkola (2008) describes Web browsers as not just a tool for accessing static HTML based content, but when combined with Web 2.0 and Mashups, a useful tool for accessing content more dynamically and frequently. The classic browsers still have rigid security options when interacting with Mashups based applications, due to its dynamic nature. Wang, Fan, Howell and Jackson (2007) suggest that the Mashups applications have either no trust between the third parties, or there is full trust between them. According to Ashley (2007), this leads to a dilemma of having to consider both security and functionality for end-user browsers. This is because the browsers at the end user level have default security features that do not address the dynamic nature of Mashups, when interacting with third parties' applications. Wang, Fan, Howell and Jackson suggest that the Mashups applications do not define trust levels between the third parties. This suggests a new security strategy is required for Mashup users.

The structure of this chapter is as follows. The first section of the chapter discusses the background of Web 2.0 technologies, with respect to business solutions. Secondly, we discuss applications developed using Web 2.0 technologies. The third section discusses the security concerns of the technologies in the context of online businesses. The final section summarizes the entire chapter by demonstrating the key boundaries of the discussion.

BACKGROUND OF WEB 2.0 TECHNOLOGIES

In 2004, the term Web 2.0 was defined for the first time, by Dale Dougherty and Craig Cline (O'Reilly, 2005). It has been defined as a new version of the Web from a usage point of view, without any technical updates for such services. The current Web 2.0 technologies, offer features for more than just displaying, or recovering, information online. The technology itself can be seen in the form of wikis, blogs, and Mashups, and these permit improved user privileges in the Web service space. Wiki systems enable an open but shared Web space for business users, where they can collaboratively contribute to complete a task. This type of Web application provides basic options, such as to add new, modify, and remove content from the Web. As such, Bean and Hott (2005) suggest that wikis acceptance in the businesses environment is not seen as a fad but a long-term investment in the future. Businesses do not only use wikis for representing their activities online, but also use them for: collaboratively writing documents, or writing research papers; as a central repository for project information, to which all project team members can contribute; writing project management documents; creating service manuals; and creating notes of meetings from distant locations. Similarly, blog systems may contain journal type entries from user groups where a number of blog applications can be easily found; these include the Google application and Blogger. Kulathuramaiyer (2007) suggests that a blog enables anyone to become a publisher of their own content, with the ability to modify content from any source.

Mashups have become a very popular Web 2.0 technology for business application development. It can be described as a method of merging existing service content or applications from multiple Web sources. Yee (2006) defined Mashups as the use of XML and Web services that reuse or remix the existing digital content and services to develop new applications or services. The Mashup, itself, can be distinguished as a Web application that seamlessly combines existing Web content from multiple sources. Mashups offer features for Web service development for businesses. Other Web 2.0 technologies are not generally associated with direct business applications; rather, they are used for social networking through enhancing user participation or collaboration. Thus, in this chapter, we highlight the use of Mashup technologies and how they can be used for business application development.

Auinger, Martin, Nedbal, and Holzinger (2008) suggest that Mashups can be both a concept and a technology for integrating Web applications or services. While the source content is normally implicit on the Web, Mashup technology helps process relevant content to be integrated whereas, existing Web service architectures would have the potential for problems, such as scalability, performance, flexibility, and ability to implement, as outlined by Dillon, Wu and Chang (2007). Web application, based on Mashups, typically adds value through benefiting users in ways that are different

Figure 1. A server-side mashup. (Adapted from Ort, Brydon, & Basler, 2002)

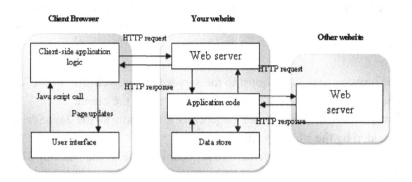

and better than the individual services they leverage (Srivastava & Koehler, 2006). According to Auinger et al., the Mashup technologies for integrating services can be classified in two primary styles, server-side Mashups and client-side Mashups. The server-side Mashups technologies integrate services and content, by acting as a proxy between a Web application on the client, typically a browser, and the other Web site that takes part in the Mashup. In a server-side Mashup, all the requests from the client go to the server, which plays a role as a proxy to make calls to the other Web site. The main task of the client in the server-side Mashup is to push information from the Web application client to the server. As defined in Auinger et al., the steps displayed in Figure 1 describe the activities of server-sided technologies, where the Web services, or content on the server, are mixed and transferred to the client throughout the HTTP protocol.

1. A user generates an event in the client, typically a Web page in a browser. The event triggers a JavaScript function in the client.
2. The client makes a request to the server on your Web site.
3. A web component, such as a servlet, receives the request and calls a method to encapsulate the code to connect and interact with the other Web site in the Mashup.
4. The proxy class processes the request, augments it as needed, and opens a connection to the Mashup site.
5. The Mashup site receives the request, processes the request, and returns data to the proxy class.
6. The proxy class receives the response and may transform it to an appropriate data format for the client. It can also cache the response for future request processing.
7. The servlet returns the response to the client.
8. A call back function updates the client view of the page.

Unlike server-side Mashups, client-side Mashups integrate services and content on the client, directly combining with the other Web site's data or functionality. The following describes this process and is also displayed in Figure 2 (Ort et al., 2007; Auinger et al., 2008).

1. The browser makes a request to the server in your Web site for the Web page.
2. The server on your Web site loads the page into the client.
3. Some action in the browser page calls a function in the JavaScript library provided by the Mashup site.
4. Based on the <script> element, a request is made to the Mashup site to load the script.
5. The Mashup site loads the script.
6. The callback function updates the client's view of the page.

APPLICATIONS OF THE TECHNOLOGIES

Many business applications have been developed using Web 2.0 technologies. The Web 2.0 applications can be viewed as a form of e-science (Fox & Pierce, 2007); e-learning, such a wikis designed for IS teaching (Kane & Fichman, 2009); e-library (Abram, 2005; Curran, Murray, & Christian, 2007); e-Government (Government 2.0 white paper, 2009); and Social networking, such as design for online communities (Ren, Kraut, & Kiesler, 2007). Fox and Pierce (2007) have suggested applications, infrastructures, and technologies for an e-Science environment. At a broader range (enterprise and distributed environment), these authors claim that Web 2.0 can

Figure 2. Client side mashup (Adapted from Ort et al., 2007)

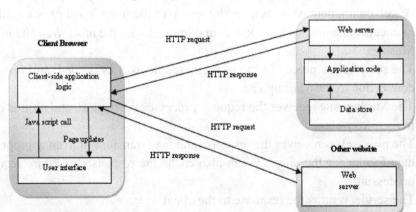

provide narrow grids for building Web services that may provide a robust managed environment.

In a recent whitepaper on government applications of Web 2.0 (Government 2.0 white paper, 2009), it has been documented that there are three key elements for Web 2.0 technologies, which are important to understand. These underlying concepts include: data access and control, participation; and customer service. Firstly, the data access and control is one of the central points of the government's concern about Web 2.0 and its implicit openness, as it provides a logical starting point for an interface through which citizens and businesses can interact. Secondly, the participation by the practitioners, customers, and employees, is the gravitational core of a Web enabled system that allows user-driven participation to actually strengthen communal knowledge. For e-democracy services of parts of the e-government system, the use of You Tube, Twitter, Flickr, Facebook, MySpace, as well as the RSS feeds can be considered as a re-invention of government services, and can be thought of as a useful new and effective way of delivering government services. Finally, with respect to customer service, Web 2.0 allows customers to individually build their own solutions by mixing available existing businesses' datasets within readily accessible tools.

Abram (2005) described a concept for Library 2.0 using Web 2.0 to automate library services. The Web 2.0 concept shifts the traditional library systems and services towards a new trend that combines e-learning modules, open access publishing, ebooks, and networking tools, including blogs, wikis and tagging. Casey and Savastinuk (2006) explain the advantages of the Library 2.0 technologies. According to them, the enabling Web 2.0 technologies offer features, such as feedback from end users in the form of reviews, ratings, or comments. Also users can customize their Web pages to include their own blogs and RSS feeds. The resulting organizational forms and strategies on display bear little resemblance to the traditional corporate model that dominated much of the preceding century.

SECURITY ISSUES

This section considers the security issues of Web 2.0 technologies, especially for Web Mashups and blogs. Hakkola (2008) suggests that two types of security issues are associated with Mashup services. The first is one arises directly from the lack of safeguards and the hostile abuse of the technology. It refers to issues related to questions about the trustworthiness of the content. Another issue exists because of the nature of Mashups, and this is discussed in the following section.

Hostile Use of Technology

According to the Hakkola (2008), the hostile use of the technology becomes an issue and a security threat because of hostile user behavior. In addition, Web 2.0 uses a browser security system called the Same-Origin Policy (SOP), which has a weakness in transferring content from other sites, while the nature of Mashup technologies is to use content from multiple destinations. OpenAjax resource (2008) suggests that there are ways to avoid SOP using Ajax proxies, dynamic script tags, and browser extensions and plugins. For example, OpenAjax resource library (2008) suggests that various ways to avoid SOP using Ajax proxies include the use of the proxy servers from the same source as the document. The proxy, in this instance, sends requests to third party services, which are hidden from view in browser. Some common vulnerability in Web 2.0 applications can be seen in terms of cross site scripting, Cross-Site Request Forgeries (CSRF), RSS Injection, Denial of Service (DoS) and non-professional developers. The following paragraph gives the details of these security concerns.

Cross-Site Scripting (XSS) is a form of attack in which confidential business content is injected with a malicious code. XSS is considered the most common dangerous attack for Web 2.0 applications (Hakkola, 2009). The attacks using XSS can be used for hacking session cookies, restricted information, altering parts of the Web content, and/or acting as a user of the browser. Cross-Site Request Forgeries (CSRF) is another form of attack that abuses trust in Web applications. For example, when a Web service remembers that the user is already logged in the system, the system does not need to check the user's identity (i.e. username and password) every time the Web content is loaded. The authentication usually functions using session cookies or HTTP authentication. Thus, CSRF breaks this trusted authentication service. This type of attacking occurs when a user logs in a trusted service, or uses other service through a trusted service or site that contains malicious code. RSS injection is also a form of attack in which RSS feed is injected with malicious code. Denial of Service (DoS) attack can appear to be sending false requests (multiple requests within a short moment of time) to the trusted service, so that the service becomes drowned with false requests. The attacker's main target is to make the service so busy that it takes too much time to answer the real requests in a timely fashion. Executing malicious JavaScript code makes this kind of attack possible. According to Wond and Hong (2007), the use of Mashups in developing Web application are truly the domain of non-professional end users, as Mashups are end user tools. According to Livshits and Erlingsson (2007), the non-professional developers do not have relevant knowledge and experience to take security issues into account. Such poorly designed applications can offer chances to attackers.

Principles in Technology Use

The basic scheme of Mashups is to reuse information sources provided from secondary sources. Mashups provide services for mixing or combining content in the application layers. This leads to issues that are not related to technology, but rather to principles and questions about the trustworthiness of other parties. For instance, the security of the content is not considered as important any more. The question that needs to be answered is how can it be known if the information provided by other parties is true or not true? There is no technical method to measure this kind of trust for users.

CONCLUSION AND FUTURE RESEARCH

This chapter discussed Web 2.0 technologies and its application areas for developing business solutions. As part of the discussion, security concerns for such technologies have been included from different sources. The security issues of the Web 2.0, from two perspectives, have been identified. These are issues arising from technology itself, and the issues arising from the non-professional development of applications. Mashups are technologies that provide compatibility with other services, and at the moment, this technology is being used without adequate provision for the development of a set of principles related to trust in the developed service. The development of these principles is difficult, as content is usually owned by the third parties. It is important that a view of this new technology, that encompasses security principles, be established, as it is impractical to invent a new technology for these purposes. The Web 2.0 technologies are developed for certain support services. The use of technology may change according to demand and this technology can suffer from security threats because there are no particular definitions, principles, or well defined architectures. This type of technology leverages and integrates the content from the existing Web applications on the Web. Apart from security issues, other issues, such as intellectual property and organizational boundaries, also need to be considered. Both of these can create implementation issues for these types of services. In addition, sensitive data may require encryption and when this data mashes up with data from other sources, there may be problems with confidentiality, or an unwillingness of a third party content providers to allow this to happen. This may interrupt the free flow of information.

REFERENCES

Abram, S. (2005). Web 2.0 - huh! Library 2.0, Librarian 2.0. *Information Outlook, 9,* 44–47.

Ashley, B. (2007). *Shaping the future of secure Ajax Mashups.* Retrieved June 2, 2009, from http://www-128.ibm.com/developerworks/library/x-securemashups/

Auinger, M. Martin, D., Nedbal, & A. Holzinger, (2008). *Mixing Content and Endless Collaboration – MashUps: Towards Future Personal Learning Environments.* Retrieved March 23, 2009, from https://online.tu-graz.ac.at/tug_online/voe_main2.getVollText?pDocumentNr=95304&pCurrPk=42744

Bean, L., & Hott, D. (2005). Wiki: A speedy new tool to manage projects. *Journal of Corporate Accounting & Finance, 16*(5), 3–8. doi:10.1002/jcaf.20128

Casey, M., & Savastinuk, L. (2006). *Library 2.0: service for the next-generation.* Retrieved March 2, 2008, from http://www.libraryjournal.com/article/CA6365200.html?q=Library + 2%E0

Curran, K., Murray, M., & Christian, M. (2007). Taking the information to the public through Library 2.0. *Library Hi Tech, 25*(2), 288–297. doi:10.1108/07378830710755036

Dillon, T. S., Wu, C., & Chang, E. (2007). GRIDSpace: Semantic Grid Services on the Web:Evolution towards a SoftGrid. In *Proceedings of the 3rd International Conference on Semantics, Knowledge and Grid,* October 29-31, Xi'an, China.

Fox, G., & Pierce, M. (2007). Web 2.0 and Grids. *In Proceedings of the 3rd International Conference on Semantics, Knowledge and Grid,* October 29-31, Xi'an, China.

Government 2.0 white paper (2009). *eGovernment social media platform deployments and future opportunities.* Retrieved June 2, 2009, from http://nass.org/index.php?option=com_search&Itemid=5&searchword=government&searchphrase=any&ordering=newest&limit=5&limitstart=0

Hakkola, J. (2008). *Mashup Security.* Research presentation. Retrieved June 2, 2009, from http://www.tml.tkk.fi/Opinnot/T-111.5550/2008/presentation_hakkola_jyrki.pdf

Kane, G. C., & Fichman, R. G. (2009). The shoemaker's children: Using wikis for IS teaching, research, and publication. *Management Information Systems Quarterly, 32*(4).

Kulathuramaiyer, N. (2007). Mashups: Emerging application development paradigm for a digital journal. *Journal of Universal Computer Science, 13*, 531–542.

Livshits, B., & Erlingsson, E. (2007). Using web application construction frameworks to protect against code injection attacks. In *Proceedings of the 2007 workshop on Programming languages and analysis for security* (pp. 95-104). New York: ACM.

O'Reilly, T. (2005). *What is Web 2.0: design patterns and business models for the next generation of software?* Retrieved June 2, 2009, from http://www.oreillynet. com/lpt/a/6228

OpenAjax Alliance. (2008). *Ajax and Mashup security.* Retrieved March 2, 2008, from http://www.openajax.org/whitepapers/Ajax%20and%20Mashup%20Security.php

Ort, E., Brydon, S., & Basler, M. (2009). *Mashups styles, Part 1: Server-Side Mashups (Sun Microsystems).* Retrieved March 23, 2009, from http://java.sun.com/ developer/technicalArticles/J2EE/mashup_1/

Pearce, J. (2008). *User collaboration in Websites.* Retrieved July 2, 2008, from http://www.nla.gov.au/nla/staffpaper/2006/jpearce.html.

Ren, Y., Kraut, R., & Kiesler, S. (2007). Applying common identity and bond theory to design of online communities. *Organization Studies, 28*(3), 377–408. doi:10.1177/0170840607076007

Srivastava, B., & Koehler, J. (2006). Web service composition - Current solutions and open problems. *IBM India Research Laboratory.* Block 1, IIT, New Delhi 110016, India. Retrieved June 2, 2009, from http://www.zurich.ibm.com/pdf/ebizz/ icaps-ws.pdf

Wang, H. J., Fan, X., Howell, J., & Jackson, C. (2007). Protection and communication abstractions for Web browsers in Mashup OS. In *Proceedings of twenty-first ACM SIGOPS symposium on Operating systems principles* (pp.1-16). New York: ACM.

Wong, J., & Hong, J. (2007). Making Mashups with marmite: towards end-user programming for the web. In *Proceedings of the SIGCHI conference on Human factors in computing systems* (pp.1435-1444). New York: ACM.

Yee, R. (2006). *Mashups, IST-Data Services.* Retrieved June 2, 2009, from http:// dret.net/lectures/services-fall06/Mashups.pdf

ENDNOTE

[1]   A Mashup is a web page or application that combines data or functionality from two or more external sources to create a new service

Chapter 8
Business Continuity Planning:
A Strategic Dilemma?

Oscar Imaz-Mairal
University of the Sunshine Coast, Australia

ABSTRACT

ICT systems are expected to be available 24/7 to internal and external users regardless of the circumstances, but the nature of uncertainty in complex and dynamic environments makes Business Continuity Planning more relevant today than ever before. Organisations providing 24/7 ICT availability become strategic dilemmas for decision makers, hence, to ensure operations, managers must balance the costs involved in providing an almost zero downtime infrastructure for information availability with the trust ICT users have on a given organization. Decision makers need to assess possible disruptions and vulnerabilities that can impact on ICT availability to all users. This chapter argues that approaches, such as virtualisation, can provide cost advantages to organizations by ensuring availability and resilience through flexible system implementation, and to achieve this objective, committed strategic managers must have arguments to defend this view.

DOI: 10.4018/978-1-60566-806-2.ch008

INTRODUCTION

The objective of this chapter is to provide a link between Business Continuity Planning (BCP) and the strategic responsibility posed to decision makers when considering the cost of producing these plans, including being ready for their implementation, and the cost of not doing it, or doing it partially. This chapter will first discuss vulnerability and disruption; second, it will discuss availability, resilience, flexibility, and strategic management commitment and the "Expected Value Paradox". Finally, this chapter will provide an argument presenting virtualization as a simple approach, still in its infancy, that promises to provide flexibility and resilience, at a fraction of the current cost. To write this chapter, research was undertaken using Proquest and multiple databases and limiting the returns by date from 2004 to 2009. The research strings used were "continuity AND virtualization", "virtualization OR availability OR resilience" (including the Australian spelling for virtualization with "s"). Earlier articles have also been included when the number of citations, or the importance of the topic discussed in them, was considered relevant. A limitation of this chapter is that search returns based on the previously mentioned search strings provided vendor based white papers, and also opinions, in the media from several professionals although the latter have not been included in this chapter. Readers could consider this limitation in different ways. For example, a gap in the literature exists and thus there is an opportunity for further research, or that vendor papers should not be considered due to their profit based intentions.

BUSINESS CONTINUITY PLANNING

Business Continuity Planning is concerned with the collection of mission critical procedures that are triggered and implemented when disaster strikes to ensure the continuance of business processes, while recovering from a given disaster (Boin & McConnell, 2007; Cerullo & Cerullo, 2004). Botha and Von Solms (2004) have defined BCP as "the complete process of developing measures and procedures to ensure an organization's disaster preparedness" (p. 329) and hence being able to continue with business as usual under any contingency.

Strategic managers are concerned with the development of capabilities and the allocation of resources to achieve organizational objectives and ensure the ongoing survival of business operations (Woodman, 2007). However, in an increasingly complex and dynamic environment, unpredictable circumstances have sometimes devastating effects on operations and survival (Zsidisin, Melnyk, & Ragatz, 2005). Computerized systems, communications and the people that interact with these systems are all susceptible of intentional and/or unintentional damage. Business customers, suppliers, and competitors rely heavily on Information Communication Technology (ICT) systems for interaction with each other and, hence, the loss of this interaction may have dramatic consequences for the survival of any firm.

BCP, to date, has focused on the impact of catastrophic events on business' operations following the 2008-9 global financial crisis (GFC), extreme weather conditions, high temperatures, torrential rains, and pandemics. This focus has put pressure on building resilience through duplication of physical resources. On the other hand, ICT threats, such as viruses and network failure, are more common and also have disastrous consequences because they impact on the information availability that businesses require to perform on a daily basis (Hawkins, Yen, & Chou, 2000; Cerullo & Cerullo, 2004). Ninety four per cent of the organisations, that have had to resort to the spirit and content of BCP, agree that BCPs have effectively contributed to reduce the impact of disruptions (Woodman, 2007). Still, many organizations do not have business continuity plans, or if they do have these plans, either lack continuous review processes or are unknown by, or are communicated poorly to, employees and stakeholders, and hence they engender reactive decision making approaches.

According to the survey conducted by The Cabinet Office and The Continuity Forum of London (Woodman, 2007), seventy three per cent of senior level managers regarded BCP highly in their responses, but only forty eight per cent agreed to have business continuity response procedures covering mission critical operations, and subsecquently the analysis of this survey recognised strategic decision making as the most salient driver for business continuity management.

Supply chain dependencies, 24/7 availability[1], customer expectations and trust, globalisation, and short product life cycles are dependent on continuous business operations (Autry & Bobbitt, 2008). If the trend remains to leave risk assessment and business continuity to security professionals, business continuity planners, or insurance professionals, the focus is likely to continue to be based on building resilience through investment on hardware resources and insurance costs (Autry & Bobbit). This approach has not proven successful in building a highly available enterprise because a strategic initiative is required to increase competitiveness and flexibility, while reducing vulnerability (Autry & Bobbitt).

VULNERABILITY & DISRUPTION

Sheffi & Rice (2005) have described vulnerability assessment as involving the answer to three questions: what can go wrong?; what is the likelihood of that happening?; and what are the consequences if it does happen?. Sheffi & Rice have further argued that any disruption has a typical profile in terms of its effect on company performance, whether that performance is measured by sales, production level, profits, customer service, or any other relevant metric. Based on the nature of the disruption and the dynamics of company's response, disruptions can be classified as "random events (including natural disasters), accidents or intentional disruptions" (Sheffi & Rice, p. 43). The likelihood of a random event ocurring can be estimated using historical data. Accidents can be estimated using a combination of historical data and industry data, while the probability of intentional disruptions is more difficult to estimate, in part, due to the lack of historical data and because likelihood is a function of the specific company's decisions and the specific actions undertaken by an organisation (Sheffi & Rice 2005).

Due to the difficulty in using metrics to assess all factors involved in vulnerability assessment, Sheffi and Rice (2005) have preferred to categorize disruptions as a function of their probability and consequences. This view implies that having a planned approach for dealing with disruptions that are difficult to predict and have a small probability of occurring, would have an immediate and significant impact on the ability of the system to meet customer demands (Zsidisin, Melnyk, & Ragatz, 2005). Thus, business continuity planning is the map that links and integrates formalized procedures and resource information. Authors such as Elliot, Swartz and Herbane (1999) proposed the view of business continuity as planning that identifies the organization's exposure to internal and external threats by implementing additional hard and soft assets. This view provides effective prevention and recovery for the organization to maintain competitive advantage and system integrity, but at extraordinary costs. Business continuity, from all these perspectives, consists of the business practices that provide focus and guidance for the decisions and actions required for a firm to prevent, mitigate, prepare for, respond to, resume, recover, restore, and transition from a crisis event by heavily investing in duplication (Shaw & Harrald, 2004). A crisis may be of many types, but in this chapter a crisis is recognized as when information availability is compromised. Resilience, flexibility and strategic management commitment are identified in the next section as positive characteristics for the 24/7 information availability of a strong organization.

AVAILABILITY, RESILIENCE, AND FLEXIBILITY

Internal and external users of information technology need to trust that the organizations they work with, or work for, keep information secure while at the same time available, confidential, and accurate because this understanding and trust has an impacting effect on sustained competitiveness (Botha & Von Solms, 2004). Design and implementation of BCP for information systems is particularly challenging as it has to consider the numerous ICT asset interactions, which tend to exist in organizations (Zambon, Bolzoni, Etalie, & Salvato, 2007). ICT business continuity planning has to guarantee that incidents affecting the ICT infrastructure do not affect the availability of ICT-dependent business processes beyond a given acceptable extent. For business continuity-management to succeed, it must provide an *always on* interconnectivity and availability. The complex factors beyond data security and physical security that influence these interrelations must be identified and, therefore, continuous, 24×7, high availability (HA) must be built into the architecture of business processes, applications and technologies (Scott & Passmore, 2005).

Downtime risks are greater with real time enterprises as all organizations may be affected in the case of a disaster, due to the interdependency existing in globalized business environments. A clear example of this situation is the global financial crisis. Therefore, business continuity plans must address *networked village* scenarios and continuity processes must integrate with diverse business processes from external environments. Business processes, with the shortest recovery time objective (RTO) and recovery point objective (RPO), rely increasingly on internal recovery technologies, such as wide-area clustering and capacity on demand, hence achieving both speed and cost-benefits (Scott & Passmore, 2005). Woodman (2007) argues that having access to alternative workplaces and/or remote working capabilities, although positive, may not be sufficient in the wake of a major disruption, and that systems should be allocated and fully tested before any disruption occurs with the key objective of providing high information availability at a reasonable price at all times (Woodman). Sheffi and Rice (2005) termed this capability as resilience. A company's resilience is a function of its competitive position and its responsiveness to all users because, in competitive markets, fast responding companies can gain market share and slow reacting organizations risk losing any existing advantage. Furthermore, companies with existing market power, that are capable of quick responses to disruption, have the "opportunity to solidify their leadership positions" (Sheffi & Rice, p. 44). The path is clearly paved; organizations can increase resilience by either "building in redundancy or building flexibility" (Sheffi & Rice, p. 44).

While some redundancy is part of every resiliency strategy, it represents sheer cost with limited benefit unless it is needed due to a disruption. Flexibility, on the other hand, can create a competitive advantage in day-to-day business operations. Strategic managers and decision makers can, therefore, justify investments in flexibility based on normal business operations without even taking into account the benefits of risk mitigation (Sheffi & Rice, 2005). There is significantly more advantage in making supply chains flexible than there is advantage in adding redundancy. Flexibility amounts to building organic capabilities that can sense threats and respond to them quickly (Sheffi & Rice). This not only increases the resilience of an organization, but it also aids to create a competitive advantage in the marketplace. Flexibility can be obtained, for example, by considering the essential elements of any supply chain: "*Material flows* from supplier through a *conversion* process, then through *distribution channels* in an upstream direction. It is controlled by various *systems*, all working in the context of the *corporate culture*" (Sheffi & Rice, p. 45). Each of these five elements offers a dimension of potential flexibility.

Strategic level managers must acknowledge this interdependency and move a step further by committing the required resources. Budget allocations, well-trained people, and well-integrated procedures aid to increase overall enterprise motivation and external user trust in the capabilities of flexible systems. The cost of commitment is high, but the cost of losing trust and capability, due to the failure to operate at a level that meets user expectations, may be even more expensive. The business environment of the twenty first century is based on resource dependencies to mitigate the impact of unforeseen consequences on complex and dynamic environments; resilient, flexible and highly available systems strengthen dependencies, but at what cost?

MANAGEMENT COMMITMENT: THE EXPECTED VALUE PARADOX

When confronting business continuity planning, decision makers find themselves amidst what Zsidisin, Melnyk and Ragatz (2005) termed "The Expected Value Paradox". Value analysis is reasonable and justified, in most cases, but in the case of business continuity planning, there are at least two limitations in relation to this investment approach. The first limitation is that the knowledge of potential events and the estimated probability of occurrence and impact are not well known and understood; secondly, the expected value approach assumes that the firm has a linear utility function[2] in relation to the impact of disruptions. Zsidisin, Melnyk and Ragatz argue that this may be possible in relation to low-level disruptions, but when catastrophic events or major disruptions occur, the linearity assumption is questionable. The impact of a catastrophic disruption, either natural or manmade, can exponentially offset any incurred costs and it is, therefore, impossible to assign value to the existing or future organizational trust. Trust may be jeopardized by neglecting investments, often considered superfluous, while ICT services and information availability operate with normality.

The responsibility for leading the processes and the decisions for business continuity lie with senior management. Woodman's (2007) analysis of a survey conducted on a sample of 1257 managers, in 2007, confirms that this is the case in seventy per cent of the cases. Resource allocation to security measures, including investment in programs to defend employees, physical assets, and intellectual property, is a necessity for security, even if the costs of security-related adaptations are weighed against other corporate goals (Sheffi & Rice, 2005). Hence, resource commitment to security and/or risk mitigation is necessary. Budget allocations may be a challenge due to the recent trend toward lean supply chains, six sigma initiatives, and overall waste reduction, but security management has a positive impact on financial performance (Zsidisin, Melnyk, & Ragatz, 2005). Risk management actions lower total costs and may reduce variability in the form of mitigation of downtime exposure (Autry & Bobbitt, 2008).

The implementation of redundant physical resources may be too costly for many organizations and, therefore, may inhibit adoption of highly available solutions (Loveland, Dow, LeFevre, Beyer, & Chan, 2008). Availability using virtualization provides value to computer systems by decreasing complexity and costs by using abstraction of physical resources, such as servers, network links and host bus adapters, into logical units (Loveland et al.). The benefits of investments in resilience and flexibility can only be realized when a disruption occurs, but sometimes these costs are difficult to justify (Sheffi & Rice, 2005). The approach promoted through virtualization for high availability reduces redundancy costs while providing 24/7 availability.

VIRTUALIZATION: A ROAD TO THE FUTURE

The most common obstacles for the implementation of business continuity and availability solutions are the securing of financial support and overcoming low corporate priorities (Hewlett-Packard, 2007). Business continuity and availability help organizations to balance cost with risk. Furthermore, adaptive infrastructure portfolios aid organizations to build and manage agile, resilient environments, while reducing operational risk and unplanned downtime. The benefit is to maintain continuous operations of critical business processes, despite a variety of challenging and threatening factors (Hewlett-Packard).

Conventional recovery approaches include tape backup, image capture, high-end replication, and server clustering, but these solutions are expensive and take too long (PlateSpin, 2007). A study conducted in 2006, identified business continuity and disaster recovery as the number one driver of virtualization technology among 150 early implementers and, hence, demonstrated a change in perceptions toward business continuity and availability solutions (Hewlett-Packard, 2007).

Virtualization, which has been used on mainframes for a long time, has now been adopted for other types of servers (Creasy, 1981). Virtualization provides a process of abstraction applied to computer resources so they can be shared readily. Virtualization includes system virtualization and resource virtualization. System virtualization applies to an entire computer system, while resource virtualization applies to specific resources (Loveland et al., 2008).

System virtualization provides a thin hypervisor layer between the physical hardware resources and the operating systems. Thus, virtualization "divides a single physical computer into multiple logical computers, or virtual servers, each running its own guest operating system" (Loveland et al. 2008, p. 592). The hypervisor multiplexes and arbitrates access to the resources of the host platform, so that they can be shared among multiple virtual servers, while enforcing a level of isolation that ensures that the others do not affect each virtual serve (Loveland et al.). Hypervisors can be implemented in server firmware or in software. Software hypervisors, sometimes called virtual machine monitors (or VMMs), are either booted natively on host hardware or run on top of a host operating system (Loveland et al., 2008). Resource virtualization operates at a lower level than hypervisors. It virtualizes individual host resources, such as network adapters and host bus adapters. Resource virtualization also can be applied to storage area networks ((Loveland et al.).

By means of deploying virtualization technology, a single physical server can operate multiple virtual machines, in which each instance of the operating system runs its own applications through a layer of software residing between the hardware and the guest operating systems. By dissolving the bonds between software and hardware, virtualization has encouraged organizations to see the data centre not as a heterogeneous mix of different servers, operating systems, applications, and data, but as a set of portable workload units. The ability to profile, move, copy, protect, and replicate entire server workloads as aggregated units between physical and virtual hosts, is helping many organizations to achieve new operational efficiencies and financial savings (PlateSpin, 2007). Therefore, virtual technology enables a service-based infrastructure to serve customers that request services rather than resources. Virtualization enables the delivery organization to adjust resources transparently to the customer, while facilitating the contracted level of service (Scadden, Bogdany, Cifford, Pearthree, & Locke, 2008).

CONCLUSION

This chapter has developed an argument relating business continuity planning and its costs by researching the literature from the perspective of availability and virtualization. The chapter has argued that the lack of business continuity plans in organizations is often due to the difficulty in justifying high resource duplication costs for the improbable possibility of a catastrophic event. Intentional and network disasters occur often and have a great impact on availability and user trust. Losing trust may have a substantial effect on organizational performance and survival. Flexibility and resilience can be achieved through virtualization. Virtualization promises to provide continuous information availability, at a fraction of the cost. To address issues of virtualization and availability, further academic research is needed investigating factors beyond data security and physical security.

REFERENCES

Autry, C. W., & Bobbitt, L. M. (2008). Supply chain security orientation: Conceptual developments a proposed framework. *The International Journal of Logistics Management, 19*(1), 42–64. doi:10.1108/09574090810872596

Boin, A., & McConnell, A. (2007). Preparing for Critical Infrastructure Breakdowns: The Limists of Crisis Management and the Need for Resillience. *Journal of Contingencies and Crisis Management, 15*(1), 50–59. doi:10.1111/j.1468-5973.2007.00504.x

Botha, J., & Von Solms, R. (2004). Acyclic approach ot business continuity planning. *Information Management & Computer Security, 12*(4), 328–327. doi:10.1108/09685220410553541

Cerullo, V., & Cerullo, M. J. (2004). Business Continuity Planning: A Comprehensive Approach. *Information Systems Management, 21*(3), 70–78. doi:10.1201/107 8/44432.21.3.20040601/82480.11

Creasy, J. R. (1981). The origin of the VM/370 Time-Sharing System. *IBM Journal of Research and Development, 25*(5), 483–490. doi:10.1147/rd.255.0483

Elliot, D., Swartz, E., & Herbane, B. (1999). Just waiting for the next big bang: business continuity planning in the UK finance sector. *Journal of applied management, 8*(1), 43-60.

Hawkins, S. M., Yen, D. C., & Chou, D. C. (2000). Disaster recovery planning: a strategy for data security. *Information Management & Computer Security, 8*(5), 222–229. doi:10.1108/09685220010353150

Hewlett-Packard. (2007, March 26). *Survey: Business Continuity and Availability Solutions a High Priority for Corporate Spending in 2007.* Retrieved March 29, 2009, from http://www.hp.com/hpinfo/newsroom/press/2007/070326a.html?jumpid=reg_R1002_USEN

Loveland, S., Dow, E. M., LeFevre, F., Beyer, D., & Chan, P. F. (2008). Leveraging virtualization to optimize high-availability systems configuration. *IBM Systems Journal, 47*(4), 591–604. doi:10.1147/SJ.2008.5386515

PlateSpin. (2007). *Consolidated Disaster Recovery Using Virtualization. Affordable Workload Protection and Recovery.* Ontario, CA: PlateSpin.

Scadden, R. R., Bogdany, R. J., Cifford, J. W., Pearthree, H., & Locke, R. A. (2008). Resilient hosting in a continuously available virtualized environment. *IBM Systems Journal, 47*(4), 535–548. doi:10.1147/SJ.2008.5386523

Scott, D., & Passmore, E. R. (2005). *Build your disaster recovery e-mail architecture before a crisis arises.* Retrieved January 2, 2009, from http://www.gartner.com/DisplayDocument?doc_cd=126490

Shaw, G. L., & Harrald, J. R. (2004). Identification of the core competencies required of executive level business crisis and continuity managers. *Journal of Homeland Security & Emergency management, 1*(1), 1-14.

Sheffi, Y., & Rice, J. B. (2005). A Supply chain view of the resilient enterprise. *MITSloan Management Review, 47*(1), 40–48.

Woodman, P. (2007, March). Business Continuity Management Survey. *Cabinet Office and The Continuity Forum*, 1-17.

Zambon, E., Bolzoni, D., Etalie, S., & Salvato, M. (2007). A model supporting Business Continuity Auditing and Planning in Information Systems. *Internet Monitoring and Protection, 2007, ICIMP 2007, Second International Conference* (pp. 33-33). San Jose.

Zsidisin, G. A., Melnyk, S. A., & Ragatz, G. L. (2005). An institutional theory perspective of business continuity planning for purchasing and supply management. *International Journal of Production Research, 43*(16), 3401–3420. doi:10.1080/00207540500095613

ENDNOTES

[1]   The Information Technology Infrastructure Library (ITIL) defines continuous operation as "An approach or design to eliminate planned downtime of an IT service" http://www.itil.org/en/shortcuts/glossarinhalt/glossarc.phpq

[2]   In a linear utility function, utility increases with reward at the same rate.

Chapter 9
Future Trends in Digital Security

Daniel Viney
University of the Sunshine Coast, Australia

ABSTRACT

This chapter discusses ICT trends of the past decade, the emergence of Web 2.0 technologies, mobile computing (as distinguished from cloud computing), the pitfalls of social networking, security considerations in the workplace, copyright and Intellectual Property considerations, and how to best control threats and vulnerabilities. We are in a period of aggressive technological growth to which there is no foreseeable end. New technologies, such as Web 2.0 and cloud computing, are emerging at an exponential rate, and as a consequence, security threats, controls, and standards are iteratively evolving. As yet, we do not know the security and privacy implications that such a rapid and wide uptake of cloud computing, and other multi-user virtual environment initiatives, and Web 2.0 technologies, will bring. In no way is this cause to panic, instead it is cause to focus on self-education, employee-education, and awareness. To put it simply, these offer our best defense to security threats. By being educated, aware, and vigilant, the majority of threats are nullified, as they are designed to prey upon those who rely on trust when reading emails, visiting Websites, and accessing site content, when navigating the World Wide Web. For example, there are millions of users who are completely unaware of threats, such as phishing, and other forms of Internet-based fraud. More than ever before, the onus is on the individual, both at home and in the workplace, to be

DOI: 10.4018/978-1-60566-806-2.ch009

responsible for maintaining best practice techniques, while utilizing digital resources to ensure that information security, individual privacy, and applicable legislation are not breached. This can only be achieved through iterative education processes, general awareness, and vigilance.

INTRODUCTION

Writing about the future is an ambitious undertaking, particularly with regard to technology. Gordon Moore, co-founder of the Intel Corporation, is one who has made an accurate prediction with a statement in 1965 that the number of transistors and resistors on a chip would double every two years (INTEL, 2005). This prediction concerning the future trends of computing capacity has become known as "Moore's Law" and a derivation of the statement, a common folk theorem, that the capacity of computing can be fitted to an exponential curve, with doubling time set close to a year and the dollar cost associated with that increase, decreasing along the same curve, is taught to Information Technology students the world over.

Whilst Moore (INTEL, 2005) was only discussing the humble computer chip, the accuracy of this prediction has seen technology become an integral part of our daily lives. There are few consumable products that one can buy these days, which do not contain a computer chip of some description. The ever decreasing cost, and ever increasing capacity of available technology, has seen rise to an almost unbelievable uptake in computing, within both the business and an individual's personal life over the past forty years, in particular the past decade.

Most of the westernized world is bordering upon having a dangerous level of technological dependence in their daily lives. If technology was to fail, as was widely feared by many in the build up to the new millennium, then we would see many businesses and essential services, including those of a financial nature and public transport infrastructure, devolve into complete disarray. However, such disruption is not only caused by a complete failure, or loss of service. For example, our uptake and dependence upon digital services, including: ecommerce, social networking, mobile computing, core business infrastructure, and cloud computing, has made us hugely vulnerable to an ever-increasing range of risks that could have immeasurable impact, should they occur. Consequently, we have borne witness to an evolution of digital security. Once upon a time, information security was less of a concern, bordering on being an afterthought; it was a cryptic discipline managed by mysterious individuals, who spoke a language that no one else understood. These days, information security is something that, although still not as widely understood as it should be, is at least a consideration of most people, be it the individual or the business. However, as computing continues to evolve and develop, so do the risks associated with it. As a consequence, digital security considerations are iteratively evolving and technologists simply must keep up.

So What is Digital Security?

First and foremost, we need to understand that the terms *information security* and *digital security* no longer simply refer to the task of keeping data concerning the business and its stakeholders confidential where appropriate, they also relate to ensuring the data stored has a high level of integrity, (that is - that it is accurate), and that the data is available and accessible upon demand. To grossly generalize: businesses need to maintain the privacy of their data to not only ensure that their core functions remain protected, that their product remains unique through protection of their intellectual property so that they can maintain a competitive edge; but also to ensure the privacy of their employees is maintained. These privacy factors include; biographical and demographic data, bank account numbers and transfer authorizations for financial institutions. Individuals also need to protect their own intellectual property, their financial data, and their privacy. In recent years, we have reached the scary realization that the onus is upon us all individually to be responsible for protecting our own identity. This is an amazing evolution that has thrown shades of ambiguity over something that we have all historically taken for granted.

What has Evolved?

The short answer to what has evolved is - everything. In the realm of digital security, we often see history repeating itself. Things may have changed slightly; old threats may have evolved to enable exploitation of new technologies, but their origins remain the same. Take the Denial of Service (DoS) attack as an example, where a target computer, database or web-service would be flooded with more data and requests than it could handle and, consequently, become inoperable. As the designers of information technology systems began to reduce the systems vulnerabilities, thus making them more robust, those perpetrating the attacks evolved their methods. This involved devising Distributed Denial of Service (DDoS) attacks, where multiple-computing devices were used simultaneously to perpetrate fresh attacks against the new, more robust target and again flood even the sturdiest systems with more requests than it could handle. This is an example of a new threat conceived and designed utilizing existing methodology.

So, what are the future trends in digital security likely to be? And importantly, how do we protect ourselves against upcoming and, currently unknown, threats? We need to realize that future threats will largely be incarnations of existing threats. For example, we need to take into account that if we become early adopters of a new technology, this will increase our levels of risk and increase the likelihood that vulnerabilities will be exploited. This is due to the competitive nature of the technology industry, where vendors and developers are constantly rushed to meet project deadlines within specific budgets. The end result of this is that many of the latest devices and software developments are rushed to the market with inadequate testing and quality control. Therefore, the latest release of an operating system is likely to have more security vulnerabilities in it than its predecessor, which has no doubt been subject to several patches and service packs containing multiple security fixes. However, there will also be new breeds of threats and vulnerabilities. There will be new exploits, that we will be vulnerable to, that are yet to be architected by the malicious individuals within the digital realm. Consequently, we need to iteratively analyze, revise and improve our identity, and access management models. Nothing is more important than keeping ourselves educated about the latest security threats, system vulnerabilities, and the controls for these threats and vulnerabilities available to us on the market or via the Web.

TRENDS

Over the past decade, we have seen several trends in the realm of information and digital security. Some have become obsolete through technological advances, whereas others have become standard to our daily business and moreover, crucial to our day-to-day activities. Within business we have seen an increasing focus upon identity management (IDM) and access provision (AP). Thompson and Thompson (2007) succinctly explain identity management as being focused upon ways in which an individual can be identified uniquely within a given environment. Access provision relates to what rights and permissions that an individual has, once identified through authentication, to data and information contained within a particular system or particular environment. Many organizations have implemented, or are moving towards, automation of this process. There are many business drivers for the implementation of mature IDM models, not only for security reasons, but also for the efficiency they can enable within business processes and business workflows and, therefore, the cost benefits that can be achieved. However, new trends in computing, such as: the increase in mobile computing, the birth of cloud computing, and the growth of social networking across Web 2.0 technologies, can make IDM and AP models harder to maintain, despite how scalable their initial design may have been.

Figure 1. Web 2.0 Meme Map (© 2005, O'Reilly. Used with permission)

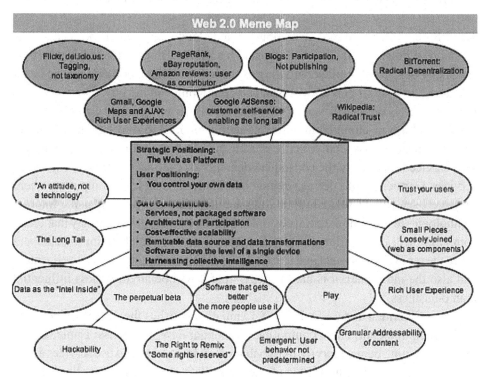

WEB 2.0 TECHNOLOGIES

The original concept, and term Web 2.0, is credited to Craig Cline and Dale Dougherty (Vice-President at O'Reilly) and it refers to a second generation of Web development and Web design, where the Web is seen as a platform that fosters communication, the secure sharing of information and data, collaboration and interoperability (O'Reilly, 2005). This new generation fosters the evolution of Web-based communities, social networking sites, wikis and personal publishing (such as Blogs, VideoBlogs, and PhotoBlogs). The graphical illustration in Figure 1 below shows Web 2.0 in a Meme Map and was developed during a brainstorming session at a O'Reilly Media conference.

A typical Web 2.0 driven Website is aesthetically pleasing, highly configurable and provides control to the end-user without them needing technical prowess. That is, Web 2.0 technologies provide the end-user with a rich user experience. Additionally, as the Meme Map above indicates, it also relates to a range of functionality and services that can be provided, such as cloud computing.

MOBILE COMPUTING VERSUS CLOUD COMPUTING

The difference between mobile computing and cloud computing is not widely understood. Whittaker (2007) wrote a post in his ZDNet Blog on the topic, where he succinctly describes mobile computing as the act of taking a portable device (such as a laptop or a smart phone) with you and computing "on the go". Cloud computing, however, is quite different. A cloud essentially is a multi-user virtual environment. The birth of cloud computing has seen vendors and developers provide an online repository for an individual's, or a business's, data, information and records. This service is driven by the consumers demand for ever-accessible, synchronized services. Gartner (2008) defines cloud computing as "a style of computing where massively scalable IT-related capabilities are provided 'as a service' using Internet technologies to multiple external customers" (p.1). Gartner goes on to say that cloud computing will be as influential as e-business. This is no small claim to make and given the rapid development and uptake of cloud computing, from both the business and also the individual, it is hard to argue that it will be anything less influential than e-business.

3Tera Chairman and CEO, Barry X Lynn, distinguishes the difference between utility computing and cloud computing (in an interview with Krissi Danielson) as cloud computing being a service that enables users to develop and use services available to them without "knowledge of, expertise with, nor control over the technology infrastructure that supports them" (Danielson, 2008, p. 1). While many people already make use of Web 2.0 driven cloud computing technologies, such as Google Apps, many do not know that they are even using a cloud, let alone being aware of the security, intellectual property and other miscellaneous risks associated with their use. Gruman and Knorr (2008) advise that cloud computing is built upon an incorporation of several technologies: Infrastructure as a Service (IaaS), Platform as a Service (PaaS), and Software as a Service (SaaS). While there are benefits to IaaS, as referred to by Lynn above, there are also many benefits to PaaS and SaaS. From the client's perspective, there is no need for an upfront investment in server hardware or software licenses. From a vendor's perspective, costs of provision are lowered by having fewer applications to maintain (Gruman & Knorr, 2008).

SOCIAL NETWORKING

The evolution of the Internet and World Wide Web over the past decade has been phenomenal. There has been an exponential rise in the use of the Web for personal publishing and social networking. Services offered by the likes of Facebook, MySpace, LinkedIn, Twitter, and Second Life, promote the development of online profiles, linking of profiles to the profiles of others and, through this, the development of increased communication channels. But as people post their latest thoughts, likes and dislikes, and their weekend stories and photos to their pages, they become vulnerable to a loss of privacy and, as mentioned earlier, increase the levels of risk associated with protecting their own identity.

However, the risks do not only lie with the protection of identity. Users of social networking sites really need to be aware that their participation can create what is analogous to a digital tattoo, where people might find that published antics of their youth come back to haunt them in later life. Social networking sites, such as Facebook and MySpace, are incredibly popular on an international scale. These days, it is far less common for someone to not have a profile on one of the many available social networking Web sites, than it is for them to have a membership with at least one of the service providers. Social networking sites are making the world smaller, allowing people to stay in contact with old friends, colleagues, and class mates, who may have moved to different locations all over the world, with just a few clicks of their mouse.

However, the very nature and success of these sites is driven by the sharing of information: people may post what they are currently doing, everyone is notified when some of their mutual friends end their relationship, photos from the weekend are uploaded, and those within them tagged with their name and links to their profile so that everyone on their friend list can see the pictures. Video and audio files can be shared, members can establish, and join groups dedicated to their differing likes, dislikes, and any cause they wish to publicly acknowledge their support of. While most social networking sites provide a level of privacy control to their users, such as the ability to stop anyone on a friends list from accessing or viewing their uploaded photos, many site members do not utilize these controls to their fullest extent, if at all. While many university and high school students might worry about family members, particularly parents, seeing some of their weekend antics immortalized in jpeg format, most do not worry about the bigger picture – that of their careers.

A study conducted by the National Association of Colleges and Employers, a professional association based in the United States, returned results that one in ten employers plan to review the social networking site profiles of their potential employees. It is worth noting, however, that 40% of those surveyed responded they were undecided as to whether or not they would use social networking sites to screen applicants (Brandenburg, 2008). A broad interpretation of this is that at least 10%, but up to 50%, of potential employers may do this right now, or will do this in the future. Another study conducted by CareerBuilder.com returned results that of 1,150 hiring managers surveyed, 12% stated that they had screened prospective employee profiles on social networking sites (CareerBuilder.com 2006).

On top of the risks associated with future job prospects, social networking sites can also impact an individual's current career. International swimming star, Stephanie Rice, is a prime example. In 2008, Swimming Australia ordered Rice to prevent public access to her Facebook profile, as the organization deemed the photos of Rice's personal life too raunchy for the public eye (Saurine, 2008). While individuals have more legal rights once employed, depending on the nature of their employment, opportunities for promotion and other assorted changes in the workplace can be hampered by the personal opinions of those managers tasked with making such decisions. Consequently, everyone should consider just how public they wish their own private lives to be.

SECURITY IN THE WORKPLACE

Digital security in the modern work environment has also evolved to become a multi-faceted discipline. Moves towards more mature identity management and role-based access management models, including those of automated provision, have become mainstream. Additionally, teams dedicated to security within ICT infrastructure, are no longer merely concerned with password expiry and directory permissions; instead they are now focusing on intrusion prevention, intrusion detection, and risk management versus risk avoidance. Security is now a more holistic discipline, including concepts such as disaster recovery, business continuity planning, and service availability. Team leaders and management are increasingly focused upon knowledge management as a discipline, their roles as custodians of data (both structured information and unstructured), and their applicable duties of care in relation to these. It is difficult to provide an example of data. Data may be, for example, a string of alphanumeric characters on a page, but the moment you look at that data within a specified context, or the moment you attribute meaning to that data, it is no longer data; it is information. Herein lies the key to securing data; store it in a way that makes attributing meaning and context to it difficult. This is easy to state, but in practice, it is far harder to achieve.

Managers within business have a duty of care, when it comes to their role as a custodian of data and information. When discussing databases, it is true that it can be hard to determine who owns the data stored within it. This is due to most databases being transactional in nature, and as such, a variety of users, systems, and interests can be involved in capturing the original information, and each user can utilize that data differently. Generally speaking, individuals do not own any data, or information about them, that is stored. However, regardless of this fact, in a legal sense, it is very arguable that if a business fails to maintain data security, resulting in a harmful misuse of that data or information, then this could amount to negligence (Awerdick, 1993). Obviously, the business is not granular enough as an entity to bear the brunt of the majority of legal action, and as such, accountability falls within the management team and senior analysts involved. That said, it is important to understand who might try to access data and information crucial to the business.

Pfleeger and Pfleeger (2003) categorize computer criminals into three identifiable cohorts: amateurs, crackers, and career criminals. Amateurs are responsible for the majority of computer-based crime. They are usually those who stumble across a perceived or real weakness within a system that allows them to access sensitive or valuable information. This category includes disgruntled employees, who may try to hijack a business as means to "get even" for a slight that they may believe they have received, or for their loss of employment. Crackers are largely comprised of high school or university students attempting to access and utilize computing systems or resources that they are not authorized to. Career criminals are those who engage in computer crime understanding exactly what they are doing and aiming for some form of profit. More recently, law enforcement agencies around the world are reporting an increase in computer crime attributable to organized crime syndicates, biker gangs, and other international groups from political and racial-hate backgrounds. It is important to note that the information security community differentiate between *crackers* and *hackers*, where hackers are individuals who use computing devices and programming in a non-malicious manner, and crackers are those who attempt to use computing devices and programming for malicious means (Pfleeger & Pfleeger, 2003).

Within the past few years, the Web has seen an emergence of *Script Kiddies* – a derogatory term used to describe a cohort of computer criminals, who perpetrate attacks on targets through the utilization of programming scripts that they have downloaded from underground Web sites. Script Kiddies have been given a derogatory name because they lack reputation in the cyber underworld as they do not have enough programming expertise to write the code required to perpetrate their attacks, instead rely on push button type tools written by others and downloaded from the Internet to initiate their attacks.

Despite there being multiple categories of computer criminals external to the workplace that can perpetrate attacks upon business, and considering the development of sophisticated security devices on most business networks and the requirement of businesses to comply to specific security standards, it is arguable that the biggest threat to the workplace is internal. The risk to the workplace that the disgruntled employee brings is heavily documented. Employees who have lost their jobs, or feel angry about a situation that has occurred in the workplace, are usually well placed to perform a range of destructive activities upon the internal network. This may be the deletion of sensitive (or otherwise important) information, destruction of computing devices and hardware, or by using means at their disposal to interrupt services and core business functions. This may also be the acquisition of sensitive information for sharing with, or the sale to, unauthorized third parties. As mentioned earlier, the prevalence of mobile computing devices in the modern world, such as USB sticks and portable external hard drives, increases the difficulty of securing data to only one location and preventing the removal of information from the workplace.

These sorts of concerns are also some of the business drivers behind the development of more mature identity management and access provision models. Such models usually are designed around the concept of role-based access and automated provisioning. Role-based access refers to an individual being provided access to all the information and resources required to perform the daily duties associated with their role in the organization, but only to those specific resources and no other. Businesses are looking to automate this process, as much as possible, for two reasons: firstly, it is an efficient and manageable process to follow upon appointing new staff and terminating existing staff; and secondly, it provides a largely fail-safe methodology for ensuring access is de-provisioned at the conclusion of an individual's employment. For example, company XYZ may utilize an Enterprise Resource Planning (ERP) system, such as PeopleSoft, to facilitate their core businesses functions, such as: planning, purchasing, marketing, sales, payroll, and human resources. If they configure the human resources component of their ERP to assign staff to a role upon the start of their employment with the business, this role can be used through a variety of means to determine file and directory permissions on the company Intranet. When the individual is no longer employed by the business, the data entry of this fact within the ERP (in conjunction with some effective dates) can automatically de-provision the access that an individual has to business resources. This is an efficient and effective approach to identity management.

However, the modern manager is not only concerned with protecting against malicious behavior from disgruntled staff or external threats, but also the other aspects of their role as a custodian of data, such as data integrity and knowledge management. The impact that a loss of data integrity, such as the storage of inaccurate financial data, can have on the business requires no explanation. However, the risks to a business from poorly managing knowledge (both tacit and explicit knowledge), and allowing poorly trained staff to access and maintain information crucial to the business, should be noted. Strong knowledge management techniques lower the impact of staff turnover and also reduce the costs of training new staff with external providers. They also have the additional benefit of supporting new staff in their transition to the workplace, increasing their initial efficiency and, therefore, reducing the varied costs to the business that can be felt through staff turnover. As always, a manager must be able to balance the cost to the business associated with implementing a solution and, also, the potential cost to the business in terms of efficiency within the workplace.

Information Security Policy and Standards

Businesses are required to comply with various information security standards and have a duty of care to communicate and educate their staff in relation to their own security policies and best practice. A common policy for businesses to enforce is that of authentication. The predominant authentication model consists of each employee having a unique username and password. Most authentication policies have a section that explicitly states the frequency with which employees must change their passwords, and also any business rules concerning the required strength of a password, such as: consisting of 8-15 characters, having a prerequisite of containing both capitalization of some alphabetical characters, and also the use of at least one number, before the system will accept the new password. Businesses must address the concerns of password strength and password reuse. Ideally, a single password would only be used for a single system, with each differing system on the network requiring a different password for access. However, this may not be the most manageable or efficient solution in practice, and as a result, most businesses are more interested in moving towards Single Sign-On solutions.

Despite the predominance of the password as the primary authentication mechanism for the majority of systems in use, we are seeing a rise in the use of biometric devices, such as fingerprint scanners, in both the business and the home. It is now common to see laptops mass produced for the average consumer, with such biometric devices included as part of the standard design. This is a vast change to the norm of five years ago, where even the simplest of biometric devices designed for home use were quite expensive and, as a consequence, infrequently used in the home environment.

On the 10th of November 2005, a high level treaty was signed between Standards Australia's National Centre for Security Standards (NCSS) and the American National Standards Institute's Homeland Security Standards Panel (HSSP). This initiative was designed to strengthen ties between standards developed within Australia and the United States of America, in order to help present unified and globally recognized peak standards aimed to protect business clients and assets, and also identify industry and community needs in terms of emerging trends in security standards (Security Standards 2005). However, businesses the world over are not only bound by their own government driven standards and policy, they are also strongly encouraged to comply with internationally recognized standards developed by the International Organization for Standardization (ISO) under their duty of care. ISO/IEC 17799 is the international standard developed by the ISO that governs the Code of Practice for Information Security Management. The ISO has developed many standards that are recognized internationally. However, more granular standards developed by governmental bodies apply to each nation. In Australia, Standards Australia supplies policy and standards for nearly all aspects of business: such as AS2805, a standard to govern Electronic Funds Transfer; AS/NZ 4360, the standard for risk management within Australia and New Zealand; and AS4539, the standard that governs authentication in Australia. This is in no way a conclusive list, but instead an example of some of the security standards that Australian managers must be aware of. Therefore, managers the world over must familiarize themselves with applicable standards and policy for their region.

COPYRIGHT AND INTELLECTUAL PROPERTY

In recent years, there have been numerous developments in relation to copyright and the Internet. The development and uptake of the Web in everyday households saw an exponential rise in piracy and other behaviors equating to copyright infringement. Businesses have had to respond by increasing their digital security to ensure that workplace networks and equipment were not used to access or facilitate file sharing. Within the past decade software, music and other digitized media companies, have been waging a war on piracy. While this endeavor is ongoing, there have been some noticeable results for legal teams representing those whose copyright has been infringed. In 2002 and 2003, the Recording Industry Association of America (RIAA) took several international Universities to court over file sharing on their networks, including: Rensselaer Polytechnic Institute, Princeton University, Michigan Technological University, Sydney University, Melbourne University and the University of Tasmania (Pearce 2003). The RIAA also put a focus in the workplace, writing to over 300 companies, providing evidence of their business networks being used for peer-2-peer file sharing (Pearce 2003). These high profile actions helped bring a focus on protection of copyright and intellectual property to the workplace.

However, this is not the only trend to have enveloped businesses. It is crucial to the modern business to record their Intellectual Property (IP) assets to specifically obtain and maintain their competitive advantage (Halpern & Vasiliadis, 2009). It was estimated in the late 1990's that up to three quarters of the Fortune 100's total market capital comprised of intangible assets, such as: copyright, patents, and trademarks (Reitzig, 2004). A decade later, it is commonplace for organizations to look for ways to not only protect, but capitalize upon their IP assets. Intellectual Property can provide a company with competitive advantage in a myriad of ways; however, according to Reitzig (2004), three of these ways are principal: incumbency through temporary technological advantage, protection of the businesses branding, and the role that the business can then play in the development of industry standards.

An argument exists, it should be noted, that businesses that actively invest in protecting their intellectual property are creating a monopoly in the market and, therefore, detracting from global pushes towards promoting fair competition in the marketplace (Nguyen & Suber, 2009). This argument is born of the fact that incumbency, through technological advantage, can create barriers of entry to a marketplace, as the cost of producing a competing product can be too high for many companies. Additionally, the use of branding and trademarks can fill a product space to reduce profitable entry points for competitors (Reitzig, 2004). Regardless of this argument, any business owner will tell you that protecting any competitive advantage, that your business may hold, is crucial for short-to-long-term success. Take Coca-Cola as an example, they have protected the ingredients (and proportions of those ingredients used in their product) as a trade secret to protect their competitive advantage, since the product was first introduced to the market as a patent medicine in 1886 (Brand Fact Sheet, nd).

Intellectual Property is also incredibly important within tertiary and higher education providers; combined they contribute a significant proportion of the world's research and development. Within the past few years, there have been several business drivers for Universities to move towards providing digitized resources and online repositories. One such driver is well documented showing the student demand for more flexible learning options to be made available to them. The modern student is older, has more responsibilities and commitments in life and, as a consequence, finds it harder to meet the 9am-5pm timetabling of classes. Flexible delivery, including streaming lectures, online classrooms, and a variety of Web-services designed to enrich the learning experience, help cater to this need. Another driver is coming from governments around the world, notably in the United Kingdom, New Zealand and Australia, who have released initiatives designed to establish a quality framework for the evaluation of research, identify emerging areas conducive to further research, promote research on both a national and international stage, and identify excellence (ARC, 2009). This particular driver requires tertiary institutions to utilize digital repositories that can provide open access to their research output in some cases, and dark, or restricted, access to more sensitive research outputs in others. As a part of these initiatives, institutions are required to record and report upon their intellectual property assets and their culturally sensitive IP assets.

What Threats will These Trends Produce?

Essentially, we are in a period of aggressive technological growth. We are seeing the emergence of new technologies on the Web (such as Web 2.0), which in turn is driving cultural change through the emergence and rapid uptake of social networking facilities available online, and the anonymity that some facilitate. As computing devices become smaller, more powerful, and cheaper, and as wireless networks become predominant, we are also seeing the emergence of new business processes and workflows, such as paperless meetings, role-based access provisioning, and web-based application interfaces - not to mention the birth of cloud computing. As we become more mobile in our computing habits and have more and more personal information about us available via the Internet, our vulnerabilities increase. From both a professional and a personal perspective, the more of our sensitive data that is stored online, the more we publish about ourselves and our daily lives, the more we are at risk to a plethora of threats, including loss of privacy, identity theft, and the loss of confidentiality surrounding our sensitive data and information.

CONTROLLING THREATS

How do we implement controls against threats that do not yet exist, or that we are unaware of? As difficult a question as this sounds, the techniques we have been using for the past decade are still the best means to control the threats facing us, and decrease the likelihood and/or impact of malicious attacks. These techniques can be summarized into four broad categories: education, awareness, vigilance and top-down support.

Education

In the workplace, the onus is upon the employer to educate the employee about digital security. Employees should be made aware of best practice techniques concerning utilizing the Internet and replying to emails, such as never sending a username and password in response to a request in email. At home, the onus is on the individual to educate themselves about latest security threats, and ways to protect themselves and their home network from these threats.

Awareness

Awareness ties in closely with, and is born of, education. However, it transcends the borders of education in that the security landscape is ever changing. New threats, or new iterations of old threats, are constantly emerging. We need to be aware of this, and recognize the need for education processes to be iterative and based upon a concept of perpetual review and improvement.

Vigilance

Vigilance is ensuring that systems are best prepared to face the online environment. This means updating antivirus and spy ware toolkits at home, ensuring Web software is patched and up-to-date. Applying operating system patches and security fixes to workstations, home computers, and servers. Vigilance also means creating and enforcing strong security policy, regularly changing passwords, and ensuring that the passwords are strong. Also, individuals should never use one password for multiple accounts across differing systems. Vigilance includes hardening systems; turning off unnecessary plug n play functionality; disabling internal windows messaging tools; hardening the IIS environment in web servers; and installing intrusion detection and intrusion prevention systems on the business network. In short, vigilance is doing what is required, in order to minimize risks and the impact those risks would have, should they ever occur.

Top-Down Support

The three broad categories above share one commonality in the work place; they need top-down support. Management simply must lead the way by enforcing and promoting best practice in the work place through implementation of strong policy, adhering to recognized national and international security standards, and ensuring business processes and business rules map to a strong security ethic. For example, enabling Virtual Private Networks for external access to work resources, enforcing regular password expiry, and setting validation rules against new passwords to ensure they are strong. If management do not strongly enforce these sorts of initiatives, then the business will simply follow suit.

CONCLUSION

We are in a period of aggressive technological growth to which there is no foreseeable end. New technologies, such as Web 2.0 and cloud computing, are emerging at an exponential rate and, as a consequence security threats, controls and standards are iteratively evolving. As yet we do not know the security and privacy implications that such a rapid and wide uptake of the cloud computing, other multi-user virtual environment initiatives, and Web 2.0 technologies, will bring. In no way is this cause to panic, instead it is cause to focus on self-education, employee-education and awareness. To put it simply, these offer our best defense to security threats. By being educated, aware and vigilant, the majority of threats are nullified, as they are designed to prey upon those who rely on trust when reading emails, visiting websites, and accessing site content, when navigating the World Wide Web. For example, there are millions of users who are completely unaware of threats, such as phishing and other forms of Internet-based fraud. We will not see the end of security threats that currently impose upon us through any means other than obsolescence, due to technological advancement. We will, however, see new iterations of these threats and also see completely new threats emerge. We will also see a rise in technology and standards to combat these threats, such as new and improved virus and spy ware protection toolkits and more frequent use of biometrics. In addition, it is likely a further increase in phishing and other Internet-based fraud activity will be seen, and a further rise in terms of threat-level to both the protection of our identity and also the protection of our privacy, through further evolution of the social networking phenomena. Businesses will be subject to more stringent reporting requirements on their intellectual property assets, and digital protection mechanisms designed to protect copyright are likely to evolve, with unknown consequences to the portable media market. More than ever before, the onus is on the individual, both at home and in the workplace, to be responsible for maintaining best practice techniques, while utilizing digital resources to ensure that information security, individual privacy, and applicable legislation, are not breached. This can only be achieved through iterative education processes, general awareness, and vigilance. The time to start is now.

REFERENCES

Australian Research Centre. (ARC, 2009). *The Excellence in Research Australia (ERA) Initiative*. Retrieved May 5, 2009, from http://www.arc.gov.au/era/default.htm

Awerdick, J. W. (1993). Who owns data in the database? [from ABI/INFORM Global Database.]. *The Practical Lawyer, 39*(4), 19. Retrieved May 27, 2009.

Borland, J. (2003). *RIAA turns up heat on tile-trading at work.* Retrieved May 28, 2009, from http://www.zdnet.com.au/news/security/soa/RIAA-turns-up-heat-on-file-trading-at-work/0,130061744,120272983,00.htm

Brand Fact Sheet. (n.d.). Retrieved May 27, 2009 from http://www.virtualvender.coca-cola.com/ft/index.jsp

Brandenburg, C. (2008). The Newest Way to Screen Job Applicants: A Social Networker's Nightmare. [from ABI/INFORM Global Database.]. *Federal Communications Law Journal, 60*(3), 597. Retrieved April 20, 2009.

CareerBuilder. (2006) *One-in-four hiring managers have used Internet search engines to screen job candidates; One-in-Ten Have Used Social Networking Sites.* (2006). Retrieved May 27, 2009, from http://www.careerbuilder.com/share/aboutus/pressreleasesdetail.aspx?id=pr331&sd=10%2f26%2f2006&ed=12%2f31%2f2006&siteid=cbpr331&sc_cmp1=cb_pr331_

Danielson, K. (2008). *Distinguishing cloud computing from utility computing.* Retrieved April 4, 2009, from http://www.ebizq.net/blogs/saasweek/2008/03/distinguishing_cloud_computing/

Gartner (2008). *Cloud computing will be as influential as E-Business.* Retrieved April 4, 2009, from http://www.gartner.com/it/page.jsp?id=707508

Gruman, G., & Knorr, E. (2008). *What cloud computing really means.* Retrieved April 4, 2009, from http://www.infoworld.com/article/08/04/07/15FE-cloud-computing-reality_1.html

Halpern, M., & Vasiliadis, V. (2009). Combating "Technology Commoditization". [from ABI/INFORM Global Database.]. *Intellectual Property & Technology Law Journal, 21*(4), 5–9. Retrieved May 7, 2009.

INTEL. (2005). *Excerpts from a conversation with Gordon Moore: Moore's Law.* Retrieved September 18, 2009, from ftp://download.intel.com/museum/Moores_Law/Video-Transcripts/Excepts_A_Conversation_with_Gordon_Moore.pdf

Nguyen, J. D., & Suber, E. F. (2009). An argument for eliminating the IP protection system. [from ABI/INFORM Global Database.]. *Business Law Today, 18*(4), 62–64. Retrieved May 8, 2009.

O'Reilly, T. (2005). *What is Web 2.0? Design patterns and business models for the next generation of software.* Retrieved April 4, 2009, from http://www.oreillynet.com/pub/a/oreilly/tim/news/2005/09/30/what-is-web-20.html

Pearce, J. (2003). *Music cos and AU universities square off over copyright claims.* Retrieved May 27, 2009, from http://www.zdnet.com.au/news/security/soa/Music-cos-and-AU-Universities-square-off-over-copyright claims/0,130061744,120273610,00.htm?feed=pt_file_sharing

Pfleeger, C., & Pfleeger, S. (2003). *Security in computing* (3rd ed.). New Jersey: Pearson Education Inc.

Reitzig, M. (2004). Management of Intellectual Property. *MITSLOAN Management Review, 45*(3). Retrieved May 28, 2009, from ABI/INFORM Global Database.

Saurine, A. (2008). *Stephanie Rice Facebook pictures censored.* Retrieved May 27, 2009, from http://www.news.com.au/dailytelegraph/story/0,22049,23468911-5001021,00.html

Standards, S. (2005). Retrieved May 5, 2009, from http://www.standards.org.au/downloads/051110_MOU_Security.pdf

Thompson, C. W., & Thompson, D. R. (2007). Identity management. [from ABI/INFORM Global Database.]. *IEEE Internet Computing, 11*(3), 82. Retrieved April 4, 2009. doi:10.1109/MIC.2007.60

Whittaker, Z. (2007). *Mobile computing vs. cloud computing*. Retrieved April 4, 2009, from http://blogs.zdnet.com/igeneration/?p=154

Compilation of References

25th International Conference Of Data Protection & Privacy Commissioners (ICDCP) (2003). Proposed Resolution on Improving the Communication of Data Protection and Privacy Information Practices. In *Proceedings of the 25th International Conference Of Data Protection & Privacy Commissioners, Sydney, 12 September 2003*. Retrieved accessed 9 January 2006, from http://www.bfdi.bund.de/cln_030/nn_535764/SharedDocs/Publikationen/EN/InternationalDS/ConferenceOfInternationalDataProtectionCommissioners2003ResolutionOnImprovingTheCommunicationOfDataProtectionAndPrivacyInformationPractices.html

Abram, S. (2005). Web 2.0 - huh! Library 2.0, Librarian 2.0. *Information Outlook, 9*, 44–47.

Adams, A., & Sasse, M. A. (1999). Users Are Not the Enemy. *Communications of the ACM, 42*(12), 41–46. doi:10.1145/322796.322806

Adelstein, F. (2006). Live forensics: Diagnosing your system without killing it first. *Communications of the ACM, 49*(2), 63–66. doi:10.1145/1113034.1113070

Afyouni, H. A. (2006). *Database security and auditing: protecting data integrity and accessibility*. Boston: Thomson Learning Inc.

Ahmad, A. (2002). The forensic chain of evidence model: Improving the process of evidence collection in incident handling procedures. *The 6th Pacific Asia Conference on Information Systems*.

Ajzen, I., & Fishbein, M. (1980). *Understanding Attitudes and Predicting Social Behavior*. Englewood Cliffs, NJ: Prentice Hall Inc.

Akester, P. (2004). Internet law: authenticity of works: authorship and authenticity in cyberspace. *Computer Law & Security Report, 20*(6), 436–444. doi:10.1016/S0267-3649(04)00088-3

Aktar, S. (2005). WLAN Performance . In Ahson, S., & Ilyas, M. (Eds.), *Handbook of Wireless Local Area Network: Applications, Technology, Security, and Standards*. Boca Raton: Taylor & Francis Group.

Alesso, H. P., & Smith, C. F. (2002). *The intelligent wireless Web*. Boston: Addison-Wesley.

Anderson, J. E., & Schwager, P. H. (2004). *SME adoption of Wireless LAN technology: Applying the UTAUT model.* Paper presented at the 7th Annual Conference of the Southern Association for Information Systems, Savannah, GE.

Anderson, T., & Twining, W. (1991). *Analysis of evidence: How to do things with facts based on Wigmore's Science of Judicial Proof.* Evanston, IL: Northwestern University Press.

Anton A. I., & Earp J. P. (2001). *A Taxonomy for Web Site Privacy Requirements.* NCSU Dept. of Comp Science Technical Report (TR-2001-14).

Anton, A. I., Earp, J. B., Vail, M. W., Jain, N., Gheen, C. M., & Frink, J. M. (2007). HIPAA's Effect on Web Site Privacy Policies. *IEEE Security and Privacy, 5*(1), 45–52. doi:10.1109/MSP.2007.7

Art.29 (2000). Opinion 4/2000 on the level of protection provided by the 'Safe Harbor Principles'. *Article 29 Data Protection Working Party of the European Union.* Retrieved May 16, 2000, from http://europa.eu.int/comm/justice_home/fsj/privacy/docs/wpdocs/2000/wp32en.pdf, accessed 9 January 2006

Ashcroft, J. (2001). *Electronic crime scene investigation: A guide for first responders.* Washington: U.S. Department of Justice.

Ashley, B. (2007). *Shaping the future of secure Ajax Mashups.* Retrieved June 2, 2009, from http://www-128.ibm.com/developerworks/library/x-securemashups/

Asia-Pacific Economic Council. (APEC, 2004). *APEC Privacy Framework.* Asia-Pacific Economic Council, November 2004. Retrieved December 16, 2008, from http://203.127.220.112/content/apec/news___media/2004_media_releases/201104_apecminsendorseprivacyfrmwk.downloadlinks.0001.LinkURL.Download.ver5.1.9

Association of Chief Police Officers (ACPO) (1999). *Association of Chief Police Officers: Good practice guide for computer based evidence.* National Hi-tech Crime Unit.

Auinger, M. Martin, D., Nedbal, & A. Holzinger, (2008). *Mixing Content and Endless Collaboration – MashUps: Towards Future Personal Learning Environments.* Retrieved March 23, 2009, from https://online.tu-graz.ac.at/tug_online/voe_main2.getVollText?pDocumentNr=95304&pCurrPk=42744

Australian Government Information Management Office. (AGIMO, 2003). *The Guide to Minimum Website Standards – Attachment C: Privacy Checklist.* Canberra: Australian Government Information Management Office. Retrieved December 16, 2008, from http://www.agimo.gov.au/practice/mws/attachments#C

Australian Law Reform Commission. (2005). *ALRC Discussion Paper 69.* Canberra: Australian Law Reform Commission.

Australian Research Centre. (ARC, 2009). *The Excellence in Research Australia (ERA) Initiative.* Retrieved May 5, 2009, from http://www.arc.gov.au/era/default.htm

Australian Security and Investments Commission. (ASIC, 2007). *Scams target you! Protect your money.* Retrieved October 28, 2008, from http://www.fido.gov.au/asic/asic.nsf/byheadline/07-51+Scams+target+you!+Protect+your+money?openDocument

Autry, C. W., & Bobbitt, L. M. (2008). Supply chain security orientation: Conceptual developments a proposed framework. *The International Journal of Logistics Management, 19*(1), 42–64. doi:10.1108/09574090810872596

Awerdick, J. W. (1993). Who owns data in the database? [from ABI/INFORM Global Database.]. *The Practical Lawyer, 39*(4), 19. Retrieved May 27, 2009.

Baase, S. (2003). *A gift of fire: Social, legal, and ethical issues for computers and the Internet.* Upper Saddle River: Pearson Education Inc.

Bajari, P & Hortaçsu, A . (2004). *Economic insights from Internet auctions Economic Literature, 42*(2), 457-486.

Baker, D. B. (2003). Wireless . In *Security for Healthcare*. San Diego: SAIC Enterprise and Health Solution.

Balter, O. (2000). How to Replace an Old Email System with a New. *Interacting with Computers, 12*(6), 601–614. doi:10.1016/S0953-5438(00)00020-5

Baraani-Dastjerdi, A., Pieprzyk, J., & Satavi-Naini, R. (1996). *Security in databases: a survey study.* Wollongong: Unpublished Survey, University of Wollongong.

Barbara, J. J. (2008). Appropriate standards and controls in computer forensics. *Forensic Magazine* (December 2007/January 2008).

Baryamureeba, V., & Tushabe, F. (2006). The Enhanced Digital Investigation Process Model. *Asian Journal of Information Technology, 5*(7), 790–794.

Bassett, R., Bass, L., & O'Brien, P. (2006). Computer forensics: An essential ingredient for cyber security. *Journal of Science and Technology, 3*(1), 26–30.

BBB. (2003). *Sample Privacy Notice.* Better Business Bureau. Retrieved December 16, 2008, from https://www.bbbonline.org/privacy/sample_privacy.asp

Bean, L., & Hott, D. (2005). Wiki: A speedy new tool to manage projects. *Journal of Corporate Accounting & Finance, 16*(5), 3–8. doi:10.1002/jcaf.20128

Becker, J. (2006). Open Source Initiative to Give People More Control Over Their Personal Online Information. *IBM Press Release*. Retrieved August 17, 2009, from http://www-03.ibm.com/press/us/en/pressrelease/19280.wss

Belanger, F., Hiller, J., & Smith, W. (2002). Trustworthiness in electronic commerce: The role of privacy, security, and site attributes. *The Journal of Strategic Information Systems, 11*(3-4), 245–270. doi:10.1016/S0963-8687(02)00018-5

Bennett, C. (1992). *Regulating Privacy: Data Protection and Public Policy in Europe and the United States*. New York: Cornell University Press.

Berk, R. A. (1983). An introduction to sample selection bias in sociological data. *American Sociological Review, 48*, 386–398. doi:10.2307/2095230

Bertino, W., Jojodia, S., & Samarati, P. (1993). Access controls in object-oriented database systems: some approaches and issues . In Bhargava, N. A. A. B. (Ed.), *Advanced Database Concepts and Research Issues (Vol. 759)*. Springer-Verlag.

Berwick, D. R., & Thompson, D. E. (1998). *Minimum provisions for the investigation of computer based offences (No. 1320-5579)*. Payneham, South Australia: National Police Research Unit.

Birdi, T., & Jansen, K. (2006). *Network Intrusion Detection: Know What You Do (Not)*. Need.

Boddington, R. G., Hobbs, V. J., & Mann, G. (2008). *Validating digital evidence for legal argument*. Paper presented at the SECAU Security Conferences: The 6th Australian Digital Forensics Conference, 1st - 3rd December 2008, Perth, WA.

Boin, A., & McConnell, A. (2007). Preparing for Critical Infrastructure Breakdowns: The Limists of Crisis Management and the Need for Resillience. *Journal of Contingencies and Crisis Management, 15*(1), 50–59. doi:10.1111/j.1468-5973.2007.00504.x

Borgner, M. S. (1994). Introduction . In Borgner, M. S. (Ed.), *Human error in Medicine*. New Jersey: Lawrence Erlbaum Associates.

Borland, J. (2003). *RIAA turns up heat on tile-trading at work*. Retrieved May 28, 2009, from http://www.zdnet.com.au/news/security/soa/RIAA-turns-up-heat-on-file-trading-at-work/0,130061744,120272983,00.htm

Boston, B. C. (March 2005). Phone viruses: How bad is it? *NewScientist Technology*.

Botha, J., & Von Solms, R. (2004). A cyclic approach ot business continuity planning. *Information Management & Computer Security, 12*(4), 328–327. doi:10.1108/09685220410553541

Brand Fact Sheet. (n.d.). Retrieved May 27, 2009 from http://www.virtualvender.coca-cola.com/ft/index.jsp

Brandenburg, C. (2008). The Newest Way to Screen Job Applicants: A Social Networker's Nightmare. [from ABI/INFORM Global Database.]. *Federal Communications Law Journal, 60*(3), 597. Retrieved April 20, 2009.

Brodsky, S. L. (2000). The expert witness: More maxims and guidelines for testifying in court. *The Journal of Psychiatry & Law, 28*(2), 289–292.

Brown, A. S., Bracken, E., Zoccoli, S., & Douglas, K. (2004). Generating and Remembering Passwords. *Applied Cognitive Psychology, 18*, 641–651. doi:10.1002/acp.1014

Burke, L., & Weill, B. (2005). *Information Technology for the Health Professions*. New Jersey: Pearson Prentice Hall.

Burkert, H. (1997). Privacy-Enhancing Technologies: Typology, Critique, Vision . In Agre, P. E., & Rotenberg, M. (Eds.), *Technology and Privacy: The New Landscape*. Boston: MIT Press.

Business Enterprise and Regulatory Reform. (BERR, 2008). *Information Security Breaches Survey*. Retrieved January 31, 2009, from http://www.pwc.co.uk/pdf/BERR_2008_Executive_summary.pdf

Caloyannides, M. A. (2001). *Computer forensics and privacy*. Norwood, Minnesota: Artech House.

Caloyannides, M. A. (2003). Digital evidence and reasonable doubt. *IEEE Security and Privacy, 1*(6), 89–91. doi:10.1109/MSECP.2003.1266366

Campbell, J., & Bryant, K. (2004). *Password composition and Security: An Exploratory Study of User Practice,* Paper presented at Australasian Conference on Information Systems, December 1-3, University of Tasmania, Hobart.

Campbell, J., Kleeman, D., & Ma, W. (2007). The Good and Not So Good of Enforcing Password Composition Rules. *Information Systems Security, 16*(1), 2–8. doi:10.1080/10658980601051375

CareerBuilder. (2006) *One-in-four hiring managers have used Internet search engines to screen job candidates; One-in-Ten Have Used Social Networking Sites.* (2006). Retrieved May 27, 2009, from http://www.careerbuilder.com/share/aboutus/pressreleasesdetail.aspx?id=pr331&sd=10%2f26%2f2006&ed=12%2f31%2f2006&siteid=cbpr331&sc_cmp1=cb_pr331_

Carrier, B. (2005). *File system forensic analysis.* Upper Saddle River, New Jersey: Addison-Wesley.

Carrier, B. D. S. Eugene. H. (2004). *An event-based digital forensic investigation framework.* Paper presented at the fourth annual Digital Forensics Research Workshop Baltimore, Maryland. Retrieved 12 October 2009 from http://www.dfrws.org/2004/index.shtml

Carrier, B. D., & Spafford, E. H. (2004). Defining event reconstruction of a digital crime scene. *Journal of Forensic Sciences, 49*(6). doi:10.1520/JFS2004127

Carrier, B. D., & Spafford, E. H. (2005). *Automated digital evidence target definition using outlier analysis and existing evidence.* Paper presented at the 2005 Digital Forensic Research Workshop (DFRWS) New Orleans, LA. Retrieved 5 September 2008 from: http://www.dfrws.org/2005/proceedings/carrier_targetdefn.pdf

Carrier, B., & Spafford, E. H. (2003). Getting physical with the digital investigation process. *International Journal of Digital Evidence, 2*(2), 1–20.

Carstens, D. S., McCauley-Bell, P., Malone, L. C., & DeMara, R. F. (2004). Evaluation of the Human Impact of Password Authentication Practices on Information Security. *Informing Science Journal, 7*(1), 67–85.

Carter, D. L. (1995). Computer crime categories: how techno-criminals operate. *FBI Law Enforcement Bulletin,* (18, May, 2005, pp.21-26).

Casey, E. (2000). *Digital evidence and computer crime: Forensic science, computers and the Internet.* London: Academic Press.

Casey, E. (2007). What does "forensically sound" really mean? *Digital Investigation, 4*(2), 49–50. doi:10.1016/j.diin.2007.05.001

Casey, E. (Ed.). (2002). *Handbook of computer crime investigation: forensic tools and technology.* London: Elsevier Academic Press.

Casey, M., & Savastinuk, L. (2006). *Library 2.0: service for the next-generation.* Retrieved March 2, 2008, from http://www.libraryjournal.com/article/CA6365200.html?q=Library+2%E0

Castano, S., Fugini, M., Martella, G., & Samarati, P. (1995). *Database Security: Addison-Wesley.* ACM Press.

Cerullo, V., & Cerullo, M. J. (2004). Business Continuity Planning: A Comprehensive Approach. *Information Systems Management, 21*(3), 70–78. doi:10.1201/1078/44432.21.3.20040601/82480.11

Chaikin, D. (2006). Network investigations of cyber attacks: The limits of digital evidence. *Crime, Law, and Social Change, 46*, 239–256. doi:10.1007/s10611-007-9058-4

Chang, I. C., Hwang, H. G., Yen, D. C., & Huang, H. Y. (2006). An empirical study of the factors affecting Internet security for the financial industry in Taiwan. *Telematics and Informatics, 23*, 343–364. doi:10.1016/j.tele.2005.11.001

Chappel, D. (2006). Introducing Windows Card Space Online. *Windows Vista Technical Articles*. Retrieved August 17, 2009, from http://msdn2.microsoft.com/en-us/library/aa480189.aspx

Chau, S., & Turner, P. (2004). *Implementing and evaluating a wireless handheld clinical care management system at an Australian aged care facility. HIC 2004*. Brisbane, Australia: HISA.

Chismar, W. R., & Wiley-Patton, S. (2006). Predicting Internet use: Applying the Extended Technology Acceptance Model to the healthcare environment . In Spil, T. A. M., & Schuring, R. W. (Eds.), *E-Health Systems diffusion and use: The Innovation, the user and the USE IT Model*. Hershey: Idea Group Publishing.

Clarke, R. (1996). Privacy, Dataveillance, Organisational Strategy. Keynote Address. In *Proceedings of the I.S. Audit & Control Association Conference; EDPAC, Perth, May 28, 1996*. Retrieved December 16, 2008, from http://www.rogerclarke.com/DV/PStrat.html

Clarke, R. (1998). *Direct Marketing and Privacy*. Xamax Consultancy Pty Ltd. Retrieved December 16, 2008, from http://www.rogerclarke.com/DV/DirectMkting.html

Clarke, R. (1999a). Internet Privacy Concerns Confirm the Case for Intervention. *Communications of the ACM, 42*(2) 60-67. Retrieved December 16, 2008, from http://www.rogerclarke.com/DV/CACM99.html

Clarke, R. (1999b). The Willingness of Net-Consumers to Pay: A Lack-of-Progress Report. In *Proceedings of the 12th International Bled Electronic Commerce Conference, Bled, Slovenia, June 7 - 9, 1999*. Retrieved December 16, 2008, from http://www.rogerclarke.com/EC/WillPay.html

Clarke, R. (2000). *Beyond the OECD Guidelines: Privacy Protection for the 21st Century*. Xamax Consultancy Pty Ltd. January 2000. Retrieved December 16, 2008, from http://www.rogerclarke.com/DV/PP21C.html

Clarke, R. (2001a). Introducing PITs and PETs: Technologies Affecting Privacy. *Privacy Law & Policy Reporter, 7*(9), 181-183. Retrieved December 16, 2008, from http://www.rogerclarke.com/DV/PITsPETs.html

Clarke, R. (2001b). Meta-Brands. *Privacy Law & Policy Reporter, 7*(11). Retrieved December 16, 2008, from http://www.rogerclarke.com/DV/MetaBrands.html

Clarke, R. (2001c). Privacy as a Means of Engendering Trust in Cyberspace. [from http://www.rogerclarke.com/DV/eTrust.html]. *The University of New South Wales Law Journal, 24*(1), 290–297. Retrieved December 16, 2008.

Clarke, R. (2002a). Trust in the Context of e-Business. *Internet Law Bulletin, 4*(5), 56-59. Retrieved December 16, 2008, from http://www.rogerclarke.com/EC/Trust.html

Clarke, R. (2002b). e-Consent: A Critical Element of Trust in e-Business. In *Proceedings of the 15th Bled Electronic Commerce Conference, Bled, Slovenia, 17-19 June 2002*. Retrieved December 16, 2008, from http://www.rogerclarke.com/EC/eConsent.html

Clarke, R. (2005a). *Privacy Statement Template*. Xamax Consultancy Pty Ltd., December 2005. Retrieved December 16, 2008, from http://www.rogerclarke.com/DV/PST.html

Clarke, R. (2005b). *About the Privacy Statement Template*. Xamax Consultancy Pty Ltd., December 2005, Retrieved December 16, 2008, from http://www.rogerclarke.com/DV/PSTAbt.html

Clarke, R. (2005c). *Evaluation of Google's Privacy Statement against the Privacy Statement Template of 19 December 2005*. Xamax Consultancy Pty Ltd., December 2005, Retrieved December 16, 2008, from http://www.rogerclarke.com/DV/PST-Google.html

Clarke, R. (2006a). *What's 'Privacy'?* Xamax Consultancy Pty Ltd., July 2006, Retrieved December 16, 2008, from http://www.rogerclarke.com/DV/Privacy.html

Clarke, R. (2006b). Google's Gauntlets. *Computer Law & Security Report, 22*(4), 287-297. Retrieved December 16, 2008, from http://www.rogerclarke.com/II/Gurgle0604.html

Clarke, R. (2006c). Make Privacy a Strategic Factor - The Why and the How. *Cutter IT Journal, 19*(11). Retrieved December 16, 2008, from http://www.rogerclarke.com/DV/APBD-0609.html

Coakes, E. (2003). Socio-technical thinking - A holistic viewpoint . In Clarke, S., Coakes, E., Hunter, M. G., & Wenn, A. (Eds.), *Socio-Technical and Human Cognition Elements of Information Systems*. Hershey: Information Science Publishing.

Cohen, F. (2006). Challenges to digital forensic evidence. Retrieved June 22, 2006, from http://all.net/Talks/CyberCrimeSummit06.pdf

Coiera, E. (2004). Four rules for the reinvention of health care. *British Medical Journal, 328*, 1197–1199. doi:10.1136/bmj.328.7449.1197

Coleman, C., & Sapte, D. W. (2003). Cyberspace security: securing cyberspace: new laws and developing strategies. *Computer Law & Security Report, 19*(2), 131–136. doi:10.1016/S0267-3649(03)00208-5

Collaborative Health Informatics Centre. (2000). *E-health - An exploratory study of health IT in Australia and New Zealand*. Milton: Collaborative Health Informatics Centre.

Collins, G. (2005). Evolving architecture drives enterprise WLAN growth. *Business Communication Review*, 28-30.

Computer Crime. (1979). *Criminal Justice Resource Manual*. United States: United States Department of Justice.

Conklin, A., Dietrich, G., & Walz, D. (2004). *Password-Based Authentication: A System Perspective*. Paper presented at the 37th Hawaii International Conference on System Sciences, Hawaii.

Connolly, C. (2008, December). The US Safe Harbor - Fact or Fiction? *Galexia Pty Ltd*. Retrieved December 16, 2008, from http://www.galexia.com/public/research/assets/safe_harbor_fact_or_fiction_2008/safe_harbor_fact_or_fiction.pdf

Creasy, J. R. (1981). The origin of the VM/370 Time-Sharing System. *IBM Journal of Research and Development, 25*(5), 483–490. doi:10.1147/rd.255.0483

Creswell, J. W., Plano-Clark, V. L., Gutmann, M. L., & Hanson, W. E. (2003). Advanced mixed methods research designs . In Tashakkori, A., & Teddle, C. (Eds.), *Handbook of Mixed Methods in Social & Behavioral Research*. Thousand Oaks: Sage Publications.

Crompton, M. (2004). Short Notices – why the Sydney resolution was adopted and progress in Australia since September 2003. In *Proceedings of the 26th International Conference on Privacy and Personal Data Protection, 14-16 September 2004, Wroclaw, Poland*. Retrieved December 16, 2008, from http://26konferencja.giodo.gov.pl/data/resources/CromptonM_paper.pdf

Crow, A. (2004). *Defining the balance for now and the future - Clinicians perspective of implementing a care coordination information systems management. HIC 2004*. Brisbane, Australia: HISA.

Culnan, M. (1993). How Did They Get My Name? An Exploratory Investigation of Consumer Attitudes Towards Secondary Information Use. *Management Information Systems Quarterly*, *17*(3), 341. doi:10.2307/249775

Culnan, M. J., & Milne, G. R. (2001). The Culnan-Milne Survey on Consumers & Online Privacy Notices: Summary of Responses. *Federal Trade Commission*. Retrieved December 16, 2008, from http://www.ftc.gov/bcp/workshops/glb/supporting/culnan-milne.pdf, accessed 9 January 2006

Curran, K., Murray, M., & Christian, M. (2007). Taking the information to the public through Library 2.0. *Library Hi Tech*, *25*(2), 288–297. doi:10.1108/07378830710755036

Danielson, K. (2008). *Distinguishing cloud computing from utility computing*. Retrieved April 4, 2009, from http://www.ebizq.net/blogs/saasweek/2008/03/distinguishing_cloud_computing/

Dasgupta, P., & Boyd, T. (2005). Security in Wireless Networks . In Ahson, S., & Ilyas, M. (Eds.), *Handbook of Wireless Local Area Network: Applications, Technology, Security, and Standards*. Boca Raton: Taylor & Francis Group.

de Paula, R., Ding, X., Dourish, P., Nies, K., Pillet, B., & Redmiles, D. F. (2005). In The Eye of The Beholder: A Visualization-Based Approach to Information System Security. *International Journal of Human-Computer Studies*, *63*, 5–24. doi:10.1016/j.ijhcs.2005.04.021

Delio, M. (2002, February). Sun Shines Light on ID Alliance. *Wired Magazine*. Retrieved August 17, 2009, from http://www.wired.com/news/business/0,1367,53859,00.html

Demougin, D., & Fluet, C. (2006). Preponderance of evidence. *European Economic Review*, *50*(4), 963–976. doi:10.1016/j.euroecorev.2004.11.002

Department of Commerce. (DOC, 2000). *Safe Harbor Overview*. U.S. Department of Commerce. Retrieved January 9, 2006, from http://www.export.gov/safeharbor/sh_overview.html, accessed 9 January 2006

Devitt, E. J., & Blackman, C. B. (1977). *Federal Jury practice and instructions* (3rd ed.). St. Paul, Minnesota: West Publishing.

Diaconis, P., & Mosteller, F. (1989). Methods for studying coincidences. *Journal of the American Statistical Association*, *84*, 853–861. doi:10.2307/2290058

Dillon, T. S., Wu, C., & Chang, E. (2007). GRIDSpace: Semantic Grid Services on the Web:Evolution towards a SoftGrid. In *Proceedings of the 3rd International Conference on Semantics, Knowledge and Grid*, October 29-31, Xi'an, China.

Dinev, T., Bellotto, M., Hart, P., Colautti, C., Russo, V., & Serra, I. (2005). Internet Users, Privacy Concerns and Attitudes towards Government Surveillance - An Exploratory Study of Cross-Cultural Differences between Italy and the United States. In *Proceedings of the 18th International eCommerce Conference, Bled, June 2005*. Retrieved January 9, 2006, from http://aisel.isworld. org/pdf.asp?Vpath=BLED&PDFpath=41Dinev.pdf

Doherty, N. F., & King, M. (2003). From technical change to socio-technical change: Towards a proactive approach to the treatment of organizational issues . In Clarke, S., Coakes, E., Hunter, M. G., & Wenn, A. (Eds.), *Socio-Technical and Human Cognition Elements of Information Systems*. Hershey: Information Science Publishing.

Doktor, R., Bangert, D., & Valdez, M. (2005). *Organizational learning and culture in the managerial implementation of clinical e-Health systems: An international perspective*. Paper presented at the 38th Hawaii International Conference on System Science, Hawaii, University of Hawaii.

Dubbold, L. (2006). Privacy and security disclosures on telecardiology Web sites. *First Monday*, *11*(5).

Earp, J. B., & Baumer, D. (2003). Innovative Web Use To Learn About Consumer Behavior and Online Privacy. *Communications of the ACM, 46*(4), 81–83. doi:10.1145/641205.641209

Earp, J., Anton, A., & Jarvinen, O. (2002). A Social, Technical, and Legal Framework for Privacy Management and Policies. In *Proceedings of the Americas Conference on Information Systems 2002*. Retrieved January 9, 2006, from http://aisel.isworld.org/pdf.asp?Vpath=AMCIS/2002& PDFpath=021101.pdf, accessed 9 January 2006

Economist (2005, December 1). Demon in the machine: Privacy laws gain support in America, after a year of huge violations. *The Economist.* Retrieved January 9, 2006, from http://www. economist.com/business/displayStory.cfm?story_id=5259499&no_na_tran=1

Edwards, K. (2005). Ten things about DNA contamination that lawyers should know. *Criminal Law Journal, 29*(2), 71–93.

Electronic Privacy Information Center. (1996). *EPIC Online Guide to Practical Privacy Tools*. Retrieved December 16, 2008, from http://www.epic.org/privacy/tools.html

Electronic Privacy Information Center. (2003). *EPIC Complaint and Request for Injunction, Investigation and for Other Relief In the Matter of Amazon.com, Inc*. Electronic Privacy Information Center. Retrieved April 22, 2003, from http://www.epic.org/privacy/amazon/coppacomplaint.html

Electronic Privacy Information Center. (2004). FTC Fails To Enforce Children's Privacy Law Against Amazon.Com. *EPIC Alert,* 11(23). Retrieved December 8, 2004, from http://www.epic. org/alert/EPIC_Alert_11.23.html

Elliot, D., Swartz, E., & Herbane, B. (1999). Just waiting for the next big bang: business continuity planning in the UK finance sector. *Journal of applied management, 8*(1), 43-60.

Emanavin, C. C. (2004). *Testing Lessig: Applying user acceptance theory to Internet use and behavior for privacy and security applications. Faculty of the Graduate School of Arts and Science*. Washington: Georgetown University.

Enfinger, F., Nelson, B., Phillips, A., & Steuart, C. (2006). *Guide to computer forensics and investigations* (2nd ed.). Boston, Massachusetts: Course Technology.

Etter, B. (2001, 21-22 June). *Computer crime.* Paper presented at the 4th National Outlook Symposium on Crime in Australia - New Crimes or New Responses, Canberra.

Etter, B. (2001b). The forensic challenges of e-crime. *Australasian Centre for Policing Research, 3*(10), 1–8.

Federal Trade Commission (1999). *Protecting Consumers Online: A Federal Trade Commission Report on the First Five Years of Its Internet Law Enforcement Program.*

Federal Trade Commission. (1998a). *Privacy Online: A Report to Congress' Federal Trade Commission.* Retrieved January 9, 2006 from http://www.ftc.gov/reports/privacy3/priv-23a.pdf

Federal Trade Commission. (1998b). *Self-Regulation Is The Preferred Method Of Protecting Consumers'Online Privacy.* Retrieved December 16, 2008, from http://www.ftc.gov/opa/1998/07/privacyh.htm, accessed 9 January 2006

Federal Trade Commission. (FTC, 2000). *Privacy Online: Fair Information Practices in the Electronic Marketplace: A Federal Trade Commission Report to Congress.* Retrieved January 9, 2006, from http://www.ftc.gov/reports/privacy2000/privacy2000.pdf

Federal Trade Commission. (FTC, 2005). *Enforcing Privacy Promises: Section 5 of the FTC Act.* Retrieved December 16, 2008, from http://www.ftc.gov/privacy/privacyinitiatives/promises.html, accessed 9 January 2006

Fisher, J. (2003). Human factors and the Systems Development Process . In Clarke, S., Coakes, E., Hunter, M. G., & Wenn, A. (Eds.), *Socio-Technical and Human Cognition Elements of Information Systems.* Hershey: Information Science Publishing.

Fiske, S. T., & Taylor, S. E. (1991). *Social cognition* (2nd ed.). New York: McGraw-Hill.

Flaherty, D. H. (1989). *Protecting Privacy in Surveillance Societies.* University of North Carolina Press.

Fleischer, P. (2005, September 7). *Protecting Customer Data in an Evolving Technology Environment.* Microsoft. Retrieved from http://www.microsoft.com/emea/presscentre/peterfleischer.mspx

Flusche, K. J. (2001). Computer forensic case study: Espionage, Part 1 Just finding the file is not enough! *Information Security Journal, 10*(1), 1–10. doi:10.1201/1086/43313.10.1.20010304/31394.6

Fox, G., & Pierce, M. (2007). Web 2.0 and Grids. *In Proceedings of the 3rd International Conference on Semantics, Knowledge and Grid,* October 29-31, Xi'an, China.

Fraud Watch, I. (2007). Internet Fraud Watch and the Internet Crime Complaint Centre. Retrieved February 28, 2009, from http://www.crime-research.org/news/20.04.2007/2627/

Freenetlaw.com. (2008). *Free privacy statement template.* Retrieved from http://www.freenetlaw.com/free-privacy-statement.php

Garg, A., Curtis, J., & Halper, H. (2003). Quantifying the financial impact of IT security breaches. *Information Management & Computer Security, 11*(2), 74–83. doi:10.1108/09685220310468646

Gartner (2008). *Cloud computing will be as influential as E-Business.* Retrieved April 4, 2009, from http://www.gartner.com/it/page.jsp?id=707508

Gauzente, C. (2004). Web Merchants' Privacy And Security Statements: How Reassuring Are They For Consumers? A Two-Sided Approach. *Journal of Electronic Commerce Research,* *5*(3). Retrieved December 16, 2008, from http://www.csulb.edu/web/journals/jecr/issues/20043/Paper4.pdf

George, E. (2004). Trojan virus defence: Regina v Aaron Caffrey, Southwark Crown Court. *Digital Investigation, 1*(2), 89. doi:10.1016/j.diin.2004.04.005

Gettes, M. R. (1999). *Shibboleth - Middleware Web Authentication Project.* Retrieved August 17, 2009, from http://shibboleth.internet2.edu/docs/shibboleth-project.html

Ghosh, A. (2004). *Guidelines for the management of IT evidence.* Paper presented at the APEC Telecommunications and Information Working Group 29th Meeting. Retrieved 5 October 2009 from http://unpan1.un.org/intradoc/groups/public/documents/APCITY/UNPAN016411.pdf

Gold, S. (2008). A newsworthy year. *Infosecurity, 6*(1), 24–28. doi:10.1016/S1754-4548(09)70008-7

Gong, R., & Chan, K. Y. (2005). Case-relevance information investigation: Binding computer intelligence to the current computer forensic framework. *International Journal of Digital Evidence, 4*(1), 1–13.

Government 2.0 white paper (2009). *eGovernment social media platform deployments and future opportunities.* Retrieved June 2, 2009, from http://nass.org/index.php?option=com_search&Itemid=5&searchword=government&searchphrase=any&ordering=newest&limit=5&limitstart=0

Gritzalis, S., & Lambrinoudakis, C. (2005). Security in IEEE 802.11 WLANs . In Ahson, S., & Ilyas, M. (Eds.), *Handbook of Wireless Local Area Network: Applications, Technology, Security, and Standards.* Boca Raton: Taylor & Francis Group.

Gruman, G., & Knorr, E. (2008). *What cloud computing really means.* Retrieved April 4, 2009, from http://www.infoworld.com/article/08/04/07/15FE-cloud-computing-reality_1.html

Gururajan, R. (2007). Drivers of wireless technology in healthcare: an Indian Study. In *Proceedings of the 15th European Conference on Information Systems (ECIS 2007), University of St Gallen, Switerland*

Gururajan, R., Rai, S., & Edward, D. (2003). *The study in the use of hand held devices in an Emergency Department for a Hospital in Western Australia.* IEEE TENCON International Conference, Bangalore.

Hakkola, J. (2008). *Mashup Security.* Research presentation. Retrieved June 2, 2009, from http://www.tml.tkk.fi/Opinnot/T-111.5550/2008/presentation_hakkola_jyrki.pdf

Halleck, J. (1996). Administrator ethical dilemma. Retrieved 23 June 2005, from http://www.cc.utah.edu/%7Enahaj/ethics/administrator.html

Halpern, M., & Vasiliadis, V. (2009). Combating "Technology Commoditization". [from ABI/INFORM Global Database.]. *Intellectual Property & Technology Law Journal, 21*(4), 5–9. Retrieved May 7, 2009.

Hamalainen, M., Pirinen, P., & Shelby, Z. (2007). Advanced Wireless ICT healthcare research . In Pirinen, P. (Ed.), *Mobile and Wireless Communications Summit, 2007.*

Havenstein, H. (2005). *Industry Focus: Wireless in Healthcare.* Techworld.

Hawkins, S. M., Yen, D. C., & Chou, D. C. (2000). Disaster recovery planning: a strategy for data security. *Information Management & Computer Security, 8*(5), 222–229. doi:10.1108/09685220010353150

Hegney, D., Eley, R., Buikstra, E., Fallon, T., Soar, J., & Gilmore, V. (2006). Australian Nurses Access and Attitudes to Information Technology - A National Survey. In H. A. Park., P. Murray, & C. Delaney (Eds.), *The 9th International Congress on Nursing Informatics (NI2006),* Seoul, Korea.

Hemsoth, C. M. (2000). Security policies: The foundation for information protection. In P. L. Davison, (Ed.), *Healthcare Information Systems.* Boca Raton: Auerbach Publications.

Hewlett-Packard. (2007, March 26). *Survey: Business Continuity and Availability Solutions a High Priority for Corporate Spending in 2007.* Retrieved March 29, 2009, from http://www.hp.com/hpinfo/newsroom/press/2007/070326a.html?jumpid=reg_R1002_USEN

Ho, H. L. (1999). A theory of hearsay. *Oxford Journal of Legal Studies, 19*(3), 403–420. doi:10.1093/ojls/19.3.403

Hoar, S. B. (2001). *Identity theft: The crime of the New Millennium* (Vol. 49).

Hoffman, D. L., Novak, T. P., & Peralta, M. (1999). Building Consumer Trust Online. *Communications of the ACM, 42*(4), 80–85. doi:10.1145/299157.299175

Holt, P. J. (2000). Biometrics. In P. L. Davidson, (Ed.), *Healthcare Information Systems.* Boca Raton: Auerbach Publications.

Hoofnagle, C. J. (2005). Privacy Self Regulation: A Decade of Disappointment. *Electronic Privacy Information Center.* Retrieved March 4, 2005, from http://www.epic.org/reports/decadedisappoint.html

Hooper, A. S. C., Bunker, B., Rapson, A., Reynolds, A., & Vos, M. (2007). Evaluating Banking Websites Privacy Statements – A New Zealand Perspective on Ensuring Business Confidence. In *Proceedings of PACIS 2007, Paper 25.* Retrieved December 16, 2008, from http://aisel.aisnet.org/pacis2007/25

Horan, T. A., Tulu, B., & Hilton, B. N. (2006). Understanding physician use of Online Systems: An empirical assessment of an Electronic Disability Evaluation System . In Spil, T. A. M., & Schring, R. W. (Eds.), *E-Health Systems Diffusion and Use: The Innovation, the User and the USE IT Model.* Hershey: Idea Group Publishing.

Hui, K., Teo, H. H., & Lee, S. (2007). The Value of Privacy Assurance: An Exploratory Field Experiment. *MIS Quartlery, 31*(3), 19–33.

Ilyas, M., & Qazi, S. (2005). Applications of WLANs in Telemedicine . In Ahson, S., & Ilyas, M. (Eds.), *Handbook of Wireless Local Area Network: Applications, Technology, Security, and Standards.* Boca Raton: Taylor & Francis Group.

Information and Privacy Commissioner. (IPCR,1995). Privacy-Enhancing Technologies: The Path to Anonymity. *Information and Privacy Commissioner* (Vol. 2). Retrieved January 9, 2006, from http://www.ipc.on.ca/web%5Fsite.eng/matters/sum%5Fpap/papers/anon%2De.htm

Information Commissioner's Office. (ICO, 2001). Compliance advice: Website Frequently asked questions. *Information Commissioner's Office,* Manchester, U.K. 26 June 2001, Retrieved January 9, 2006, from http://www.ico.gov.uk/documentUploads/Website%20FAQ.pdf

INTEL. (2005). *Excerpts from a conversation with Gordon Moore: Moore's Law.* Retrieved September 18, 2009, from ftp://download.intel.com/museum/Moores_Law/Video-Transcripts/Excepts_A_Conversation_with_Gordon_Moore.pdf

Ives, B., Walsh, K. R., & Schneider, H. (2004). The Domino Effect of Password Reuse. *Communications of the ACM, 47*(4), 75–78. doi:10.1145/975817.975820

Jain, A. K., Ross, A., & Prabhakar, S. (2004). An introduction to biometric Recognition. *IEEE Transactions on Circuits and Systems for Video Technology, 14*(1), 4–20. doi:10.1109/TC-SVT.2003.818349

Jamalipour, A. (2003). *The Wireless Mobile Internet: Architectures, Protocols and Service.* West Sussex: John Wiley & Sons Ltd.

Janes, S. (2000). The role of technology in computer forensic investigations. *Information Security Technical Report, 5*(2), 43–50. doi:10.1016/S1363-4127(00)02006-9

Jensen, C., & Potts, C. (2004). Privacy Polices as Decision-Making Tools: An Evaluation of Privacy Notices. In *Proceedings of CHI 2004, April 24-29, 2004, Vienna, Austria.*

Johnson, B. C. (2002). *Wireless 802.11 LAN Security: Understanding the Key Issues.* Boston: Systems Expert Corporation.

Johnson, C. (2004). *Realising value from Health technology investments: Improving the selection and delivery of a portfolio of projects. HIC 2004.* Brisbane, Australia: HISA.

Jordan, E., & Silcock, L. (2005). *Beating IT risks.* Chichester: John Wiley & Sons Ltd.

Journal, I. S. A. C. A. 1. Retrieved November 26th 2009 from http://www.isaca.org/Template.cfm?Section=Home&CONTENTID=52143&TEMPLATE=/ContentManagement/ContentDisplay.cfm

Kane, G. C., & Fichman, R. G. (2009). The shoemaker's children: Using wikis for IS teaching, research, and publication. *Management Information Systems Quarterly, 32*(4).

Kavanaugh, C. (2000). The future of automated patient identification, car coding, and smart cards. In P. L. Davidson, (Ed.). *Healthcare Information Systems.* Boca Raton: Auerbach Publications.

Kawaguchi, A., Russell, S., Qian, G., Miayata, C., & Becerra, J. (2005). Integrated WLAN Deployment: Implementation of a Mobile Wireless Diabetes Management System . In Ahson, S., & Ilyas, M. (Eds.), *Handbook of Wireless Local Area Network: Applications, Technology, Security, and Standards.* Boca Raton: Taylor & Francis Group.

Kenneally, E. E. (2004). Digital logs—proof matters. *Digital Investigation, 1*(2), 94–101. doi:10.1016/j.diin.2004.01.006

Khan, M. F. (2005). WLAN Security: Issues and solution . In Ahson, S., & Ilyas, M. (Eds.), *Handbook of Wireless Local Area Network: Applications, Technology, Security, and Standards.* Boca Raton: Taylor & Francis Group.

Kim, D. (2005). Cognition-Based Versus Affect-Based Trust Determinants in E-Commerce: Cross-Cultural Comparison Study. In *Proceedings of International Conference on Information Systems.* Retrieved December 16, 2008, from http://aisel.isworld.org/pdf.asp?Vpath=ICIS/2005&PDFpath=WBISA03.pdf

Kobsa, A., & Teltzrow, M. (2005). Impacts of Contextualized Communication of Privacy Practices and Personalization Benefits on Purchase Behavior and Perceived Quality of Recommendation. In *Proceedings of Workshop: Beyond Personalization, IUI'05, January 9, 2005, San Diego, California, USA*. Retrieved January 9, 2006, from http://www.cs.umn.edu/Research/GroupLens/beyond2005

Koehler, J. J., & Thompson, W. C. (2006). *Mock jurors' reactions to selective presentation of evidence from multiple-opportunity searches*. American Psychology-Law Society: Division 41 of the American Psychological Association.

Kong, J., Gerla, M., Prabhu, B. S., & Gadh, R. (2005). An overview of network security in WLANs . In Ahson, S., & Ilyas, M. (Eds.), *Handbook of Wireless Local Area Network: Applications, Technology, Security, and Standards*. Boca Raton: Taylor & Francis Group.

Kruse, W. H. J. (2002). *Computer forensics: Incident response essentials*. Indianapolis: Addison-Wesley.

Kulathuramaiyer, N. (2007). Mashups: Emerging application development paradigm for a digital journal. *Journal of Universal Computer Science, 13*, 531–542.

Lapointe, L., Lapointe, L., & Fortin, J. P. (2006). The Dynamics of IT Adoption in a Major Change Process in Healthcare Delivery . In Spil, T. A. M., & Schuring, R. W. (Eds.), *E-Health Systems Diffusion and Use: The Innovation, the User and the USE IT Model*. Hershey: Idea Group Publishing.

Lee, M. K. O., & Turban, E. (2001). A Trust Model for Consumer Internet Shopping. *International Journal of Electronic Commerce, 6*(1), 75–91.

Leiwo, J. (1999). *Observations on information security crisis*. Bangkok: King Mongkut's Institute of Technology.

Lemos, R. (2008). Lax security leads to child-porn charges [Electronic Version]. *Security Focus*. Retrieved 22 November 2008 from http://www.securityfocus.com/brief/756.

Lichtenstein, S., Swatman, P. M. C., & Babu, K. (2002). Effective Online Privacy Policies. In *Information Systems: Enabling Organisations and Society: Proceedings of 13th Australasian Conference on Information Systems, Victoria University, Melbourne, Australia*.

Lichtenstein, S., Swatman, P. M. C., & Babu, K. (2003). *Narrowing the Gap Between Privacy Policy and Practice: Guidelines and Framework for Integrating Online Privacy Policy With Practic*. Working Paper 2003/05, School of Information Systems, Deakin University, Melbourne, Australia.

Livshits, B., & Erlingsson, E. (2007). Using web application construction frameworks to protect against code injection attacks. In *Proceedings of the 2007 workshop on Programming languages and analysis for security* (pp. 95-104). New York: ACM.

Losavio, M., Adams, J., & Rogers, M. (2006). Gap Analysis: Judicial experience and perception of electronic evidence. *Journal of Digital Forensic Practice, 1*, 13–17. doi:10.1080/15567280500541462

Loveland, S., Dow, E. M., LeFevre, F., Beyer, D., & Chan, P. F. (2008). Leveraging virtualization to optimize high-availability systems configuration. *IBM Systems Journal, 47*(4), 591–604. doi:10.1147/SJ.2008.5386515

Lu, J., Yu, C. H., Liu, C., & Yao, J. E. (2003). Technology Acceptance Model for Wireless Internet. *Internet Research: Electronic Networking Applications and Policy.*

Luddy, W. J. Jr, & Wolk, S. R. (1986). *Legal aspects of computer use. Prentice Hall.* Prentice Hall.

Ma, W., Campbell, J., Tran, D., & Kleeman, D. (2007). A Conceptual Framework for Assessing Password Quality. *International Journal of Computer Science and Network Security, 7*(1), 179–185.

Maine Medical Center. (2002). *Wireless security and management in healthcare organization.* Portland: Maine Medical Center.

Man, S., Hong, D., Hayes, B., & Matthews, M. (2004). *A Password Scheme Strongly Resistant to Spyware* (pp. 94-100). Paper presented at the International Conference on Security and Management, Las Vegas, USA.

Mann, W. C. (2005). Aging, disability, and independence: Trends and perspectives . In Mann, W. C. (Ed.), *Smart Technology for Aging, Disability, and Independence.* New Jersey: John Wiley & Sons Incorporated Publication. doi:10.1002/0471743941.ch1

Marcella, A. J., & Greenfield, R. S. (Eds.). (2002). *Cyber forensics: A field manual for collecting, examining and preserving evidence of computer crimes.* Boca Raton, Florida: CRC Press Ltd.doi:10.1201/9781420000115

Markel, M. (2008). Safe harbor and privacy protection: a looming issue for IT professionals. *IEEE Transactions on Professional Communication, 49*(1), 1–11. doi:10.1109/TPC.2006.870462

Mattord, H. J., & Whitman, M. E. (2003). *Principles of information security: preparing tomorrow's information security professionals.* Boston, Massachusetts: Thomson Learning, Inc.

Mattord, H. J., & Whitman, M. E. (2004). *Management of information security.* Boston: Thomson Learning.

Mayfield, R., & Cvitanic, J. (2001) Mathematical Proofs of Mayfield's Paradox: A Fundamental Principle of Information Security. *Information Systems Control Journal, 2.* Retrieved from http://www.isaca.org/Template.cfm?Section=Home&CONTENTID=17181&TEMPLATE=/Content-Management/ContentDisplay.cfm

Meinert, D. B., Peterson, D. K., Criswell, J. R., & Crossland, M. D. (2006). Privacy Policy Statements and Consumer Willingness to Provide Personal Information. *Journal of Electronic Commerce in Organizations, 4*(1), 1–17.

Mercuri, R. (2005). Challenges in forensic computing. *Communications of the ACM, 48*(12), 17–21. doi:10.1145/1101779.1101796

Meyers, M., & Rogers, M. (2004). Computer forensics: The need for standardization and certificate. *International Journal of Digital Evidence, 3*(2).

Milne, G. R., & Culnan, M. J. (2002). Using the content of online privacy notices to inform public policy: a longitudinal analysis of the 1998-2001 U.S. web surveys. *The Information Society, 18*(5), 345–359. doi:10.1080/01972240290108168

Milne, G. R., Culnan, M. J., & Green, H. (2006). A Longitudinal Assessment of Online Privacy Notice Readability. *Journal of Public Policy & Marketing, 25*(2), 238–249. doi:10.1509/jppm.25.2.238

Misra, S. K., Wickramasinghe, N., & Goldberg, S. (2003). Security challenge in mobile health-care setting. *Wireless I.T. Committee Meeting.* Cleveland: Information Technology Association of Canada.

Mocas, S. (2004). Building theoretical underpinnings for digital forensics research. *Digital Investigation, 1*(1), 61–68. doi:10.1016/j.diin.2003.12.004

Mohay, G. M. (2003). *Computer and intrusion forensics.* Boston: Artech House Inc.

Morris, G. (1990). *Computer security and the law.*

Morse, J. M. (2003). Principles of mixed methods and multimethods research design . In Tashak-kori, A., & Teddlie, C. (Eds.), *Handbook of Mixed Methods in Social & Behavioral Research.* Thousand Oaks: Sage Publications.

Myers, R. D., Reinstein, R. S., & Griller, G. M. (1999). Complex scientific evidence and the jury. *Judicature Genes and Justice: The Growing Impact of the New Genetics on the Courts, 83*(3).

Nezovic v Minister of Immigration and Multicultural and Indigenous Affairs (2003).

Nguyen, J. D., & Suber, E. F. (2009). An argument for eliminating the IP protection system. [from ABI/INFORM Global Database.]. *Business Law Today, 18*(4), 62–64. Retrieved May 8, 2009.

Nikishin, A. (2004). Malicious software – past, present and future. *Information Security Technical Report, 9*(2). doi:10.1016/S1363-4127(04)00020-2

Nisbett, R. E., & Ross, L. (1980). *Human inference: Strategies and shortcomings of social judgment.* Englewood Cliffs, NJ: Prentice Hall.

Nisbett, R. E., Krantz, D. H., Jepson, C., & Kunda, Z. (1983). The use of statistical heuristics in everyday inductive reasoning. *Psychological Review, 90,* 339–363. doi:10.1037/0033-295X.90.4.339

Nykanen, P. (2006). E-Health Systems: Their use and visions for the future . In Spil, T. A. M., & Schuring, R. W. (Eds.), *E-Health Systems Diffusion and Use: The innovation, the user and the USE IT Model.* Hershey: Idea Group Publishing.

O'Moore, R. (1995). The conception of a Medical Computer System . In Van Gennip, E. M. S. J., & Talmon, J. (Eds.), *Assessment and Evaluation of Information Technologies in Medicine.* Amsterdam: IOS Press.

O'Reilly, T. (2005). *What is Web 2.0? Design patterns and business models for the next generation of software.* Retrieved April 4, 2009, from http://www.oreillynet.com/pub/a/oreilly/tim/news/2005/09/30/what-is-web-20.html

Office of the Federal Privacy Commissioner. (2000). *Guidelines for Federal and ACT Government Websites.* Office of the Federal Privacy Commissioner, Sydney, Australia, Retrieved December 16, 2008, from http://www.privacy.gov.au/internet/web/index.html

Oleschuk, V. (2003). *Wireless Security and Health Care Information Systems.* Grimstad: Agder University College.

OpenAjax Alliance. (2008). *Ajax and Mashup security.* Retrieved March 2, 2008, from http://www.openajax.org/whitepapers/Ajax%20and%20Mashup%20Security.php

Oppliger, R. (2003). Microsoft. NET Passport: A Security Analysis. *Computer, 36*(7), 29-35. Retrieved August 17, 2009, from http://csdl2.computer.org/persagen/DLAbsToc.jsp?resourcePath=/dl/mags/co/&toc=comp /mags/co/2003/07/r7toc.xml&DOI=10.1109/MC.2003.1212687

Organisation for Economic Cooperation and Development. (1980). *OECD Guidelines on the Protection of Privacy and Transborder Flows of Personal Data.* Organisation for Economic Cooperation and Development, Paris. Retrieved December 16, 2008, from http://www.oecd.org/document/18/0,2340,en_2649_201185_1815186_1_1_1_1,00.html

Organisation for Economic Cooperation and Development. (2000a). *Developing a Privacy Policy and Statement.* Organisation for Economic Co-operation and Development, Paris, 2000. Retrieved December 16, 2008, from http://www.oecd.org/document/1/0,2340,en_2649_34255_28863233_1_1_1_1,00.html

Organisation for Economic Cooperation and Development. (2000b). *OECD Privacy Statement Generator.* Organisation for Economic Co-operation and Development, Paris, 2000, Retrieved December 16, 2008, from http://www.oecd.org/document/39/0,2340,en_2649_34255_28863271_1_1_1_1,00.html

Ort, E., Brydon, S., & Basler, M. (2009). *Mashups styles, Part 1: Server-Side Mashups (Sun Microsystems).* Retrieved March 23, 2009, from http://java.sun.com/developer/technicalArticles/J2EE/mashup_1/

Palmer, G. L. (2001). *A road map for digital forensic research.* Paper presented at the First Digital Forensic Research Workshop (DFRWS), Air Force Research Laboratory, Rome Research Site.

Palmer, G. L. (2002). Forensic analysis in the digital world. *International Journal of Digital Evidence, 1*(1).

Palmer, J. W., Bailey, J. P., & Faraj, S. (2000). The Role of Intermediaries in the Development of Trust in the WWW: The Use and Prominence of Trusted Third Parties and Privacy Statements. *Journal of Computer-Mediated Communication, 5*(3).

Pearce, J. (2003). *Music cos and AU universities square off over copyright claims.* Retrieved May 27, 2009, from http://www.zdnet.com.au/news/security/soa/Music-cos-and-AU-Universities-square-off-over-copyright claims/0,130061744,120273610,00.htm?feed=pt_file_sharing

Pearce, J. (2008). *User collaboration in Websites.* Retrieved July 2, 2008, from http://www.nla.gov.au/nla/staffpaper/2006/jpearce.html.

Perry, D. (2006, May 29). Can single sign-on be simple sign-on? *The Register.* Retrieved August 17, 2009, from http://www.theregister.co.uk/2006/05/29/simple_sso/

Pett, M. A., Lackey, N. R., & Sullivan, J. J. (2003). *Making sense of factor analysis: The use of factor analysis for instrument development in health care research.* Thousand Oaks: SAGE Publications.

Pfleeger, C., & Pfleeger, S. (2003). *Security in computing* (3rd ed.). New Jersey: Pearson Education Inc.

PlateSpin. (2007). *Consolidated Disaster Recovery Using Virtualization. Affordable Workload Protection and Recovery.* Ontario, CA: PlateSpin.

Pollitt, M. M. (2001, 16-19 October 2001). *Report on digital evidence.* Paper presented at the 13th INTERPOL Forensic Science Symposium, Lyon, France.

Pospesel, H., & Rodes (jnr), Robert. E. (1997). *Premises and conclusions: Symbolic logic for legal analysis.* New Jersey: Prentice-Hall, Inc.

Project For Rural Health Communications and Information Technologies (1996). Telehealth in rural and remote Australia. *Report of the Project for Rural Health Communications and Information Technologies.* Moe, Monash University: Australian Rural Health Research Institute.

Pruitt, S. (2005, April 4). Europe takes lead on improving online privacy notices. *The Industry Standard.* Retrieved December 16, 2008, from http://www.thestandard.com/internetnews/002774.php

Quaddus, M., Fink, D., Gururajan, R., & Vuori, T. (2005). *Driver and inhibitors of the adoption of wireless handheld technology in the healthcare industry: Views from selected WA stakeholders. HIC 2005.* Melbourne, Australia: HISA.

Quinn, S. (2005). Examining the state of preparedness of information technology management in New Zealand for events that may require forensic analysis. *Digital Investigation, 2*(4), 276–280. doi:10.1016/j.diin.2005.10.005

Ratha, N. K., Connell, J. H., & Bolle, R. M. (2001). Enhancing Security and Privacy in Biometrics-Based Authentication Systems. *IBM Systems Journal, 40*(3), 614–634. doi:10.1147/sj.403.0614

Regan, K. (2001, June 15). Does Anyone Read Online Privacy Policies? *E-Commerce Times.* Retrieved December 16, 2008, from http://www.ecommercetimes.com/story/11303.html

Regan, P. (2003). Privacy and Commercial Use of Personal Data: Policy Developments in the United States. *Journal of Contingencies and Crisis Management, 11*(1), 12–18. doi:10.1111/1468-5973.1101003

Reitzig, M. (2004). Management of Intellectual Property. *MITSLOAN Management Review, 45*(3). Retrieved May 28, 2009, from ABI/INFORM Global Database.

Ren, Y., Kraut, R., & Kiesler, S. (2007). Applying common identity and bond theory to design of online communities. *Organization Studies, 28*(3), 377–408. doi:10.1177/0170840607076007

Review of the Evidence Act 1995. (2004). Australian Law Reform Commission. Issues Paper 28. Retrieved 5 October 2009 from http://www.austlii.edu.au/au/other/alrc/publications/issues/28/

Rhodes, K. (2004). Operations Security Awareness: The Mind Has No Firewall. *Computer Security Journal, 16*(2), 27–36.

Rogers, M. K., & Seigfried, K. (2004). The future of computer forensics: A needs analysis survey. *Computers & Security, 23*(1), 12–16. doi:10.1016/j.cose.2004.01.003

Rosencrance, L. (2000a, September 18). Amazon Loses 2 Partners Over Privacy Policy. *Computerworld.* Retrieved January 9, 2006, from http://www.computerworld.com/cwi/story/0,1199,NAV47_STO50529,00.html

Rosencrance, L. (2000b, December 11). Amazon.com's Privacy Policies in Spotlight Again, U.S., U.K. Probes Urged. *Computerworld*. Retrieved January 9, 2006, from http://www.computerworld. com/cwi/story/ 0,1199,NAV47_STO54993,00.html

Rotman, L. (2005). Internet2 collaborates with Microsoft to Enable Interoperability of Federated Authentication Software. *I2 News Archive*. Retrieved August 17, 2009, from http://lists.aarnet. edu.au/pipermail/middle-l/2005-December/000074.html

Rowlingson, R. (2004). A ten step process for forensic readiness. *International Journal of Digital Evidence, 2*(3).

Rubinfeld, D. L., & Sappington, D. E. M. (1987). Efficient awards and standards of proof in judicial proceedings. *The Rand Journal of Economics, 18*(2), 308–315. doi:10.2307/2555555

Rudy, I. A. (1996). A Critical Review on Research on Electronic Mail. *European Journal of Information Systems, 4*, 198–213. doi:10.1057/ejis.1996.2

Saferstein, R. (1998). *Criminalistics: An introduction to forensic science* (6th ed.). Upper Saddle Rive, NJ: Prentice Hall.

Saks, M. J., & Koehler, J. J. (2005). The coming paradigm shift in forensic identification science. *Science, 309*(5736), 892–895. doi:10.1126/science.1111565

Salden, A. H., Hesselman, C., Van Eijik, R., Tokmakoff, A., Bargh, M., De Heer, J., & Benz, H. (2005). Mobile WLAN application services . In Ahson, S., & Ilyas, M. (Eds.), *Handbook of Wireless Local Area Network: Applications, Technology, Security, and Standards*. Boca Raton: Taylor & Francis Group.

Saurine, A. (2008). *Stephanie Rice Facebook pictures censored*. Retrieved May 27, 2009, from http://www.news.com.au/dailytelegraph/story/0,22049,23468911-5001021,00.html

Scadden, R. R., Bogdany, R. J., Cifford, J. W., Pearthree, H., & Locke, R. A. (2008). Resilient hosting in a continuously available virtualized environment. *IBM Systems Journal, 47*(4), 535–548. doi:10.1147/SJ.2008.5386523

Schaper, L., & Pervan, G. (2004). A model of information and communication technology acceptance and utilization by Occupational Therapists. *Decision Support in an Uncertain and Complex World: The IFIP TC8/WG8.3, International Conference 2004*, Curtin University of Technology.

Schneier, B. (1996). *Applied cryptography: protocols, algorithms, and source code in C* (2nd ed.). New York: John Wiley Sons, Inc.

Schneier, B. (2000). *Secrets and lies: digital security in a networked world*. New York: Wiley Computer Publishing.

Schneier, B. (2004, August 19, 2004). Opinion: Cryptanalysis of MD5 and SHA: Time for a new standard: Crypto researchers report weaknesses in common hash functions. *Computerworld*.

Schwaig, K. S., Kane, G., & Storey, V. C. (2004). Privacy, fair information practices and the fortune 500: the virtual reality of compliance. *Database, 36*(1), 49–63.

Schwaig, K. S., Kane, G., & Storey, V. C. (2006). Compliance to the fair information practices: How are the Fortune 500 handling online privacy disclosures? *Information & Management, 43*(7), 805–820. doi:10.1016/j.im.2006.07.003

Sciannamea, M. (2005). *Study says WLAN growth to triple within two years*. therfidwebblog.

Scott, D., & Passmore, E. R. (2005). *Build your disaster recovery e-mail architecture before a crisis arises*. Retrieved January 2, 2009, from http://www.gartner.com/DisplayDocument?doc_cd=126490

Shaw, G. L., & Harrald, J. R. (2004). Identification of the core competencies required of executive level business crisis and continuity managers. *Journal of Homeland Security & Emergency management, 1*(1), 1-14.

Sheffi, Y., & Rice, J. B. (2005). A Supply chain view of the resilient enterprise. *MITSloan Management Review, 47*(1), 40–48.

Sheridan, T. B., & Thompson, J. M. (1994). People versus computers in medicine . In Bogner, M. S. (Ed.), *Human Error in Medicine*. New Jersey: Lawrence Erlbaum Associates.

Silverstone, H., & Sheetz, M. (2007). *Forensic accounting and fraud investigation for non-experts*. New Jersey: John Wiley & Sons, Inc.

Sinnot, D. (2004). *Wireless insecurity*. ProActive Network and Security.

Slade, R. (2004). *Software forensics: Collecting evidence from the scene of a digital crime*. New York: McGraw Hill.

Sleek, S. (2000). Good e-recordkeeping saves you money, protects you from liability. *Digital Discovery and e-Evidence, 1*(1), 4-5.

Smith, H. J., Milberg, S. J., & Burke, S. J. (1996). Information Privacy: Measuring Individuals' Concerns About Organizational Practices. *Management Information Systems Quarterly, 20*(2). doi:10.2307/249477

Sommer, P. (1998). *Intrusion detection systems as evidence: Recent advances in intrusion detection*. London: Computer Security Research Centre, London School of Economics & Political Science. Retrieved February 28, 2009, from http://www.raidsymposium.org/raid98/Prog_RAID98/Full_Papers/Sommer_text.pdf

Sommer, P. (2000). Digital footprints: Accessing computer evidence. [Special Edition]. *Criminal Law Review (London, England)*, 61–78.

Spafford, E. H. (1992). Opus: Preventing Weak Password Choices. *Computers & Security, 11*(3), 273–278. doi:10.1016/0167-4048(92)90207-8

Spenceley, C. (2003). *Evidentiary treatment of computer-produced material: a reliability based evaluation*. Sydney: University of Sydney.

Srivastava, B., & Koehler, J. (2006). Web service composition - Current solutions and open problems. *IBM India Research Laboratory*. Block 1, IIT, New Delhi 110016, India. Retrieved June 2, 2009, from http://www.zurich.ibm.com/pdf/ebizz/icaps-ws.pdf

Stambaugh, H., Beaupre, D., Icove, D. J., Baker, R., Cassaday, W., & Williams, W. P. (2000). *State and local law enforcement needs to combat electronic crime*. Retrieved 22 November 2008 from http://www.ncjrs.gov/txtfiles1/nij/183451.txt

Standards, S. (2005). Retrieved May 5, 2009, from http://www.standards.org.au/downloads/051110_MOU_Security.pdf

Stanford, V. (2001). Pervasive Health Care Applications Face Tough Security Challenges. *Pervasive Computing. IEEE, 1*, 8–12. doi:10.1109/MPRV.2002.1012332

Stanton, J. M. (2003). Information Technology and privacy: A boundary management perspective . In Clarke, S., Coakes, E., Hunter, M. G., & Wenn, A. (Eds.), *Socio-Technical and Human Cognition Elements of Information Systems*. Hershey: Information Science Publishing.

Stanton, J. M., Stam, K. R., Mastrangelo, P., & Jolton, J. (2005). Analysis of End User Security Behaviours. *Computers & Security, 24*(2), 124–133. doi:10.1016/j.cose.2004.07.001

Stephenson, P. (2000). *Investigating computer-related crime*. Boca Raton, Florida: CRC Press.

Streza, R. (2003). Discovery unplugged: Should internal e-mails be privileged confidential communications? *Defense Counsel Journal, 70*(1), 36–41.

Suomi, R. (2006). Introducing electronic patient records to hospitals: Innovation adoption paths . In Spil, T. A. M., & Schuring, R. W. (Eds.), *E-Health Systems Diffusion and Use: The Innovation, the User and the USE IT Model*. Hershey: Idea Group Publishing.

Talbot, D. (2006). Simplified Sign-On. *MIT Technology Review*, March/April 2006. Retrieved August 17, 2009, from http://www.technologyreview.com/read_article.aspx?ch=specialsection s&sc=emerging&id=16474

Tapper, C. (1999). *Cross and Tapper on evidence* (9th ed.). London: LexisNexis Butterworths.

Tapper, C. (2004). *Cross & Tapper on evidence* (10 ed.). London: LexisNexis Butterworths.

The Productivity Commission. (2005). *Impacts of advances in medical technology in Australia: Productivity Commission Research Report*. Melbourne.

TheAge. (2005). NSW speed cameras in doubt. August 10.

Thompson, C. W., & Thompson, D. R. (2007). Identity management. [from ABI/INFORM Global Database.]. *IEEE Internet Computing, 11*(3), 82. Retrieved April 4, 2009. doi:10.1109/MIC.2007.60

Thompson, D. E., & Berwick, D. R. (1998). *Minimum provisions for the investigation of computer based offences*. Payneham, South Australia: National Police Research Unit.

Tillers, P. (2005). Picturing factual inference in legal settings. In *Gerechtigkeitswissenschaft: Kolloquium aus Anlass des 70: Geburtstages von Lothar Philipps*. Berlin.

Tobin, W. A., & Thompson, W. C. (2006). Evaluating and challenging forensic identification evidence. *Champion Magazine* (July, p.12).

Trček, D., & Trobec, R., Pavesić and Tasič, J. F. (2007). Information systems security and human behaviour. *Behaviour & Information Technology, 26*(2), 113–118. doi:10.1080/01449290500330299

Treasury Board of Canada Secretariat. (2004, November 5). *Directive on Government of Canada Web Site privacy policies*. Treasury Board of Canada Secretariat, Ottawa. Retrieved January 9, 2006, from http://www.tbs-sct.gc.ca/gos-sog/impl-rep/impl-rep2000/imp.report71/att-pj_e.htm

Truste (2004). Your Online Privacy Policy. *Truste*. Retrieved January 9, 2006, from http://www.truste.org/pdf/WriteAGreatPrivacyPolicy.pdf

Truste (2005, August). TRUSTe Guidance on Model Web Site Disclosures. *Truste*. Retrieved January 9, 2006, from http://www.truste.org/docs/Model_Privacy_Policy_Disclosures.doc

Turisco, F. (2000). Mobile computing is the next technology frontier for Health Providers. *Healthcare Financial Management, 55*, 78–82.

Unamed. (1994). (H. C. Lee Ed.). *Crime scene investigation.* Taoyuan: Central Police University Press.

Unamed. (1999). *Association of Chief Police Officers: Good practice guide for computer based evidence.* Retrieved 5 October 2009. from. http://www.7safe.com/electronic_evidence/ACPO_guidelines_computer_evidence_v4_web.pdf

Unamed. (2000). *The virtual horizon: meeting the law enforcement challenges: developing an Australasian law enforcement strategy for dealing with electronic crime: scoping paper.* Paper presented at the Police Commissioners' Conference - Electronic Crime Working Party 2000, Adelaide. Retrieved 5 October 2009 from http://www.acpr.gov.au/publications2.asp?Report_ID=102

Unamed. (2005b). Australian Law Reform Commission: Review of the Evidence Act 1995. Submission E 17. Retrieved 5 October 2009 from http://www.austlii.edu.au/au/other/alrc/publications/reports/102/

Unnamed. (2003). *Guidelines for the management of IT evidence: A handbook (HB171).* Sydney: Standards Australia International Ltd.

Ur Rehman, T. (2005). IP Mobility . In Ahson, S., & Ilyas, M. (Eds.), *Handbook of Wireless Local Area Network: Applications, Technology, Security, and Standards.* Boca Raton: Taylor & Francis Group.

US Federal Trade Commission. (2007). *Consumer fraud and identity theft complaint data for 2006,* data accessed from Consumer Sentinel and Identity Theft Clearinghouse. Retrieved March 20, 2008, from http://www.tamingthebeast.net/blog/ecommerce/internet-fraud-statistics-0207.htm.

Venkatesh, V., Morris, M. G., Davis, G. B., & Davis, F. B. (2003). User acceptance of Information Technology: Towards a unified view. *Management Information Systems Quarterly, 27*, 425–478.

Versel, N. (2008). *Use of mobile and wireless technology jumps in hospitals.* Digital Health Care.

Volonino, L. (2003). Electronic evidence and computer records. *Communications of the Association for Information Systems, 12*, 457–468.

Vu, K. L., Proctor, R. W., Bhargav-Spantzel, A., Tai, B., Cook, J., & Schultz, E. E. (2007). Improving Password Security and Memorability to Protect Personal and Organizational Information. *International Journal of Human-Computer Studies, 65*, 744–757. doi:10.1016/j.ijhcs.2007.03.007

Walker, J., & Whetton, S. (2005). Health informatics in action: Rural and remote health . In Whetton, S. (Ed.), *Health Informatics: A Social-Technical Perspective.* Oxford: Oxford University Press.

Wall, C., & Paroff, J. (2004). Cracking the computer forensics mystery. *UtahBar Journal, 17*(7).

Walton, D. N. (2000). Argumentation and theory of evidence . In *New trends in criminal investigation and evidence* (*Vol. 2*, pp. 711–732). Antwerp: Intersentia.

Wang, H. J., Fan, X., Howell, J., & Jackson, C. (2007). Protection and communication abstractions for Web browsers in Mashup OS. In *Proceedings of twenty-first ACM SIGOPS symposium on Operating systems principles* (pp.1-16). New York: ACM.

Wang, H., Lee, M. K. O., & Wang, C. (1998). Consumer privacy concerns about Internet marketing. *Communications of the ACM, 41*(3), 63–70. doi:10.1145/272287.272299

Warren, L. (1997). *Radio National Transcripts: Santa, smog, and speed! The Law Report*. Australia: Australian Broadcasting Corporation.

West-Brown, M. J., Stikvoort, D., Kossakowski, K.-P., Killcrece, G., Ruefle, R., & Zajicek, M. (2003). *Handbook of Computer Security Incident Response Teams (CSIRTs)* (2nd ed.). Pittsburgh, PA, USA: CMU/SEI.

Whetton, S. (2005a). The health care environment and Health Informatics . In Whetton, S. (Ed.), *Health Informatics: A Social-Technical Perspective*. Oxford: Oxford University Press.

Whetton, S. (2005b). What is Health Informatics? In Whetton, S. (Ed.), *Health Informatics: A Social-Technical Perspective*. Oxford: Oxford University Press.

Whetton, S., & Showell, C. (2005). Tools: Promises and Pitfalls . In Whetton, S. (Ed.), *Health Informatics: A Social-Technical Perspective*. Oxford: Oxford University Press.

Whitcomb, C. M. (2002). An historical perspective of digital evidence: A forensic scientist's view. *International Journal of Digital Evidence, 1*(1).

Whitman, M. E., & Mattord, H. J. (2005). *Principles of information security* (2nd ed.). Boston, Massachusetts: Thomson Learning.

Whitman, M. E., & Mattord, H. J. (2009). *Principles of Information Security* (3rd ed.). Thomson Course Technology.

Whittaker, Z. (2007). *Mobile computing vs. cloud computing*. Retrieved April 4, 2009, from http://blogs.zdnet.com/igeneration/?p=154

Wiedenbeck, S., Waters, J., Birget, J. C., Brodskiy, A., & Memon, N. (2005). PassPoints: Design and longitudinal evaluation of a graphical password system. *International Journal of Human-Computer Studies, 63*, 102–127. doi:10.1016/j.ijhcs.2005.04.010

Williams, P. (2002). *Organized crime and cyber-crime: Implications for business*. Retrieved 9 February 2009, from http://www.cert.org/archive/pdf/cybercrime-business.pdf

Wong, J., & Hong, J. (2007). Making Mashups with marmite: towards end-user programming for the web. In *Proceedings of the SIGCHI conference on Human factors in computing systems* (pp.1435-1444). New York: ACM.

Wong, K. D. (2005). *Wireless Internet Telecommunications*. London: Artech House.

Woodman, P. (2007, March). Business Continuity Management Survey. *Cabinet Office and The Continuity Forum*, 1-17.

Workman, M., Bommer, W. H., & Straub, D. (2008). Security Lapses and the omission of information security measures: A threat control model and empirical test. *Computers in Human Behavior, 24*, 2799–2816. doi:10.1016/j.chb.2008.04.005

Wu, K., & Wu, X. (2007). A wireless mobile monitoring system for home healthcare and community medical services. In X. Wu (Ed.), *Bioinformatics and Biomedical Engineering, 2007. ICBBE 2007. The 1st International Conference.*

Xu, Y., Tan, B., Hui, K. L., & Tang, W. K. (2003). Consumer Trust and Online Information Privacy. In *Proceedings of the International Conference on Information Systems, 2003.* Retrieved January 9, 2006, from http://aisel.isworld.org/pdf.asp?Vpath=ICIS/2003&PDFpath=03CRP45.pdf

Yan, J., Blackwell, A., Anderson, R., & Grant, A. (2004). Password Memorability and Security: Empirical Results. *IEEE Security & Privacy, 2*(5), 25–31. doi:10.1109/MSP.2004.81

Yang, T. A., & Zahur, Y. (2005). Security in WLANs. In Ahson, & M. Ilyas (Eds.), *Handbook of Wireless Local Area Network: Applications, Technology, Security, and Standards.* Boca Raton: Taylor & Francis Group.

Yapp, P. (2001). Passwords: Use and Abuse. *Computer Fraud & Security, 9*(1), 14–16. doi:10.1016/S1361-3723(01)00916-2

Yasinsac, A., Erbacher, R. F., Marks, D. G., Pollitt, M. M., & Sommer, P. M. (2003). Computer forensics education. *IEEE Security & Privacy, 1*(4), 15–23. doi:10.1109/MSECP.2003.1219052

Yee, R. (2006). *Mashups, IST-Data Services.* Retrieved June 2, 2009, from http://dret.net/lectures/services-fall06/Mashups.pdf

Young, J. R. (2006). Security lapses common at colleges. *The Chronicle of Higher Education, 53*(10).

Zambon, E., Bolzoni, D., Etalie, S., & Salvato, M. (2007). A model supporting Business Continuity Auditing and Planning in Information Systems. *Internet Monitoring and Protection, 2007, ICIMP 2007, Second International Conference* (pp. 33-33). San Jose.

Zeeshan, A. (2003). *Wireless security in health care.* SA, Australia: University of South Australia.

Zikmund, W. G. (2003). *Business Research Methods.* Ohio, Thomson: South Western

Zsidisin, G. A., Melnyk, S. A., & Ragatz, G. L. (2005). An institutional theory perspective of business continuity planning for purchasing and supply management. *International Journal of Production Research, 43*(16), 3401–3420. doi:10.1080/00207540500095613

Zviran, M., & Haga, W. J. (1999). Password Security: An Empirical Study. *Journal of Management Information Systems, 15*(4), 161–185

About the Contributors

Don Kerr, PhD, is an Associate Professor of Information Systems at the University of the Sunshine Coast. His research interests include assessing and monitoring the level of online fraud amongst senior citizens, the development and evaluation of decision support systems and the evaluation of the implementation of enterprise resource planning systems with particular emphasis on training and security. He has published 76 peer reviewed papers in both agricultural and management journals and conferences over the past 20 years.

John G. Gammack (PhD Cambridge, 1988) is an adjunct Professor at Murdoch University in Perth, and also at Griffith University in Queensland, Australia. He has around 200 internationally recognised publications mostly concerning informatics, and was lead author of the first popular textbook in this general field. Professor Gammack is a former head of both IT and management schools, and was research director for cross-university interdisciplinary groups specialising in Internet studies and in user and societal (IT) needs. Currently John spends time at various Chinese institutions as a visiting faculty member, and continues his research in informatics and digital life.

Kay Bryant is an independent contractor with experience in information systems. She has extensive academic experience in teaching information systems. Her research covers information systems and data security and includes publications in the Australasian Journal of Information Systems and Expert Systems with Applications.

***

Richard Boddington teaches and researches information security and cyber forensics at Murdoch University. He commenced his career with the London Metropolitan Police, was appointed a Detective Chief Inspector with the Royal Hong Kong Police Special Branch, later becoming an Intelligence Officer with the Australian Security Intelligence Organisation. More recently, he was a senior investigation analyst with the Western Australian Department of Treasury & Finance. He is currently completing his PhD student at Murdoch researching the use of expert systems in digital evidence validation. Richard operates a security consultancy working with the mining industry as well as cyber forensic analysis for the legal fraternity and private clients.

Kevin Curran BSc (Hons), PhD, SMIEEE, FBCS CITP, SMACM, FHEA is a senior lecturer in Computer Science at the University of Ulster and group leader for the Ambient Intelligence Research Group. His achievements include winning and managing UK & European Framework projects and Technology Transfer Schemes. Dr Curran has made significant contributions to advancing the knowledge and understanding of computer networking and systems, evidenced by over 450 published works. He is perhaps most well-known for his work on location positioning within indoor environments, pervasive computing and internet security. His expertise has been acknowledged by invitations to present his work at international conferences, overseas universities and research laboratories. He is a regular contributor to BBC radio & TV news in the UK and is currently the recipient of an Engineering and Technology Board Visiting Lectureship for Exceptional Engineers and is an IEEE Technical Expert for Internet/Security matters. He is listed in the Dictionary of International Biography, Marquis Who's Who in Science and Engineering and by Who's Who in the World.

Declan Walsh has a BEng in Electronics and Computer Systems from the University of Ulster. He is currently doing an MSc in Nanoelectronics at The University of Manchester.

Jennifer Caldwell (BSC) is a graduate in Computer Science of the University of Ulster. She is currently working for the Western Health and Socail Care Trust in Londonderry in their IT department.

Marcella Gallacher (BSC) is a graduate in Computer Science of the University of Ulster. She is presently working in IT and here research interests include distributed systems, multimedia and Internet Technologies

Roger Clarke is a consultant with particular expertise in eBusiness, information infrastructure, and dataveillance and privacy. His work encompasses corporate strategy, government policy, and public advocacy. He spent 1984-95 as a senior academic, and continues as a Visiting Professor at U.N.S.W. (in cyberspace law and policy) and the A.N.U. (in computer science). He has been a Board member of the Australian Privacy Foundation since its inception in 1987, and is currently its Chair.

John Campbell is Professor of Information Systems in the Faculty of Information Sciences and Engineering at the University of Canberra. His research interests include IT governance and business alignment; user information systems security practices; evaluating IT investments; IT policy development; individual, organizational and societal impacts of telework; virtual organizations, communities and teams; and information systems research methods. He has published articles in Information Systems Journal, Information & Management, Data Base for Advances in Information Systems, Behaviour & Information Technology, Journal of Organizational Computing and Electronic Commerce, and the Australasian Journal of Information Systems.

Raj Gururajan is a Professor in Information Systems in the Faculty of Business at the University of Southern Queensland, Australia. His main area of research is user behaviour issues in using wireless technology, the management of technology and the diffusion of technology at enterprise level. Currently he is applying these interests to health settings. He has published over 100 refereed articles, won over $2 million in grant income, manages six funded projects and supervising over 10 PhD students. He also holds 3 national competitive grants (ARC) in health informatics.

Abdul Hafeez-Baig holds a PhD in the domain of healthcare and information systems from USQ and master's degrees in MIS and MBA from Griffith University, Brisbane, Australia. Since joining USQ in 2004, he has published many referred publications in the domains of health and education regarding technology management. Abdul is very conversant with wireless technology as well as emerging technologies and learning management systems. He teaches information systems concepts to both undergraduate and postgraduate students, including MBA students. Abdul also has numerous publications in academic and scholarly journals, and has a vast array of scholarly conference papers, all of which have revolved around the domain of information systems. Abdul has extensive experience in the area of information systems, especially with regards to the healthcare sector. He is particularly interested in wireless healthcare applications, systems analysis and design, adoption, the infusion and diffusion of information technology, M-learning and E-Commerce, outsourcing, networking, health care and information technology, and the re-engineering of business processes.

Shah Jahan Miah received his PhD in information systems from Griffith University Australia. His current research areas include DSS development in industries, IS development methods, and web-based solution development. Shah has lead authored more than 20 papers in different IS areas. He has published in the journals include *Expert systems with Applications* and *Knowledge Based Systems*, and presented his research in the conferences include *Americas Conference on Information Systems (AMCIS)* and *Australasian Conference on Information Systems (ACIS)*. Dr. Miah is currently working as a lecturer in informatics at University of the Sunshine Coast (USC) Queensland Australia.

Oscar Imaz-Mairal studied Business Information Systems at the University of the Sunshine Coast where he then completed a Masters in Business Administration. Oscar is now a PhD candidate at the same University. Oscar has had 25 years of Business experience in areas as diverse as banking, hospitality and property development holding the position of CEO for a group of construction and development companies where he focused on business process efficiency and total quality management.

Daniel Viney, BICT ITIL PRINCE2, is the Research Information Systems Coordinator & a systems analysis, design and project management tutor at the University of the Sunshine Coast. His research interests include digital security, cloud computing and social networking. In the business sector, Daniel specialises in "bridging the communication gap" between technology and business and he has extensive experience in developing and maintaining web services, learning management systems, content management systems, digital repositories, research management systems and training delivery.

Index

high availability (HA) 167, 169
hotmail 78, 82
hypertext markup language (HTML) 153
hypertext transfer protocol (HTTP) 155,
    158

I

identity management (IDM) 176, 180, 182
Identity Provider 79
Infocard 78, 79
information and communication technolo-
    gies (ICT) 9, 29, 130, 132, 147,
    163, 165, 166, 167, 168, 173, 180
information security 174, 175, 181, 183,
    188
Information Technology Infrastructure
    Library (ITIL) 172
information technology (IT) xiii, 2, 5, 6, 7,
    8, 9, 12, 13, 14, 15, 16, 17, 21, 22,
    29, 32, 34, 35, 36, 63, 65, 68, 69,
    85, 88, 89, 143, 145, 146, 147, 148,
    149, 150, 174
information technology (IT) security 2,
    15, 16, 17, 32
information technology service (ITS) 8, 9,
    10, 11, 12, 14, 29
infrastructure as a service (IaaS) 178
Intel Corporation 78, 174
intellectual property (IP) 173, 184, 185,
    189

J

jurisdiction 24

K

keyloggers 3

L

laser beams 130
legal precedents 49, 60
library 2.0 157, 160
Limewire 45
local area networks (LAN) v, ix, xiv, 129,
    137, 145, 147
local hierarchies 24

logic bomb 3

M

malicious software (malware) 1, 3, 5, 12,
    13, 18, 19
management commitment 164, 166
mashups 152, 153, 154, 155, 156, 157,
    158, 159, 160, 161, 162
meta-brands 86
metrics 166
Microsoft .NET Passport 78
misdemeanors 44, 55
mobile computing 173, 174, 176, 178, 182
Moore, Gordon 174, 189
MSN 76, 78
murder scene 25
MySpace 157

N

National Geographic 97, 98, 100
networked village 167
network logs 44
New South Wales Road Traffic Authority
    (RTA) 51
non-technical attacks 50
non-volatile memory 40
NVIVO 138

O

OASIS 78
operating systems 170
organisation for economic cooperation and
    development (OCED) 85, 90, 94,
    99, 104, 109, 110

P

password composition 112, 113, 114, 115,
    117, 118, 119, 120, 125, 126
password management 112, 113, 114, 125,
    126
password reuse 113, 114, 117, 121, 123,
    124, 125
password security 112, 113, 114, 115, 125,
    126
peer-to-peer (P2P) application 45